# Interpreting Mr Keynes

# Interpreting Mr Keynes
## The IS–LM Enigma

*Warren Young*

WESTVIEW PRESS
Boulder, Colorado

Copyright © England by Warren Young

Published in 1987 by Polity Press,
Dales Brewery, Gwydir Street, Cambridge CB1 2LJ, UK.

Published in 1987 in the United States by

WESTVIEW PRESS
Frederick A. Praeger, Publisher
5500 Central Avenue
Boulder, Colorado 80301

Young, Warren, 1949–
Interpreting Mr. Keynes.
1. Keynesian economics.   2. Keynes, John Maynard,
1853–1946.   3. IS–LM model (macroeconomics)   I. Title.
HB99.7.Y68   1986   330.15′6      87–10535
ISBN 0–8133–0533–0

Printed in Great Britain

# Contents

# Acknowledgements

This book is dedicated to Sir Roy Harrod. I am very grateful to Lady Harrod for allowing me to quote from his letters. I hope that his fundamental contribution to the discovery and development of the IS–LM approach will now finally be recognized. Prof. James Meade's contribution to the IS–LM approach has also gone unrecognized up to now. I am indebted to him for enabling me to put the Harrod–Hicks–Meade IS–LM approach in its proper perspective. Prof. Sir John Hicks has also been most helpful by kindly answering questions I put to him in correspondence, and by allowing his letters to Meade and Robertson to be reproduced and quoted here.

Prof. Partha Dasgupta and his father Prof. A. K. Dasgupta have been of great assistance, the former by his continuing active interest in my work, the latter by kindly allowing me to interview him about his early work.

Prof. Arthur Brown and his son Prof. William Brown have been of immense help in my efforts; the former by very kindly allowing me to interview him and reproduce his original notes from the September 1936 Oxford conference, the latter through his constant encouragement and interest in my work.

Many have assisted me in trying to put the history of the IS–LM approach together. I wish to thank Prof. S. Dennison for his kindness and co-operation in sending material from the Robertson papers and very kindly giving permission to quote from Sir Dennis Robertson's letters. Prof. Lord Kaldor has been of great help, by granting interviews and access to his correspondence. I am also very grateful to Prof. David Champernowne and Prof. Brian Reddaway for granting interviews also and for clearing up many unresolved questions, through both discussion and correspondence. Prof. George Shackle and Prof. Ludwig Lachmann have also been most helpful by providing their recollections of what took place at the Oxford conference in September 1936. Prof. Jan Tinbergen has also very kindly allowed me to quote from his letters. Prof. Lord Kahn has kindly allowed me to quote Keynes's reply to Meade on his IS–LM paper and Prof. Don Moggridge has kindly allowed me to quote from Hawtrey's letters.

Maurice Allen's role in modern economics has yet to be told, and I am grateful to him for allowing me to quote here parts of his unpublished essay 'Marginalia on the Quantity Theory'. Others who have kindly replied to my queries on the 1936 Oxford conference include Prof. Sir Henry Phelps-Brown, Prof. C. Clark, Dr H. Robinson and Dr R. Bretherton.

Prof. Tom Rymes, Prof. Peter Temin, Dr Peter Clarke, Prof. Tony Thirlwall and Prof. Marc Blaug have also helped with their encouragement and comments and Prof. Liz Durbin kindly sent me copies of Harrod's letters to her father, the late Evan Durbin.

Ed Nissan, Barry Goss, Albert Arouh, Omar Hamouda, Vani Boorah, Mike Landesmann, Björn Hansson, Roy Rotheim and David and Margaret Toase – and their warm friendship – helped me get through a cold year in Cambridge.

I also wish to thank the President of Wolfson College; the Master, Fellows and Registrar of my college, Churchill; and the members of the Faculty of Economics and Politics, University of Cambridge, for their hospitality during my period as visiting scholar, 1985–6.

Dr A. Raspin, the Archivist (special collections) of the British Library of Economics, and the Archivist of the Archives Centre, Churchill College, Cambridge, have also been of great assistance.

Last but not least Dr Geoff Harcourt has been a constant inspiration and his encouragement has led me through many dark days when I thought I had lost my way on the IS–LM trail.

But above all I have to thank my long-suffering wife Sara and daughters Shani and Natalie, who allowed me to spend so much time away from home engaged in 'hagiography'.

I am solely responsible for any errors and omissions in this book, but can only hope that my efforts will spur others to try and 'see where the feet grow' as regards the origins and development of core concepts in modern economic thought.

# Preface

There is an old African saying to the effect that 'what goes around, comes around'. This adage applies to most branches of knowledge, but it is especially apt regarding *Methodenstreit* in modern economic thought. Perhaps the most puzzling controversy involves the IS–LM approach and its relation to Keynes's *General Theory*. For, if one takes the recent attack on IS–LM made by Kahn in his book *The making of Keynes's General Theory* at face value, it would seem that the debate over the representation of Keynes's model of macroeconomic behaviour has come full circle: from Keynes's somewhat ambivalent stance on Hicks's IS–LM representation, to Kahn's absolute rejection of it almost fifty years later. Indeed, as we shall see, the origins and development of the IS–LM approach and its subsequent effect on economic thought have been, up to now, an enigma. In this book, I hope to shed some new light upon this relatively uncharted area in the history of economic thought – problems that have not been studied even though the IS–LM approach has been called by some 'the core of modern macroeconomics'.

The introductory chapter presents the reasons for and background to the study and outlines the key issues. These include the nature of IS–LM, its origins and development, Keynes's attitude towards it and IS–LM as a case study in the history of thought.

Chapter 1 deals initially with the chameleonic nature of Keynes's *General Theory*. This was the result of a lack of consensus about the representation of Keynes's central message in the General Theory group, and its subsequent split into two variant approaches – that of Joan Robinson and Kahn, who reject IS–LM-type representations outright, and that of Harrod and Meade, which enabled the IS–LM approach to develop eventually into its 'Hicks–Hansen' version. The stress Keynes put upon uncertainty – which so disturbed economists – and the reaction of the economics profession to this in the form of a search for continuity and certainty which culminated in the IS–LM approach, is also discussed briefly. The first section of this chapter concludes with a new perspective on Keynes's 1937 *Quarterly Journal of Economics* paper which restated the importance of uncertainty.

The second section of chapter 1 surveys the published correspondence between Keynes and Harrod, and Hicks's exchange with Keynes concerning their respective papers. Relevant exchanges between Keynes and Harrod on the *General Theory* are also analysed. This section also deals with Meade's 'simplified model of Keynes' system' from the perspective of Meade's subsequent published interpretation of his approach. The third section of chapter 1 deals specifically with the 1936 Oxford conference and what can be called 'the IS–LM papers'. The focus is on what was perhaps the most important meeting in the history of economics, the symposium on Keynes's *General Theory* held on Saturday morning, 26 September 1936, which opened the sixth European Conference of the Econometric Society held in Oxford. At this symposium, three 'classic and still famous critiques of the General Theory' – in the words of George Shackle, who attended the meeting – were given by Harrod, Hicks and Meade respectively. The material presented here is based upon previously unpublished correspondence and textural evidence, participants' recollections and reactions to the symposium. While this material sheds new light on the preparation, initial effects and aftermath of the IS–LM papers given at the meeting, it also raises the question of multiple discovery with regard to the origins and development of the IS–LM approach itself. The final section of chapter 1 focuses on the similarities and differences between the originators of the IS–LM approach and the reasons for the divergence in the General Theory group, which was rooted in variant views of the Keynesian revolution and of the nature, scope and method of conceptual change in economics.

Chapter 2 deals with evidence concerning antecedents to and variants of the IS–LM approach. The first section analyses what may be the earliest attempt at a 'reconciliation' between Keynes and 'the orthodox theory' – an unpublished essay written in 1934 by Maurice Allen, an Oxford contemporary of Meade. The second section deals with the IS–LM-type approaches evident in Redda-way's 1936 review of Keynes's *General Theory* and in Lange's system (1938), which Keynes, it seems, also acknowledged as being similar to the ideas he expressed in the *General Theory*. The third section deals with the equations and diagrams presented in Champernowne's June 1936 *Review of Economic Studies* paper. The fourth and final section focuses on Harrod's equational represen-tation of Keynes's *General Theory* which circulated in Oxford in Hilary Term, 1936 and was subsequently presented in Harrod's paper at the September 1936 Oxford conference and published – prior to Hicks's paper – in *Econometrica*. This section also presents evidence concerning the existence of Harrod's 'Trade Cycle group', which assisted in the diffusion of his interpretation of Keynes's *General Theory* and in developing his approaches to the trade cycle and dynamic theory.

Chapter 3 concentrates on the phenomenon that diagrams not only seem to assist, but may even accelerate, the acceptance of concepts in economics. The first section outlines possible alternative derivations of the IS–LM diagram from material extant at its conception, in addition to Hicks's versions of its derivation. The second section discusses the combined role of equations and diagrams and their effect on economic thought and economists in the context of the IS–LM approach and its earliest exponents, Lerner and Kaldor, in the pre-war period. This section also presents new evidence concerning Kaldor's use of IS–LM to refute Pigou on the wage–employment nexus in 1937, Robertson's role in the development of Kaldor's paper and his view of IS–LM, and Hicks's involvement in the Keynes–Pigou–Kaldor exchange. The third section deals with Hansen's role in the institutionalization of IS–LM as Keynes's General Theory. The fourth section focuses on Timlin's 1942 presentation of the Keynes–Lange system – forgotten by most economists – and Modigliani's 1944 paper, which laid the basis for the 'neo-classical synthesis'.

Chapter 4 surveys the 1936–7 and 1951–2 correspondence between Harrod and Hawtrey on Keynes's *General Theory*, Hawtrey's *Capital and Employment*, and Harrod's *Trade Cycle*. The first section reviews their early correspondence on Keynes's *General Theory* and Harrod's *Trade Cycle*. The second section deals with their 1951 correspondence on the *General Theory* and Harrod's *General Theory* diagram, the only diagram to appear in Keynes's book. In the third section, Harrod's influence on Hawtrey's view of

Keynes's *General Theory* is discussed. The fourth section deals with their respective views on the efficacy of fiscal and monetary policy from the perspective of Hawtrey's interpretation of Keynes's *General Theory* views and Harrod's IS–LM interpretation of them.

Chapter 5 focuses on both early and recent re-evaluations and critiques of Keynes's *General Theory* and the IS–LM approach. The first section deals with Hicks IS–LM diagrammatics and his 1950 account of the derivation of his diagram. The second section discusses the Clower–Leijonhufvud reinterpretation of Keynes, and places it in the perspective of its little-known forerunner, the Keynes–Lange system outlined by Timlin. The third section surveys the post-Keynesian attack on IS–LM and places Hicks's 'explanations' of his IS–LM approach in perspective. The final section of the chapter deals with recent controversies in economics and the role played in these by the IS–LM approach. In chapter 6 I attempt an overview of the history of the IS–LM approach and reach some conclusions concerning its significance as a case study in the history of economic thought. The first part sums up the evidence on the origins and development of the IS–LM approach. The second section focuses on the split in the General Theory group and Keynes's reaction to IS–LM and summarizes the evidence in this regard. The third section deals with the question of whether the IS–LM approach is the 'revealed preference' and 'trained intuition' of the economics profession, or should be seen as only one 'suggested interpretation'. The fourth and final section of this chapter deals with the IS–LM case from the comparative perspective of other diagrammatic representations in economics, and suggests an alternative way for dealing with the origins and development of core concepts in modern economics by means of a 'grounded' history of economic thought.

# Introduction

## IS–LM: chimera or Keynes's central message?

### Background

In his 1984 Hicks Lecture, Solow raised a number of questions about the nature, origins, development and role in economic analysis of what he called 'the IS–LM model'. The IS–LM diagram – which some economists have termed 'the core of modern macroeconomics', and others see as the essence of what Joan Robinson called 'Bastard Keynesianism' – first appeared in Hicks's April 1937 *Econometrica* article entitled 'Mr. Keynes and the "Classics": A Suggested Interpretation'. This article was based on a paper that Hicks originally gave at the September 1936 Econometric Society meeting in Oxford. According to Solow, this paper was 'the origin, as everyone knows, of the IS–LM model'. He continued that 'to a large extent the IS–LM model for almost fifty years has been Keynesian economics', qualifying this, however, by adding 'though only a part of Keynesian economics it is fair to say'. He also cited Tobin's description of 'the IS–LM apparatus as "the trained intuition of many of us" '.[1]

In his lecture, Solow asked 'Why was it precisely J. R.'s [Hicks's] paper that wormed its way into our imagination and our intuitions?' Solow then attempted an answer by counterpointing Hicks's interpretation of Keynes's *General Theory* to those of Harrod and Meade. In Solow's words 'At the very same meeting of the Econometric Society in Oxford in September 1936, there were three papers that tried to extract a model from the *General Theory*, not just one. Roy Harrod's was published before J. R.'s in the January [1937] issue of *Econometrica*, and James Meade's appeared shortly afterward in the detailed Report of the Oxford meeting'. Solow continued 'It is not too far-fetched to say that the same basic equations could be detected in all three versions. At some celestial level of abstraction, they could be described as identical products. But it was the IS–LM model that established itself as our trained intuition'.[2]

Solow then posed the additional question 'What . . . was the source' of IS–LM's 'survival value?', and attempted an acceptable answer:

> If economics were really a science – in the aggressive sense – as most modern economists think it is, then there would be little or nothing to choose among alternative models so long as one way or another they contain the same equations, and thus have the same implications. Either there would be nothing to choose, or else we would choose on fundamentally trivial grounds. But suppose economics is not a complete science in that sense, and may even have very little prospect of becoming one. Suppose all it can do is help us to organize our necessarily incomplete perceptions about the economy, to see connections the untutored eye would miss, to tell plausible stories with the help of a few central principles. Suppose, in other words, that economics is 'a discipline, not a science' . . . in that case what we want a piece of economic theory to do is precisely to train our intuition, to give us a handle on the facts . . . IS–LM survived because it proved to be a marvellously simple and useful way to organize and process some of the main macroeconomic facts.[3]

What stands out among the points Solow raised are first, his reference to the 'detailed Report of the Oxford meeting' and secondly his reference to Meade's paper and observation that Harrod's and Meade's papers were similar to Hicks's. To take the first point – if one actually looks at the 'detailed Report of the Oxford meeting' to see whether there was any discussion of the papers given by Hicks, Harrod and Meade, two things stand out. First, the list of participants at the Oxford meeting – and at what was essentially a symposium on Keynes's system – reads almost like a *Who's Who* of modern economics. Secondly, the 'detailed Report' of the symposium on Keynes contains only a summary of Meade's paper and brief reference to a 'discussion' on stability. This is the extent of the 'detail' about the symposium on Keynes.[4]

Thus, although this symposium was arguably one of the most important in the history of modern economic thought – and occurred at a conference which could also be claimed as one of the most important meetings of economists ever – almost nothing is reported of participants' comments on or reactions to the papers presented at the symposium, or relating to discussion of Hicks's and Harrod's papers. A fuller account of what actually took place, is essential to the history of economic thought, especially as Hicks's IS–LM diagram became 'the trained intuition' of most of the economics profession.

Interestingly, the impact of conference papers on both participants and those who have seen or heard about the papers in their pre-publication form, and the importance of discussion at scientific meetings, can readily be seen in physics – an area of scientific inquiry which many economists have taken as a 'role-model' for their own profession. For example, Niels Bohr, one of the founders of modern physics and the new quantum theory, became interested in the latter, according to Max Jammer, after hearing a report of discussions at the First Solvay Conference held in Brussels in 1911, from Lord Rutherford. Moreover, as Jammer relates 'after reading the proceedings that his brother Maurice, the secretary of the meeting, had to prepare', Louis de Broglie, the originator of wave-particle duality in matter, 'became so excited' that, in de Broglie's words 'I decided to devote all my efforts to investigate the real nature of the mysterious quanta . . . whose profound meaning had not yet been understood'. The importance of the discussions that took place at the Fifth and Sixth Solvay meetings (1927 and 1930) – and the famous Einstein–Bohr debates on the nature of the new physics – have been widely documented. They still shape the course of development of modern physics today.[5]

The papers raise a number of problems. Meade's paper – as Harrod's – was published before Hicks's, and appeared in the *Review of Economic Studies* in February 1937. Now, if the equations in all three papers are similar and, as Solow puts it, 'at some celestial level of abstraction, they could be described as identical products', then the question can be asked: were they independent interpretations of Keynes's *General Theory* or was there a degree of 'cross-fertilization' of ideas? Moreover, how did Keynes react to the respective interpretations of his *General Theory*?

Other questions arise from Solow's lecture, for example: does the IS–LM diagram represent the 'trained intuition' of economists or is it just, as Hicks put it in 1937, 'a suggested interpretation'? And, if it is the 'trained intuition' of economists, how, when and why did it come to dominate the analytic techniques of macroeconomic analysis and, for that matter, does it still 'rule the roost'?

In order to answer these and related questions, it is necessary to focus on four things: the nature of IS–LM; the origins and development of IS–LM; the reaction to IS–LM, especially by Keynes; and the role in and impact of IS–LM on modern economics, as a case study in the history of economic thought. To do this, we must first set out the key issues in each of these topics.

## Key issues

### *What is IS–LM?*

The IS–LM diagram is familiar to all economists. Indeed, those who have chosen to teach undergraduates the 'macro-principles' of economics or 'macroeconomics' use this diagram to explain and analyse both macroeconomic phenomena and policy prescriptions and alternatives. At another level, economists have engaged in controversies about whether this diagram is a valid representation of Keynes's *General Theory* and have also argued amongst themselves and defended their respective macroeconomic world-views – whether 'Keynesian' or 'Monetarist' – using IS–LM.

Hicks's IS–LM diagram enables the economist to express concomitantly the interrelationships between fundamental macroeconomic variables such as income, interest rate, investment, saving and the demand for and supply of money. The diagram consists of two curves 'IS' and 'LM' drawn in a coordinate framework, with 'income' as the horizontal and 'interest' as the vertical axes respectively. In the IS–LM diagram as it appeared in Hicks's 1937 *Econometrica* article, the LM curve – or as Hicks originally called it, the LL curve – was drawn on the basis of an equation of the form

$$M = L\ (I,\ i)\ \text{(Equation 1)}$$

where M represents the 'demand for money', I is 'total income', and i is the 'rate of interest'. Thus, as Hicks put it 'against a given quantity of money', i.e. money supply, this 'equation . . . gives us a relation between income (I) and the rate of interest (i). This can be drawn out as a curve (LL) which will slope upwards, since an increase in income tends to raise the demand for money, and an increase in the rate of interest tends to lower it.'[6]

Hicks then goes on to draw his IS curve on the basis of two additional equations:

$$I_x = C\ (i)\ \text{(Equation 2)}$$
$$I_x = S\ (I)\ \text{(Equation 3)}$$

where $I_x$ is the 'value of investment, or simply investment', i is the 'rate of interest' and I is 'total income'. According to Hicks, these equations 'taken together give us another relation between income and investment'. Hicks then says, parenthetically, 'the marginal-efficiency-of-capital schedule determines the value of investment at any given rate of interest, and the multiplier tells us what level of income will be necessary to make savings equal to that value of investment'. Hicks ends his derivation by saying 'The curve IS can therefore be drawn showing the relation between income and interest which must be maintained in order to make saving equal to investment. Income and the rate of interest are now determined together at P, the point of intersection of the curves LL and IS' (see figure I.1) Later, however, Hicks 'generalizes' equations 2 and 3 by inserting income into both.[7]

On this basis, Hicks proceeds to a diagrammatic outline of his derivation of what he calls 'the generalized General Theory'. By assuming that total money income is given, Hicks draws both a curve representing 'at that given income' – in money terms – the marginal efficiency of capital, and a curve representing the supply of saving. In his view, the intersection of these curves determines the interest rate for that 'given income' which equalizes savings and investment. Given this, according to Hicks, the IS curve now represents 'the relation between income' and what he calls 'the corresponding investment rate of interest'.[8]

Hicks then proceeds to 'generalize' his LL curve. He does this by relaxing the assumption of a given money supply and substituting the idea of a 'given monetary system'. In this case, the LL curve not only represents 'the relation between income' and what Hicks calls 'the "money" rate of interest', but the elasticity of the LL curve now depends 'on the elasticity of the monetary system (in the ordinary monetary sense)'.[9]

Thus, Hicks summarizes what he terms the 'little apparatus' he 'invented':

As before, income and interest are determined where the IS and LL curves intersect–where the investment rate of interest equals the money rate. Any change in the inducement to invest or the propensity to consume will shift the IS curve; any change in liquidity preference or monetary policy will shift the LL curve. If, as a result of such a change, the investment rate is raised above the money rate, income will tend to rise; in the opposite case, income will tend to fall; the extent to which income rises or falls depends on the elasticities of the curves.

Hicks justifies using his diagram by pointing to the 'things we can get out of our skeleton apparatus'. Nevertheless, while claiming it to be just a 'slight extension of Mr Keynes's similar skeleton', Hicks mentions, albeit briefly, problems in his use of 'income' in his 'generalized General Theory' or 'suggested interpretation' of Keynes.[10]

A number of issues emerge from a careful reading of Hicks's

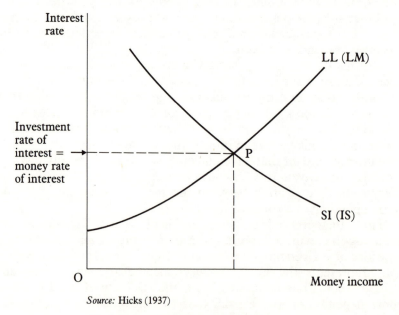

*Source:* Hicks (1937)

*Notes:* Real income appears on the horizontal axis
        only after Lange (1938), Timlin (1942)
        and Modigliani (1944)

**Figure I.1** The SILL (IS–LM) diagram (1937)

article. These concern the nature of the IS–LM diagram or, as Hicks preferred to call it, his SILL diagram: how the diagram was expressed; and how the diagram was derived by Hicks. With regard to the first point, it is clear that both the generalized SI and LL curves, and SILL diagram, are notional constructs, a mapping of composite functions onto a coordinate system, and not the diagrammatic representation of the individual functional relationships from which they are derived. The SI and LL curves can neither be actually specified nor estimated through the use of statistical techniques to obtain measures of the 'shape' and 'elasticities' of the respective curves. These must be assumed notionally. Both Hicks's construct SILL diagram and the shapes and elasticities of the SI and LL curves are the result of a series of sophisticated thought-experiments by which Hicks was able to conflate in one diagram what he took to be the 'essence' of Keynes's *General Theory*.

Briefly then, Hicks's SILL diagram rests on a simultaneous equation approach to Keynes's *General Theory*, the equations of which – when combined into notional composite functions via a series of thought-experiments – enable us to draw SI and LL curves. These curves, when mapped onto a coordinate system (which can be, and has been called 'income–interest space') then give Hicks's well-known SILL or IS–LM diagram.[11]

But the question may then be asked: how did Hicks arrive at his thought-experiments and thereby at his notional system? In addition, both Hicks's equations and the curves and diagram he based on them are expressed in nominal, i.e. money terms. And yet, the IS–LM approach that economists know – and teach – today is usually expressed in 'real' terms. How, when and why did this transition come about? Finally, what are the natures of the 'interest rate' and 'income' axes in Hicks's diagram: do they represent 'notional' or 'composite' variables, or are they, as Joan Robinson would have put it, 'fudges'?

About the second and third points one may ask: was Hicks's diagram a singular and unique representation of Keynes's *General Theory* or – in view of Solow's observation on the similarity between Hicks's, Harrod's and Meade's interpretations – was it the outcome of a more widespread contemporary approach to interpreting Keynes's *General Theory*, i.e. what can be called 'the IS–LM approach'? Furthermore, is Hicks's diagram alone to be considered the IS–LM approach, or can the IS–LM approach be said to arise from a combined equational – diagrammatic approach? Moreover, where did the equations that Hicks used to draw his curves and diagram come from? Finally, in light of Solow's observation on the equations in Hicks's, Harrod's and Meade's papers we may ask whether these equations were the product of Hicks's 'intuition' alone, or whether they were part of an IS–LM-type approach to Keynes's *General Theory* that was also held by Roy Harrod and James Meade?

### The origins and development of the IS–LM approach: puzzles and personalities

In his paper 'Mr. Keynes and Traditional Theory' which he read to the symposium on Keynes at the September 1936 Oxford meeting, Harrod asserted that there was 'no authorized version of Keynes'. As Solow noted however it was Hicks's 'suggested interpretation' that became the accepted and standard representation of Keynes's *General Theory*. In fact, since the publication of Hicks's article, both Harrod's and Meade's papers have been more or less overlooked by most observers and historians of economic thought. This is readily attested to by the distinct lack of reference to them in the literature, during the past two or three decades and even previously, for example in Hicks's 1937 article itself! On the other hand, Hicks's article is among the most cited references in the economic literature and has been reprinted often – both in collections of readings and in a number of collections of Hicks's works compiled by Hicks himself.[12]

Thus, while most economists have probably read Hicks's paper, or have at least 'looked it over', it is doubtful whether many have even looked at Harrod's or Meade's. Indeed, some economists may not even be aware that they exist, while others may not know when and where they were published. It is not surprising, therefore, that even such an astute observer as Solow would have 'discovered' the similarities between Hicks's, Harrod's and Meade's papers only recently, since neither the economics profession nor historians of economic thought have previously posed the crucial question about the main analytical and teaching tool of so many economists, i.e. what are the origins of the IS–LM approach and how did it develop?

Interestingly, the economics literature contemporary with the early interpretations by Harrod, Meade and Hicks reveals other

'IS–LM-type' approaches to Keynes's *General Theory* as early as June 1936, for example by Champernowne and Reddaway – the former in terms of both equations and diagrams; the latter, equations only. Moreover, Hicks's IS–LM diagram was already being used by Kaldor at the end of 1937 to put across Keynes's argument and refute Pigou on the problem of wages and employment. Also, by 1938 Lange had already expressed the IS–LM equations in 'real terms'.[13]

The circumstantial evidence suggests that the IS–LM approach was more widespread than even Solow realized. But, if this is so a number of puzzles appear, concerning the major personalities involved in the origins and development of the IS–LM approach. First, was there any interchange of ideas between the early interpreters of Keynes? Second, if there was, to what degree did they influence each other? Third, in view of the fact that both Harrod and Meade were part of what can be called the General Theory group – which consisted of Kahn, the Robinsons, Harrod and Meade – yet (according to Solow) they both took an IS–LM view of Keynes's *General Theory*, in contrast to the other members, we may ask whether there was a split in the General Theory group, and, if there was, did anybody notice it at the time? Finally, how did such a split influence Keynes's reaction to IS–LM, and what was his reaction to the 'IS–LM approach' which, it would seem, was actually quite widespread at the time?

### Keynes and IS–LM: acceptance or ambivalence?

In February 1937, Keynes published what was ostensibly a reply to critics of his *General Theory* – for example Robertson and Viner – who had earlier set out their critiques in the *Quarterly Journal of Economics (QJE)*. Keynes's reply has been reprinted a number of times – in abridged form – and cited often. The first part of his 1937 *QJE* article, however, and especially the concluding portion, has not been analysed in depth by historians of economic thought. After addressing his replies to the authors of the critiques published earlier in the *QJE*. Keynes wrote:

There are other criticisms also which I should be ready to debate. But tho I might be able to justify my own language, I am anxious not to be led, through doing so in too much detail, to overlook the substantial points which may, nevertheless, underlie the reactions which my treatment has produced in the minds of my critics. I am more attached to the comparatively simple fundamental ideas which underlie my theory than to the particular form in which I have embodied them, and I have no desire that the latter should be crystallized at the present stage of the debate. If the simple basic ideas can become familiar and acceptable, time and experience and the collaboration of a number of minds will discover the best way of expressing them.

Keynes then re-emphasized uncertainty as one of the cardinal elements of his *General Theory*.[14]

In September 1937, Keynes again stressed uncertainty as a central theme. Indeed, in his essay 'The Theory of the Rate of Interest' which appeared in *Lessons of Monetary Experience*, Keynes wrote that in his *General Theory*

The rate of interest and the marginal efficiency of capital are particularly concerned with the indefinite character of actual expectations; they sum up the effect on men's market decisions of all sorts of vague doubts and fluctuating states of confidence and courage. They belong, that is to say, to a stage of our theory where we are no longer assuming a definite and calculable future.[15]

Now the question immediately follows: how did Keynes initially react to the (quite widespread) 'IS–LM approach'? If he did accept it, was it on its merits, or did he tacitly agree with it to enable him to put across his 'simple fundamental' and 'basic ideas', as he called them? There have been widely divergent views about Keynes's reaction to IS–LM. Some observers – including Hicks – asserted that Keynes accepted it, while others – for example Kahn – claim that Keynes did not protest enough when it first appeared. What then *was* Keynes's considered reaction to the 'suggested, interpretation' by Hicks and others, and how, when and in what form did he express it?[16]

### *IS–LM as a case study in the history of economic thought: problems and perspectives*

In view of Solow's observations and the issues raised above, a study of the IS–LM approach is, without doubt, long overdue. But we are faced at the outset with a distinct lack of information and documentation about its origins and development. Thus, both further documentary evidence and reconstruction of events are required in order to understand the evolution of the IS–LM approach.

It is clear that more is involved here than a study of how Hicks developed his diagram. According to the conventional approach to the history of thought, that would be enough. And indeed, as we will show, Hicks's own accounts of how he came to the diagram are sufficiently problematic to pose questions about its genesis.

In my view, the emphasis should be on the origins and development of the IS–LM concept, focusing on the interaction between the people involved and the concept itself. We will ground our study of the IS–LM concept by tracing its origins and development through a variety of sources and by focusing on the IS–LM approach as a whole, rather than on IS–LM in the narrower framework of what has been called 'Hicksian economics' or the 'economics of Hicks'.[17]

To sum up, we can only attempt to determine whether IS–LM represents Keynes's central message or is, as some would call it – emulating Keynes – a chimera, after an in-depth study of the development of the IS–LM approach. To do this, however, we must deal with the nature of Keynes's *General Theory* and whether there was a split in the General Theory group. Then we will attempt to reconstruct what actually occurred at the symposium on Keynes where Hicks, Harrod and Meade gave their respective papers and it is to these issues that we now turn.

# 1

# The nature of Keynes's *General Theory*, the IS–LM papers and the Oxford conference, September 1936

## The nature of Keynes's *General Theory* and its outcome

### *The* General Theory *as chameleon*

Keynes's *General Theory* has been described in many ways, for example, as disturbing, revealing, liberating, revolutionary and even kaleidoscopic. While the last term, used by Shackle, comes close to reflecting the explicit qualitative aspect of Keynes's work, in my view the most appropriate description of it is chameleonic. I prefer this term because, while the external appearance of the *General Theory* can be deemed a constantly changing pattern, it seems to have an intrinsic versatility that changes according to its background, or that of the respective observer. Where the problem lies, then, is the lack of consensus amongst economists on the fundamental nature of the *General Theory* and its structure. This is not surprising, however, in light of the fact that those involved in the evolution of Keynes's *General Theory*, i.e. the members of the General Theory group – Kahn, the Robinsons, Harrod and Meade – and Keynes himself, did not form a homogeneous unit. This is especially evident with respect to the 'central message' they were trying to get across, as seen in the case of Keynes's change of mind about the structural nature of the conceptual model he was presenting. For example, in his 1932 lectures, Keynes claims that in a monetary economy 'all the factors are interdependent and hence simultaneous equations'. Likewise, in his 1933 lectures on 'the monetary theory of production', Keynes presented a system of equations; these equations according to him, 'showing that the rate of interest is the determining factor as to the volume of employment or the income of the community in an entrepreneur economy'. The equational system Keynes proposed in these lectures – as recorded by both Fallgatter and Bryce, who attended them in the Michaelmas term – is readily seen to be simultaneous in nature. Keynes then warns us not to overemphasize these equations since they 'are merely a means of exposition, and not a productive tool. The real tool is thought, and they are not a substitute for it, but at most a guide, or embodiment'. His caveat notwithstanding, the equational representation presented by Keynes in his 1933 lectures does go some way towards the IS–LM approach, even though this equation system cannot be found in the published version of the *General Theory*, although it appears, in somewhat different form, in the 1934 draft of the *General Theory*.[1]

The reasons for Keynes pulling back from the simultaneous equation representation of his proposed system are still not clear. Moreover, at least two members of the General Theory group – Harrod and Meade – went on to represent the 'central message' of the *General Theory* in this way in the papers they gave at the same meeting where Hicks revealed his now famous diagrammatic representation of Keynes's system. My efforts, however, have not been directed towards interpreting Keynes's *General Theory*; this must be left to the economics profession itself. What can be said at this point is that the chameleonic nature of Keynes's work seems to have enabled economists of his time – and up to the present day – to interpret the *General Theory* in a number of ways, ranging from the IS–LM approach to the post-Keynesian interpretation. Keynes's *General Theory* actually stands probably somewhere in the middle, although economists seem to disagree as to where the middle ground really is. The IS–LM approach, on the other hand, its origins and the reasons for its adoption by the economics profession, still pose questions that must be answered if economists – and the public at large – are to understand the development of modern economic thought.

### The split in the General Theory group

The story begins essentially with the General Theory group itself. In contrast to its later Oxford counterpart – Harrod's Trade Cycle group – the collection of young academics that formed the General

Theory group can hardly be said to have constituted a unified whole, either in terms of overall world-view or attitudes towards the system being developed by their collective efforts with Keynes. While there may have been consensus regarding the overall purpose of Keynes's *General Theory*, a basic cleavage existed between the members of the group over whether the approach they were developing was a determinate system which could be expressed in the form of simultaneous equations or a system fraught with uncertainty and animal spirits. The composite outcome of their divergent views can be seen in Book IV of the *General Theory* and its respective chapters, where Keynes's system swings from the investment schedule of chapter 11, to the uncertainty and animal spirits of chapter 12 and back to the determinate system of chapter 18 with its restatement of the General Theory. The split in the General Theory group, in effect, pulled Keynes in two directions at once, and thus the ambiguities and ambivalence of the *General Theory* are not surprising.[2]

An additional example of the split in the General Theory group is evident in Meade's textbook based on the *General Theory* entitled *Economic Analysis and Policy*, first published in 1936. In this book, as in his paper 'A Simplified Model of Mr. Keynes' System', Meade takes a simultaneous equation approach to the *General Theory*. Although his book does not contain a formal equation system, an equation set something like the form proposed in his 'simplified model' can be derived from his statements on the determination of income, saving, investment and the rate of interest.

Robertson seems to have been the first to notice the split in the General Theory group, and as early as May 1937. In a letter to Meade dated 25 April 1937, Robertson wrote

A pupil of mine complained to me yesterday of a passage in your book and on looking it up found that I also had complained in the margin, and had thought of raising it with you some time. On p. 73, you say 'Let's suppose that when wages fall 10%, prices fall 10% and see what happens' and the reader, always ready to oblige, says 'Right let's suppose'. Then at the bottom of p. 74 we are told that 'we have seen' that a cut in wages will only affect employment through the rate of interest. You quietly assume that you have proved something which at the time you didn't even claim to prove, but only asked us to believe for the sake of fun! The reader has been hoodwinked, the question shelved!

Meade, referred to his paper 'A Simplified Model of Mr. Keynes' System', emphasizing its treatment of wages by way of reply, to which Robertson answered, in a letter dated 9 May 1937:

Many thanks for your further explanations about wages. I think my difficulty was not with the assumption $\pi = 1$ [ $\pi$ 'measures the elasticity of expected future yields to changes in the present profitability of industry'], which seems to me the natural one to make, but with the roundabout method – assuming something will happen (the 10% fall in prices) which there's no reason to think will happen, and then saying the reverse of this situation will only happen because of a fall in the rate of interest. It seems to me that either we must tell the story step by step, in which case there is nothing wrong with the 'classical' argument (Pigou, Th. of Unemp! pp. 101–2, Viner QJE Nov'36, 162). Or we must go straight to the new position of equilibrium, in which we find the schedule of marginal efficiency of capital raised (given $\pi = 1$) as well as (probably) the rate of interest fallen. In neither case is there anything inconsistent between your result and the 'orthodox' view that employment is increased because, with the old volume of employment, there would be an excess of price over marginal cost (Cf. also Hawtrey, Capital and Employment, p. 223). I.e. once more you seem to me to be abandoning JMK rather than expounding him![3]

In an interview with James Meade some fifty years after the publication of the *General Theory*, he recounted his view of it:

I saw it as a general consistent structure; a determined system given expectations. And of course Maynard Keynes was very insistent that expectations were very variable. But given expectations, I saw it as a coherent system of simultaneous determination in a macro situation . . . I also saw it as very old hat and didn't learn anything from the book . . . I think I knew the structure of the *General Theory* broadly speaking long before the *General Theory* was published.

It was Harrod, however, who was the driving force behind the determinate simultaneous equation approach. This is evident both from his correspondence with Keynes on the *General Theory* in 1935 and in various pronouncements to the group of young Oxford dons he led from 1936 onwards (see chapter 2). For Harrod, this approach was part of a quasi-deterministic economic *Weltanschauung* as exemplified in his subsequent presidential address to Section F of the British Association in August 1938, entitled 'Scope and Method of Economics'. In this lecture, published in the September 1938 issue of the *Economic Journal*, Harrod discussed the need to derive general laws and fundamental equations in economics in order to be able both to bring about change and affect its form. Nowhere in his survey of what he termed the economic criterion; static theory; dynamic economics; and empirical studies; are the crucial role and effects of uncertainty in economics dealt with. Moreover, although expectations are mentioned, their importance is minimized. In Harrod's world-view, then, economic phenomena take place *in vacuo* or on a 'frictionless surface', unaffected by the human frailties of being vexed by uncertainty and subject to the whim of 'animal spirits'.[4]

### *IS–LM and the quest for continuity and certainty–the ideological setting*

The decade 1928–38 was – with the exception of the World Wars – possibly the most turbulent era in modern history. Indeed, as the historian David Thomson has noted, during this decade prosperity collapsed, democracy was eclipsed and peace demolished. But above all, the period was characterized by the breakdown of the liberal *laissez-faire* outlook that had developed during the century between 1830 and 1930.[5]

It is indeed a historical quirk that in what was probably the nadir of the depression, in 1931, the group of young academics called the 'Circus' – acting as Keynes's sounding-board – provided him with the initial feedback and constructive criticism he required to develop the 'central message' of what later became the *General Theory*. Between 1932 and 1936, Keynes and the General Theory group – Kahn and the Robinsons at Cambridge and Harrod and Meade at Oxford – both refined Keynes's ideas and spread the *General Theory*'s central message, developing alternate representations according to their ideological predilections.

The Cambridge branch of the General Theory group stressed the overriding revolutionary character of Keynes's ideas and their complete break with orthodox theory, emphasizing the importance of uncertainty and expectations in determining the outcome of economic phenomena. The Oxford branch, while accepting that the *General Theory* constituted a fundamental revision of economic thinking, saw it not as irreconcilable with the orthodox mainstream of economic thought, but as a substantially improved and more general way of explaining economic phenomena. According to this view, the *General Theory* could be considered as a higher stage of economic understanding in the evolution of economic thought which encompassed earlier theory, rather than a total break with previously held theory.[6]

This view is especially evident in Harrod's interpretation of Keynes's *General Theory*, ranging from his correspondence with Keynes in 1935–6 and in his subsequent paper 'Mr. Keynes and Traditional Theory', to his correspondence with Hawtrey in 1951 on the nature of the *General Theory*, and his presentation of Keynes's ideas and the 'Keynesian revolution' in his later work. It can also be seen in Meade's paper on the 'Keynesian revolution'. These examples will be discussed in detail below. Suffice it to say that this aspect of the split in the General Theory group was reflected in the reaction to the *General Theory* amongst economists, providing fertile ground for acceptance of what became known as the IS–LM approach.[7]

The published version of the *General Theory* has been described as disturbing, unsettling and even shocking to those who were not already converted or were opposed to its central message. Indeed – besides the members of the General Theory group itself – some leading economists had, by 1936, seen various drafts of chapters of the *General Theory*. A number of economists – mainly advanced research students and young lecturers – had also participated in seminars on its content held by Kahn and Joan Robinson in Cambridge or discussions on it led by Harrod in Oxford. Most economists, however, had no advance warning of what to expect from Keynes's *General Theory*, and when it was published, it brought diverse reactions, ranging from immediate acceptance of its central message and related tenets by some, to their outright rejection by others.[8]

The majority of 'working economists', however, seemingly did not know how to digest Keynes's new book and remained in a state of what may be called 'conceptual inertia' until the IS–LM approach was expounded in the papers of Harrod, Hicks and

Meade, at the symposium on Keynes's *General Theory* at the European meeting of the Econometric Society held at New College, Oxford, on Saturday morning, 26 September 1936, with the papers subsequently published in *Econometrica* and the *Review of Economic Studies* in January, February and April 1937. The reception given to the IS–LM approach was noteworthy, in so far as it rapidly became the most widely accepted representation of Keynes's *General Theory*, even though the core of the Cambridge branch of the General Theory group refused to accept its validity then and even half a century later.[9]

Briefly, the IS–LM approach was the conceptual manifestation of the quest for continuity and certainty in economics based on the predisposition towards order and determinacy which constituted the prevalent ideological tendency at the time; a reaction to the intellectual crisis brought about by the breakdown of what can be called the 'abstract ideas at the centre' that characterized the period 1830–1930.[10]

### *Keynes's 1937* Quarterly Journal of Economics *paper and the restatement of uncertainty*

In my view, the most puzzling aspect of the reaction to the *General Theory* is Keynes's 1937 *Quarterly Journal of Economics* paper; a reply to his critics and also to the reviews of the *General Theory* in the *Quarterly Journal of Economics* (*QJE*). The question which has remained unanswered, however, is why Keynes focused upon uncertainty as the main theme in his summary presentation of the *General Theory* in the 1937 paper, stressing its crucial role in economic analysis and thought.[11]

Interestingly, the most plausible explanation for Keynes's restatement of uncertainty here is implicit in Kahn's recent attack on the IS–LM approach in his book *The Making of the General Theory*. According to Kahn, 'it is tragic that Keynes made no public protest' when the IS–LM approach 'and related diagrams and algebra . . . began to appear'. But, if we assume that Keynes was aware of the implications of Harrod's and Meade's representation of the *General Theory*, to say nothing of Hicks's, then his 1937 *QJE* paper also would be addressed to them. This assumption is based on the fact that Keynes had seen the first two papers even before the September 1936 Oxford conference, as we will show, and Hicks sent the latter paper to Keynes on 16 October 1936. The *QJE* review symposium on the *General Theory*, – in which Viner, Robertson, Leontief and Taussig gave critiques – only appeared in November 1936. It is therefore highly probable that Keynes took the opportunity offered by the 1937 *QJE* paper to address not only his critics and the specific *QJE* reviews but the IS–LM approach as presented by Harrod, Hicks and Meade respectively. Keynes's re-emphasis on uncertainty as the main theme of the *General Theory* is not therefore surprising or out of place. Rather, he is pointing out the main shortcoming of the IS–LM approach which does not, and cannot, take uncertainty into account, since accepting uncertainty in the IS–LM system means that systemic equilibrium does not necessarily occur, nor is the existence of equilibrium necessarily assured, this being the outcome of all possible states of the economy, including those considered as being of a 'special' nature.[12]

In an interview with Prof. Arthur Brown – who attended the 1936 Oxford conference and was in contact with both the members of the Sub-faculty of Economics in Oxford and the members of the Institute of Statistics at the time – recalled finding the 1937 *QJE* paper 'surprising'. Upon first reading it:

I found it surprising because I thought it was stressing the thing which the circle I was in – although we were aware of Chapter 12 and animal spirits, a marvellous Chapter, and all that was part of the game – hadn't fitted into our scheme except as a general qualification – our scheme being IS–LM or something like that – a sort of Marshallian qualification of the thing which gives you the bones but is altogether too sharp and hard to represent the real world. One accepts that a four-equation system doesn't represent the real world exactly, and Chapter 12 – long-term expectations, animal spirits and uncertainty is an important gloss on this – that's all a very important qualification, but the real centre – where most parts of the *General Theory* come together – is in these four equations. I was surprised because the qualification – although one would not belittle the qualification as insignificant or gimmicky – is being raised above what we thought was the structural heart of the thing. We were surprised that the author of the *General Theory* – who had made the crucial steps of putting income into the savings function and reinterpreting the function of interest in such a way that you could write down a system which enabled you to understand the possibility of an underemployment equilibrium which didn't exist in the scheme of thought in which we had been brought up – the author of that had said, well really and truly, the most important point is that the future is totally unknown and the expectations that people form about it are influenced mostly by things that are perhaps irrelevant to it.[13]

In an interview, George Shackle gave his views on the relation between the 1937 *QJE* paper and IS–LM. With regard to the *QJE* paper, he said 'I would call it the third edition; there was the *Treatise*, the *General Theory*, and at last Keynes realized what the central nerve of his theory was and he put it in the *QJE*, and in fact, in one absolutely explosive paragraph'. When asked, Shackle also acknowledged that 'it may also be a reply to Hicks and IS–LM.' He went on to say 'I have a feeling that Keynes really came round to the realization of what his central theme was and put it down . . . he was no doubt moved to think about it again by these critiques, and having to answer the criticisms he naturally put an even more forceful version of the *General Theory* into the *QJE*.' When asked if the core of the *QJE* paper was the emphasis on uncertainty, Shackle replied 'I certainly think so.' Finally, when questioned as to whether he agreed with the contention that Keynes's basic and implicit response to IS–LM is the *QJE* article, he replied 'that is my view exactly.'[14]

What Keynes thought of the IS–LM approach, however, remains unresolved and is subject to various interpretations. This is because of his ambiguous reaction to the earlier versions of the IS–LM approach which preceded Hicks's presentation and Keynes's response to Hicks's paper itself. It would seem, therefore, that the origins of the IS–LM approach, its subsequent effect on economists, the economics profession and economic inquiry has been the fundamental enigma in the development of modern economic thought.[15]

### Keynes, Harrod, Hicks and Meade – published correspondence and the structure of the IS–LM papers

*Harrod's IS–LM paper and the Keynes–Harrod correspondence*

A close study of the Keynes–Harrod correspondence in the period prior to the publication of both the *General Theory* and Harrod's interpretation of it, namely 'Mr. Keynes and Traditional Theory', reveals that Harrod consistently advocated a synthesis between Keynes's approach to the determination of the interest rate and that of the classical theory. Harrod suggested to Keynes that if the classical savings function were replaced by a function which included both income and interest, and further, if the equilibrium levels of these variables were determined simultaneously by inclusion of the liquidity preference function, then Keynes's interest rate approach would be 'accommodated' to that of the classical theory. Keynes initially replied to Harrod's suggestions in his often-mentioned but, in my view, inadequately quoted letter of 27 August 1935. In it Keynes reproached Harrod repeatedly on these points, but to no avail. For example, Keynes saw the tendency in Harrod 'to appear to accept' what Keynes called his 'constructive part', but perceived that Harrod also attempted 'to find some accommodation between this and deeply cherished views' (i.e. the traditional theory). Keynes wrote further that he had 'only half shifted' Harrod away from the traditional theory and that Harrod was preoccupied 'with the old beliefs'. In addition, Keynes claimed that what Harrod held to be his view was a misperception, or, in Keynes's words 'a view . . . which you think to be my view'. According to Keynes, 'the main point' was that the interest rate is not 'the factor which, allowing for changes in the level of income, brings the propensity to save into equilibrium with the inducement to invest'. Rather, the interest rate 'is the price which brings the demand for liquidity into equilibrium with the amount of liquidity available. It has nothing to do with saving'. Keynes continued to rebuke Harrod, going so far as to say 'my own firm conviction is that your mind is still half in the classical world', and concluded that he hoped to be 'able to convince' Harrod 'that the classical theory of the rate of interest has to be discarded in toto, and is incapable of rehabilitation in any shape or form'.[16]

Harrod responded to Keynes's letter of 27 August in a somewhat roundabout manner on 30 August 1935, and outlined on the first page of his letter what he took Keynes's view to be, namely that investment is determined by the marginal efficiency of capital and the interest rate, and that the interest is determined by liquidity preference and the quantity of money. On this basis, Keynes replied on 10 September that he absolved Harrod of misunderstanding his theory since 'It could not be stated better than on the first page of your letter.'[17]

A year later, on 24 August 1936, Harrod sent Keynes a draft of 'Mr. Keynes and Traditional Theory'. In a covering letter, Harrod wrote that he intended to open his presentation with the caveats that Keynes was 'in no way responsible' for his 'interpretation and might not accept it', and that his paper was 'a very freehand sketch, stressing what seems to me important and not what might seem to you, not even what I think would seem to you, important in your contribution'.[18]

Keynes's response to Harrod of 30 August 1936 is somewhat problematic since, at first glance, Keynes seems to approve of Harrod's interpretation. The beginning of the letter suggests that what Harrod presents is 'instructive and illuminating', Harrod having 're-oriented the argument beautifully'. In the body of the letter, however, Keynes reiterates his 'notion of interest as being the meaning of liquidity preference which', according to Keynes, 'became quite clear' in his mind 'the moment' he 'thought of it', so that 'the proper definition of the marginal efficiency of capital linked up one thing with another.' Harrod's reply of 3 September 1936 is instructive. First, he mentions Keynes's recognition that Harrod had reoriented his theory and takes this as unqualified and complete approval, in Harrod's words 'of the form into which I have cast your theories'. It is only in the middle of Harrod's letter that we see him acknowledge Keynes's reference to liquidity preference, with 'But I probably ought to recast the part about liquidity preference to bring it more into line with your definitions.'[19]

The final form of Harrod's paper was published in *Econometrica* in January 1937. After a brief introduction to the generally accepted theory, Harrod makes the first point of his synthetic approach: in his view 'Keynes' conclusions need not be deemed to make a vast difference to the general theory . . . [since] whether they entail a substantial modification of the more general theory depends on how that is stated.'[20]

Despite Keynes's admonitions, however, Harrod constructed a system in which saving is determined jointly by income and the interest rate, and the interest rate is determined jointly by liquidity preference, the money supply and the level of income. The determination of interest rate is especially important in this respect, since while it contradicts the relationship specified by Harrod (in his letter to Keynes of 30 August 1935) as being Keynes's notion of interest rate determination, it does not contradict the form of interest rate determination advocated consistently by Harrod, both prior to the publication of the *General Theory* and over the next three decades.[21]

Harrod justifies his proposed savings function and interest rate equation by saying first that 'it may be assumed that people save a larger amount from a larger income, the relation of the amount which people choose to save to the rate of interest is a matter of controversy.' He further acknowledges that 'in Keynes' view the level of income has a more important effect on the amount which people choose to save than the rate of interest.' Harrod continues 'However, there is no need to pick a quarrel here. The rate of interest may be brought back into this part of the picture without affecting the main arguments [*sic*].' As for the interest rate equation [or, as Harrod puts it, the liquidity preference equation], Harrod claims that 'probably . . . the level of income ought to be inserted in this equation.' He is, however, fully aware that he has violated Keynes's notion of interest rate determination but justifies this by saying 'it is not necessary to give a final pronouncement on the significance of the liquidity preference equation. It appears that, even if some modification is required in this . . . equation, which determines the rate of interest, a type of analysis similar in its general structure to that of Keynes may be maintained.'[22]

Before comparing Harrod's representation of Keynes's system with the model Hicks proposed and with that of Meade, one must first find the rationale underlying Harrod's model. This is easy when we know what we are looking for, since Harrod provides us with his view of the economic world in 'Mr. Keynes and Traditional Theory'. The problem has been that few economists have bothered to read Harrod's paper carefully or compared with the system Keynes proposed in the *General Theory* itself. Harrod states his rationale in concise and lucid terms when describing his proposed system as a whole:

The matter may be put thus: the savings/interest equations suffice to determine the level of activity, subject to the proviso that the quantity of money which appears in the liquidity preference equation is a known quantity; and this will be known if the price level . . . is known. The equations in the general field suffice to determine the price level, subject to the proviso that the level of activity is known. Thus there is after all mutual dependency.

This is exactly what Harrod wanted, i.e. a system where not only do 'all the old pieces reappear', albeit 'in different places', but 'where the mutual interdependency of the whole system remains'. The interdependent and reversible nature of Harrod's symmetric savings function serves as a clear illustration of this.[23]

### Hicks's IS–LM paper and the Keynes–Hicks correspondence

Hicks did not attempt to put the mantle of Keynes's approval on his approach and straightforwardly subtitled his 1937 paper 'A Suggested Interpretation'. While Keynes admits (in his letter acknowledging receipt of Hicks's paper) that he had 'at one time . . . tried the equations', as Hicks had done, 'with income in all of them' – and indeed, in the 1934 draft of the *General Theory* we can see a symmetric form for his equations – it would seem that Keynes intuitively recognized the implications of such an approach, so that the final version of his system as it appears – albeit in literary form – in the *General Theory* is asymmetric, as will be shown below. Hicks, replying to Keynes, remained 'impenitent about including income in the marginal efficiency of capital equation', and also stressed his 'desire to separate the essential content of your theory from its formal arrangement'. Finally, Hicks wrote 'I am a convinced liquidity preference man; but I do covet some freedom of choice about the way (or ways) the doctrine shall be expressed.' In the paper itself, then, Hicks justifies the inclusion of income in all the equations of his proposed system on the basis of 'mathematical elegance', or, in other words, as Patinkin has noted, income is included in all three equations as a result of Hicks's 'advocacy of . . . symmetry'.[24]

### Meade's IS–LM paper and Keynes's system

Before counterpointing Keynes's system as presented in the *General Theory* with the systems proposed by Harrod and Hicks respectively, an additional approach – in the form of a 'simplified model of Mr Keynes' system' – must also be considered. The reason for this is straightforward. At the 1936 Oxford conference, James Meade rounded out the discussion of Keynes's *General Theory* by presenting a paper of the same title, which later appeared in the February 1937 issue of *Review of Economic Studies*. Meade's paper is important in the following respects. First, not only did he abstract Keynes's system into a two-sector model, but he also expressed it in symbolic and mathematical terms. Secondly, as in the case of Hicks and Harrod, Meade's proposed system is essentially a system of symmetrical simultaneous equations. Thirdly, the key problem again is Meade's treatment of the interest rate and investment and their place in Keynes's system, as in the Hicks and Harrod approaches to the *General Theory*. Finally, a careful perusal of Meade's paper and its mathematical appendix shows that the underlying form of his model is identical to that of Harrod and Hicks.[25]

Some four decades after presenting his paper at what was probably the most significant conference of economists this century, Meade contributed a short piece entitled 'The Keynesian Revolution' to a collection of essays on Keynes. In this essay, Meade outlined what he calls the 'essence of Keynes' intellectual' or 'theoretical revolution'. In his view, 'one rather simple and precise relationship which is the quintessence of Keynes' intellectual innovation' can be singled out. According to Meade, 'Keynes' intellectual revolution was to shift economists from thinking normally in terms of a model of reality in which a dog called savings wagged his tail labelled investment to thinking in terms of a model in which a dog called investment wagged his tail labelled savings.' While Meade's canine analogue is colourful, it must be placed in the context of his view that under certain conditions the 'savings wagging investment' model 'would hold', for example 'in a period of full employment'. It can be said, therefore, that Meade views Keynes's system as valid only 'in a period of mass unemployment'. This is seen clearly when he writes that 'the Treasury view [of the 1920s and early 1930s] was applying to conditions of mass unemployment a mode of thought that was suitable for conditions of full employment.' In Keynes's words, Meade, as Harrod, was also 'half in the classical world'.[26]

Meade's earlier paper can now be put into the context of his overview of Keynes's contribution to economics. The paper consists of two parts – text and a mathematical appendix. The connection between them, in the case of the critical 'unknown', i.e. the rate of interest, is tenuous. Furthermore, the key function in the mathematical appendix – equation 6 relating investment to income via the proportion of income saved – is both 'overburdened' and 'underspecified'. In addition, its crucial influence on the system notwithstanding, the importance of this equation is understated, to say the least. The link between these points can be seen by a close reading of the paper. First, while Meade does not specify any explicit functional relationship between investment and the rate of interest in the equational system of the mathematical appendix, such a relationship is both implied and described in the text. For example, if 'a rise in the rate of interest is necessary to preserve equilibrium as employment increases, this means that a chance increase in incomes, profits and employment would stimulate investment more than savings, so that some discouragement of investment by a rise in the rate of interest would be necessary to preserve equilibrium'. He then suggests keeping the rate of interest down to increase 'the incentive to invest' and concludes with the description of a situation where 'the rate of interest cannot . . . rise sufficiently to diminish investment.'[27]

Despite having established a link between investment and the rate of interest in the text of his paper, Meade does not specify any formal functional relationship between them in the mathematical appendix. Rather, he specifies an investment function of the form:

$$xp [x] = sY \text{ (Equation 6)}$$

where $x$ = output of capital goods, $p [x]$ = the price of a unit of capital goods, $s$ = the proportion of income saved and $Y$ = total income (I use $Y$ here, and not 'I' as Meade did), so that $xp [x]$ = 'the amount spent on newly produced capital goods', or investment. This is the extent to which he specifies both investment and savings functions, although a consumption relationship is established but not included formally in his proposed equation system (equations 1–8).[28]

With regard to interest rate determination Meade claims outright in his mathematical appendix that 'the rate of interest equals the marginal efficiency of capital' (equation 7), although in both text and equation 8 he relates the interest rate implicitly to the money supply, liquidity preference and income. For example, under certain conditions, 'in order to preserve equilibrium as employment increases . . . unless the rate of interest is kept down by an increased supply of money, the incentive to save would grow more rapidly than the incentive to invest, so that an expansion would be impossible.' Under alternate conditions, if 'a chance expansion of employment and incomes . . . increase the incentive to invest . . . much more than the incentive to save . . . an actual diminution in the supply of money would be required to raise interest rates sufficiently to maintain equilibrium'. By equating interest with the marginal efficiency of capital in his mathematical appendix, however, Meade has implicitly gone against the spirit of Keynes's *General Theory* in this respect (cf. Keynes's appendix to chapter 14 of the *General Theory*). In part III of this appendix Keynes writes: 'for investment is stimulated either by a raising of the schedule of the marginal efficiency or by a lowering of the rate of interest. As a result of confusing the marginal efficiency of capital with the rate of interest, Professor von Mises and his disciples have got their conclusions exactly the wrong way round.' Since it is doubtful whether Meade was a disciple of von Mises when writing his article or afterwards, it cannot be said that he deliberately took a line contrary to Keynes on determination of the rate of interest. His underlying position here, as on investment, must be reconstructed in light of the text of his article and his later attitudes towards both issues. In other words, we must determine 'what Meade really meant'.[29]

I have already cited some relevant text on determination of the rate of interest, in which Meade recognizes the effect of the money supply and income on interest rate. According to him, the liquidity preference schedule also affects the interest rate in a situation in which, if money supply is kept constant 'any chance increase in incomes and expenditure' brings about 'an increased volume of business activity' leaving 'less of the given stock of money to be held in excess of the requirements to finance current transactions'. In this case, 'the ratio between the value of non-liquid property and the amount of "idle money" will increase, which will cause the rate of interest to rise.' He continues 'this in itself will diminish the incentive to invest so that there is less probability that the incentive to invest will increase more than the incentive to save in consequence of any chance increase in total incomes.'[30]

With respect to the latter issue Meade states in 'The Keynesian Revolution', that 'investment is in fact influenced primarily by outside or "exogenous" influences such as the confidence and expectations of businessmen.' This, in conjunction with his linkage of investment with interest rate, provides a complete investment function along the lines of Keynes's approach in the *General Theory* itself, i.e. that investment is a function of given capital stock, the state of expectations and the rate of interest. At this point we can say that Meade sees the rate of interest as being determined by liquidity preference, money supply and income. I maintain in addition (in view of his approach in the text of his paper), that the interest rate can easily be appended to the right-hand side of Meade's investment function, that is, if this approach is taken at face value. The composite investment–savings function that results from integration of Meade's text and mathematical appendix is then

$$I = s\,(Y, i)$$

where $I$ = investment, $s$ = proportion of income saved and $Y$ = income. This composite function can be split into a savings function of the form

$$S = f\,(Y, i)$$

and an investment function of the form

$$I = \varphi\,(K, E, i)$$

i.e. that investment is determined by the interest rate in conjunction with given capital stock and the state of expectations, savings being determined by income and the interest rate accordingly.[31]

### The IS–LM paper's equational systems and Keynes's General Theory

Meade's 'simplified model of Keynes' system' can now be placed alongside the Harrod and Hicks approaches and counterpointed to the system Keynes presented in the *General Theory* according to Kahn and Joan Robinson. This is done in symbolic form in figure 1.1 Notice the identical nature of the Harrod, Hicks and Meade systems, all of which are in direct contrast to Keynes's system as interpreted by Kahn and Robinson. According to Harrod, Hicks and Meade, the equilibrium levels of interest rate, income, investment and saving are determined simultaneously, given that the quantity of money and liquidity preference are known, in addition to the marginal efficiency of capital (MEC). Or, as Harrod puts it, 'if the schedules expressing the marginal productivity of capital [= MEC] the propensity to consume and the liquidity preference are known and the total quantity of money in the system is known also, the amount of investment, the level of income, and the rate of interest, may readily be determined.'[32]

In Keynes's *General Theory* system, on the other hand according to Kahn and Robinson, interest is determined independently by function $\psi$ ; given interest, investment is determined independently

| Keynes *General Theory*, 1936 (according to Kahn and Joan Robinson) | Harrod 'Mr Keynes and Traditional Theory' (Jan. 1937) | Hicks 'Mr Keynes and the Classics' (April 1937) | Meade 'A Simplified Model of Keynes' System' (Feb. 1937) |
|---|---|---|---|
| $Y = C + I$<br>$C = f(Y)$<br>$I = \phi(\overbrace{K, E, i}^{MEC})$<br>$i = \psi(LP, \bar{M})$ | $Y = C + I$<br>$S = f(Y, i)$<br>$I = \psi(\underbrace{MEC}, i)$<br>$K, E$<br>$i = \chi(LP, \bar{M}, Y)$ | $Y = C + I$<br>$S = f(Y, i)$<br>$I = \phi(\overbrace{K, E, i}^{MEC})$<br>$i = \psi(LP, \bar{M}, Y)$ | $Y = C + I$<br>$S = F(Y, i)$ $\Big\}\ I = s(Y, i)$<br>$I = \varphi(\overbrace{K, E, i}^{MEC})$<br>$i = \phi(LP, \bar{M}, Y)$ |
| (Income in terms of 'wage-units') | | ('Nominal income' rate of money wage per head given) | |

**Figure 1.1** Equational structure of the IS–LM papers and the *General Theory*

*Notes:*

\* All three papers given at Econometric Society meeting, Oxford, September 1936.

Y = income; C = consumption; I = investment; K = capital stock;
E = expectations; S = saving; s = proportion of income saved;
MEC = marginal efficiency of capital; LP = liquidity preference;
M̄ = quantity of money; i = interest rate.

by function $\phi$ ; given investment, income and consumption are determined accordingly. In Keynes's words 'saving and investment are the determinates of the system, not the determinants. They are the twin results of the system's determinants, namely, the propensity to consume, the schedule of the marginal efficiency of capital, and the rate of interest.' Thus, contrary to Harrod's assertions, his proposed system is diametrically opposed to that of Keynes, being symmetric and characterized by interdependencies and simultaneous relations, while Keynes's is asymmetric, characterized according to Kahn and Robinson by independently determined functions and causally structured relations.[33]

The Hicks system is also characterized by symmetry, interdependence and simultaneity, in contrast to the way in which Kahn and Robinson viewed Keynes's *General Theory* system. The Hicks system, however, had been widely accepted as the 'Keynesian model', at least until 1974. For in that year Pasinetti – and Hicks himself – began to question the validity of IS–LM as the standard interpretation of Keynes's *General Theory*. In a 1976 *Festschrift* for Georgescu-Roegen, Hicks acknowledged further the conceptual limitations of his IS–LM approach as the standard Keynesian system. Things came to a head in 1980 with Hicks's 'reinterpretation' of IS–LM and presentation of it not as the standard Keynesian system but as a notional construction with limited expositional and analytical efficacy. These points will be discussed in more detail in chapter 5.[34]

Over the same period (1976–80), however, Patinkin continued to assert that the Hicks system was 'accepted' by Keynes himself and thereby valid 'as the standard interpretation of the *General Theory*'. In his view this is because 'the revealed preference of the profession is actually for the more formal [i.e. symmetric] style of presentation of the analysis that Keynes used in his 1934 draft, as against his presentation in the final form of the *General Theory*'. As we will show, however, the IS–LM interpretations were neither 'accepted' nor 'rejected' by Keynes. Rather, he preferred to remain ambivalent; and this, so as to enable the members of the General Theory group to disseminate his 'fundamental' and 'basic' ideas.[35]

### The 1936 Oxford conference and the IS–LM papers

*New textual evidence*

It is indeed strange that the events leading up to the presentation of the IS–LM papers have never been studied in detail. It may be that publication of the Keynes–Harrod correspondence in Keynes's collected writings and publication and discussion of the Keynes–Hicks correspondence, first by Hicks himself and then in Keynes's collected works, satisfied the curiosity of those who write the history of economic thought. However, as we will see, there are anomalies in the Keynes–Hicks correspondence which must be dealt with. In addition, the events surrounding Meade's paper seem to have been overlooked entirely, even though the relationship between the IS–LM papers may hinge on it.

HICKS'S PAPER

A careful rereading of the Keynes–Hicks correspondence is a good starting-point from which to identify anomalies and pose questions that have never been asked before. Indeed, the answers to these questions should throw totally new light on the development of the IS–LM approach.

In Hicks's letter of 2 September 1936 in reply to Keynes's (in response to his review of the *General Theory*), he concludes 'After a vacation spent mostly on other things, I have just been getting back to these matters, with a view to preparing for the symposium on your book which I am taking part in at the Econometric Society in Oxford at the end of the month. So it was really useful to get your letter.' Keynes answered Hicks on 8 September 1936, but received no reply until Hicks's letter dated 16 October 1936. In it Hicks writes

The scandalously long time which I have taken before replying to your last letter is mostly to be explained by the enclosed paper [the draft of which has not survived according to the editor of Keynes's collected writings]. Actually when I got your letter, I was on holiday; then, when I got back, I had to finish this paper against time; then when I had finished the paper and given it, I wanted to rewrite it; and it was not until all that was done that I felt able to reply to your letter, since the paper itself contains some portion of my reply . . . I shall be most interested to know if you disagree – with this or much of the rest of this stuff.[36]

Keynes did not answer Hicks until almost six months later when, in his often-cited reply dated 31 March 1937 he wrote: 'At long last

I have caught up with my reading and have been through the enclosed. I found it very interesting and really have next to nothing to say by way of criticism.' Keynes continued, however, 'On one point of detail. I regret that you use the symbol I for income. One has to choose, of course, between using it for income or investment. But, after trying both, I believe it is easier to use Y for income and I for investment. Anyhow we ought to try and keep uniform in usage.' Hicks replied on 9 April 1937, 'I had hardly hoped that you would be so much in agreement with it; but I am delighted to find that you are.' Hicks continued:

> I am sorry about using I for income. The fact was that I hadn't the ghost of an idea (until Dennis Robertson told me about it a couple of months ago when he read the paper) that there was any particular sanctity about Y, and that it hadn't just been drawn out of a hat. Other people, I find, are in the same case; so that I doubt if there is much chance of getting consistency in notation.[37]

The major anomaly evident in the Keynes–Hicks correspondence involves the form of the equations and notation utilized by Hicks and its relationship to that in Harrod's and Meade's papers. Another anomaly involves the degree to which information was exchanged between Keynes, Harrod, Hicks and Meade prior to the symposium on Keynes's system. Indeed, while Harrod's paper was prepared some time before the conference – for example, Keynes not only read it but commented upon it prior to its presentation – Hicks's paper was not circulated in advance. Thus, it would seem that none of the symposium's participants saw Hicks's paper before it was presented.[38]

The first question arising from these anomalies is straightforward. If the equational representation of Keynes's system in all three IS–LM papers is identical, how did this come about? Furthermore, how is it that the notation in Hicks's and Meade's papers is identical, while that in Harrod's paper is different, whereas the explicit form of equations in Hicks's paper is the same as in Harrod's? But the crucial and unasked question – indeed, the key to understanding the development of the IS–LM approach – is: did Hicks see either Harrod's or Meade's paper, or both, before the symposium, and to what extent, if any, was there an exchange of information between the authors of the IS–LM papers?[39]

Before presenting new textual evidence which answers these

questions, one point must be made clear. Hicks never claimed to have originated the IS–LM equations. Indeed, some would argue that they are already implicit in Keynes's 1933 lectures and in the 1934 draft of the *General Theory* itself. Moreover, as we will show, they can even be found in print in one form or another prior to the September 1936 conference. In addition, the IS–LM equations as they appear in Harrod's paper were seen by Keynes at least a month before the conference, and may have been the subject of discussion in Oxford as early as a month after the publication of the *General Theory* itself. On the other hand, Hicks does claim originality for the IS–LM diagram presented in his paper, but this is a separate issue that will be dealt with in more detail in chapter 3. Suffice it to say that IS–LM-type equations were part of the 'analytical tool-kit' of some economists closest to Keynes – if not Keynes himself – even before the IS–LM papers were given at the Oxford conference.[40]

In a letter to James Meade dated 6 September 1936,[41] Hicks wrote:

Dear Meade,

Harrod has asked me to send his paper on to you, and I take the opportunity of returning your own paper at the same time.

I am sorry not to have returned your paper before, but I was waiting till I saw Harrod's before I decided what to write myself, and I didn't know how much of yours I should want until then. Now I have got a good deal of my paper done, and can manage without that from now on. I am taking up a number of Harrod's points, but making my paper on the whole rather critical of Keynes. I have got some maths in my paper, and have been careful to use your symbols, so as not to cause unnecessary confusion.

As I am just going away for a holiday, I am afraid I shan't get my paper done until about 2 days before the meeting; consequently I shall be obliged to produce it out of a hat and not circulate it first. I am sorry for this, but it is not altogether my fault.

Yours,
John R. Hicks

It is evident from the letter (see figure 1.2) that not only did Hicks see both Harrod's and Meade's papers, he waited to see what Harrod had written before even starting his own paper. Moreover, not only did Hicks take up 'a number of Harrod's points', but, it would seem, Harrod's equation system also. However, as Hicks says, he used Meade's notation rather than Harrod's, i.e. 'i' instead of 'Y' for interest, and 'I' for income. Hicks's reference to 'other people' not using 'Y' for income, in his letter to Keynes of 9 April 1937, probably refers to both Meade and Harrod. While this letter provides answers to the questions posed above, it also raises the issue of the origin of Hicks's SILL diagram (see chapter 3).[42]

MEADE'S PAPER

A number of major issues concerning Meade's 'simplified model' have never been resolved. First, Keynes's attitude to Meade's paper is still a puzzle, since only his reactions to Hicks's and Harrod's papers have been published. Furthermore, while Hicks's paper was not circulated, Harrod's was, but whether Meade saw it before the conference has not been considered. In addition, whether Meade's paper was circulated prior to the conference, and the reaction to it, has never been documented. Finally, the reason for Meade's paper not appearing in *Econometrica* – in contrast to those of Harrod and Hicks – has not been discussed.[43]

To take the first point: in a postcard to Meade dated 14 September 1936, Keynes wrote 'Thanks for the copy of your paper. It's excellent. I have no criticisms to suggest.' On whether Meade saw Harrod's paper: Harrod sent Meade a note dated 12 September, telling him 'I have got another copy of this in hand. But would you keep it carefully, just in case I want another copy for any purpose between now and Sept. 26.' It seems that Meade had asked Harrod for a copy of his paper, not knowing that he had already asked Hicks to forward it to Meade after reading it.[44]

Now, while Meade saw Harrod's paper prior to the conference, he completed his own beforehand. This is confirmed by the fact that Phelps-Brown had sent Meade's paper on to Tinbergen – who attended the conference – in early September 1936. Indeed, Tinbergen's letter to Meade dated 18 September 1936 foreshadows the discussion on the stability of Meade's 'simplified model' that later took place at the symposium. In his letter Tinbergen wrote:

> Mr. Phelps-Brown was kind enough to send me a copy of the interesting paper you have prepared for the Oxford meeting of the Econometric society . . . I read it with great interest and hope to make a thorough study of it; it is very illuminating.
> I found, however, one point to which I should like to draw

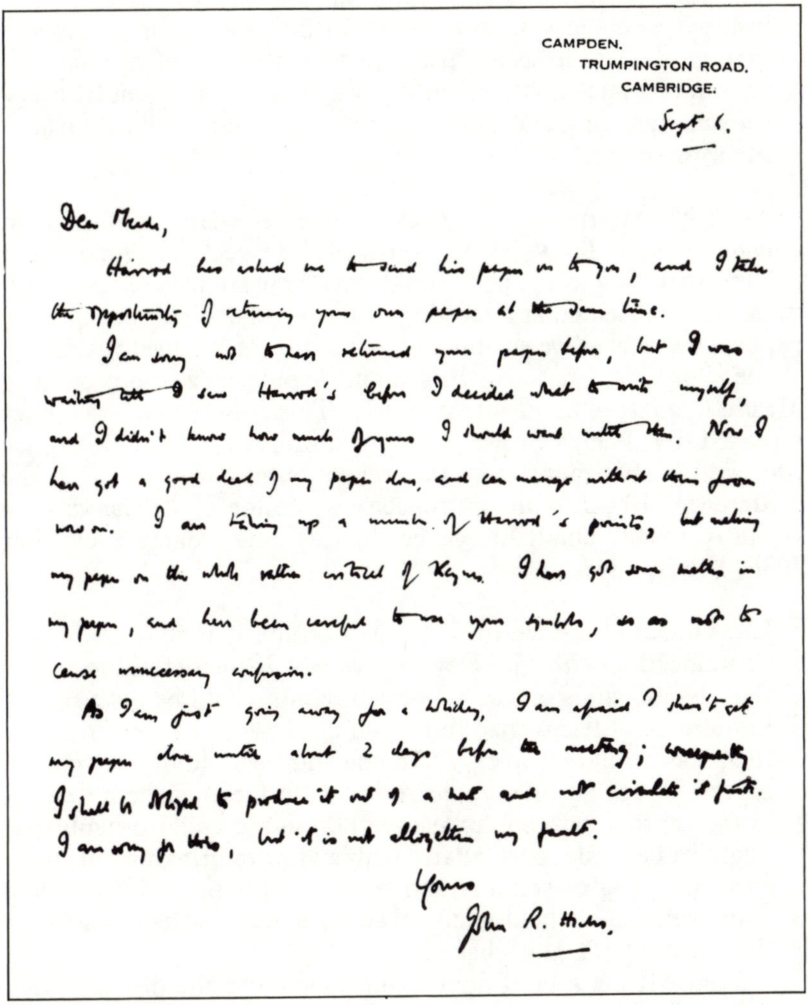

CAMPDEN.
TRUMPINGTON ROAD.
CAMBRIDGE.

Sept 6.

Dear Meade,

Harrod has asked me to send his paper on to you, and I take the opportunity of returning your own paper at the same time.

I am sorry not to have returned your paper before, but I was waiting till I saw Harrod's before I decided what to write myself, and I didn't know how much of yours I should want until then. Now I have got a good deal of my paper done, and can manage without them from now on. I am taking up a number of Harrod's points, but making my paper on the whole rather critical of Keynes. I have got some thanks in my paper, and have been careful to use your symbols, so as not to cause unnecessary confusion.

As I am just going away for a while, I am afraid I shan't get my paper done until about 2 days before the meeting; consequently I shall be obliged to produce it out of a hat and not circulate it first. I am sorry for this, but it is not altogether my fault.

Yours
John R. Hicks.

**Figure 1.2** Hicks's letter to Meade, 6 September

From the Meade Collection, British Library of Political and Economic Science,
London School of Economics

your attention. As far as I can see, your statement on the stability of the system is open to doubt. In general I deny that it is possible to determine whether a system is stable or not with the help of merely static equations. In order to solve that question one would have to know all the lags that have to be inserted into the system in order to make it dynamic. As a matter of fact, it seems possible to make out of the same system of static equations different dynamic systems of which the one shows a stable and the other an unstable equilibrium at the same point.[45]

As both Harrod's and Hicks's papers were published in *Econometrica* in January and April 1937 respectively, one could assume that Meade's paper should have appeared there also as all three were presented at a meeting of the Econometric Society. The paper, however, as we shall see, was the subject of a lively exchange at the symposium between Frisch and Meade, Frisch objecting to Meade's interpretation of stability. This discussion was later reported by Phelps-Brown in the summary of the conference proceedings, but more about this below. Some two weeks after the conference, Frisch – in his capacity as editor of *Econometrica* – wrote to Meade about his paper. In this letter, dated 8 October 1936, Frisch said:

I was much interested in your paper on the stability questions in connection with Mr. Keynes' system. If the definition and the fundamentals of the stability situation could be discussed in more exact terms than those you use in your paper, I think the paper would be an excellent one and I should be very glad to see it appear in *Econometrica*. I feel rather definitely, however, that before it appears a thorough-going overhauling ought to be made, particularly with a view to bringing out the exact meaning of stability and the assumptions under which your conclusions hold good. May I suggest that you discuss this matter with Marschak?

I am writing a brief note trying to sum up the discussions that took place at Oxford on stability. I shall probably submit this for the review of economic studies. I shall send you a copy of the MS when it is ready.[46]

The note Frisch mentioned, however, never appeared in *Review of Economic Studies* (*RES*). What did appear there was Meade's paper itself; this since Meade did not rewrite it along the lines Frisch suggested. Rather, it seems he sent it on to Ursula Hicks, then an editor of *RES*, who responded in a letter dated 30 November 1936:

> I have not written to you before about your article for the Review, because I thought you would be very busy . . . I feel I ought not to wait any longer, as we are counting on it for the next number (when we shall have a number of articles on Keynes).
>
> The point I want to write about is this. I think a good many of us felt at Oxford that at a first reading the paper was very difficult to understand. I believe it is almost entirely a matter of detail and arrangement, and if you read it over now critically yourself after an interval of a month or two, I feel sure you will agree with me. What is wanted is to clear the main text (by means of such devices as footnotes for side issues, and an appendix for mathematical working) so that the problem, argument and conclusions stand out crystal clear. As I should like to spare our readers the bother we had, and also to run no risks of their missing your really important conclusions, I am going to list a few points, but naturally I must leave the form of emmendation [*sic*] to your own judgement.[47]

This letter shows that the structure of the paper Meade gave at the symposium on Keynes was somewhat different from its published version. It is interesting to note at this point that Meade recollects his paper being turned down by Keynes for publication in the *Economic Journal* (*EJ*) because of lack of space and other considerations. According to Meade, Keynes wrote to him saying that while he agreed with it and 'that it was a true representation of the *General Theory*', he was sorry that he couldn't publish it since not only was the *EJ* 'inundated and absolutely full of commentary on the *General Theory*', but that he 'was already publishing a simplified account of the *General Theory* in the EJ', which Meade recalls Keynes said was by Reddaway. Meade now thinks that Keynes may have just been trying to put him off at the time, since Reddaway's review of the *General Theory* came out in the *Economic Record* of June 1936 (see chapter 2). In any event, no written rejection by Keynes addressed to Meade is to be found in Meade's correspondence.

More significant, however, is Meade's recollection of the development of his conference paper. According to him, he 'wrote something like it in about 1934' in draft form. He also recalls that 'When the *General Theory* came out, I wrote it up . . . I had in my mind this idea of writing a simple model of determination of employment . . . before the *General Theory* was published.' In Meade's view, 'the macro-model [in *Economic Analysis and Policy*] is not basically different in structure . . . I don't think that the thought behind that [*Economic Analysis and Policy*] differs in any respect whatsoever from the thought behind this ["A Simplified Model of Mr. Keynes' System"].'[48]

HARROD'S PAPER

The major unresolved question concerning Harrod's paper is why it was published in *Econometrica* at all. Indeed, in his letter to Harrod of 30 August 1936, Keynes wrote 'I should much like to have your paper for the E.J. My only ground for hesitation is the personal embarrassment of how much space as editor I can properly give to discussions of my own stuff. In December I am expecting something from Ohlin. Would next March be too late from your point of view?.' Harrod's reply of 3 September 1936, was 'I should be perfectly happy for it to appear in the Journal next March.'[49]

The reason for Harrod's decision to publish in *Econometrica* rather than in *EJ* is not clear. One may surmise, however, that Harrod wanted to establish the priority of his paper by its publication in *Econometrica* of January 1937, since if it were published in the March 1937 issue of *EJ*, it would have appeared at about the same time as Hicks's paper. It is interesting to compare Keynes's attitude to Harrod's paper – which he offered to publish in *EJ* – with his attitude to Hicks's paper. In his letter of 31 March 1937 cited above, Keynes writes 'I think you mentioned that the article is to appear shortly. In what journal is it coming out, Econometrica, perhaps?.' In contrast, in a previously unpublished letter to Harrod dated 7 October 1936, Keynes wrote 'I'm rather sorry that your paper is to appear in Econometrica . . . I fancy that neither Pigou nor Kahn, nor Joan Robinson take it in.' Whether Keynes was expressing regret at Harrod's paper not being published in *EJ*, or that the people mentioned would not see it since they did not subscribe to or read *Econometrica* is a moot point.

It is important to remember here that neither Keynes nor Kahn nor Joan Robinson attended the Oxford meeting at which the papers given by Harrod, Hicks and Meade respectively – according to Kahn and Robinson at least – shunted economics off the main-line message of Keynes's *General Theory* onto the 'erroneous' IS–LM track.[50]

*Participants' recollections and reactions*

THE CONFERENCE

In the October 1937 issue of *Econometrica*, Phelps-Brown reported on the Sixth European meeting of the Econometric Society which took place between 25 and 29 September 1936. This conference was attended by some sixty economists from ten countries – the majority of whom were already, or went on to become, leaders of the economics profession. Shackle, who attended, has described it as 'a momentous meeting' and a 'star-studded gathering'. A cursory glance at the attendance list published in *Econometrica* reads like a *Who's Who* of the founders of modern economics. Only a few leading figures did not attend, for example Hawtrey, Kahn and Joan Robinson, who, as Keynes noted, did not 'take in Econometrica', and Kaldor and Robertson, who were in America at the time. Keynes, according to his correspondence with Harrod, was 'reading a paper to the economic club at Stockholm on about the same date', although before preparing his own presentation, he wrote to Harrod on 30 August 1936 'But I now feel that I should like to read them your paper instead!.'[51]

Some twenty papers were presented at the conference according to the proceedings compiled by Phelps-Brown, and can be divided into seven major areas:

1 The symposium on Keynes – papers by Harrod, Hicks and Meade
2 Macrodynamics and econometric theory – papers by Frisch and Tinbergen
3 Statistical methods – regression, correlation and scatter analysis – papers by Allen, Neyman and Georgescu-Roegen
4 International trade and national income analysis – papers by Lerner, Wisniewski and Clark
5 Economic systems – structure, wages and unemployment and trade cycle theory – papers by Haavelmo, Bijl, Akerman
6 Economic measurement – cost of living, money flexibility,

income distribution and depreciation – papers by Staehle, Frisch, Champernowne, Gibrat

7 Time series and mathematical modelling – papers by Menders-hausen, Hamburger, Bolza.[52]

The largest group of participants came from the London School of Economics (LSE) and University of London [18], and the second largest from Oxford – the University and Institute of Economics and Statistics [11]. Cambridge was represented by only about half that number [5], those attending being mathematically inclined faculty members and research students. British participants also came from Manchester, Leeds, Aberdeen and Exeter. Only two participants from the United States attended, but European participation was significant, composing a third of the conference. The largest European contingent was six Dutch – including Tinbergen; followed by four Poles – including Michal Kalecki; three Swiss; two Norwegians – including Frisch; two French; and two Swedes – including Lindhal. Italy and Austria were represented by one participant each, but these were the well-established economists del Vecchio – who was on the council of the Econometric Society – and Bolza.[53]

The overall role of the 1936 conference in the development of modern economic thought is problematic, for while it can be considered to have provided a blueprint for teaching and research that extended over the next half-century, its importance has been almost completely overlooked by most economists – including a few who even attended the conference itself. On the one hand, illustrations of the former case can be seen in Colin Clark's recollection that he had discussed quarterly economic models at the conference with Harold Barger, while Shackle recollects Harrod gathering a group around him for an informal discussion of his view on the trade cycle, but more about this below.[54]

On the other hand, Lachmann came away disappointed from the symposium on Keynes, while Phelps-Brown, some fifty years later, was surprised that the 1936 Econometric Society meeting held 'an important place in the history of economic thought', this due in part to his 'not having been able to enter at the time into the discussion of theory', his interests being 'in statistical applications and enquiries'. It is understandable then, that in his report of the conference proceedings in *Econometrica* in October 1937, Phelps-Brown's summary of the symposium on Keynes, for example, is quite brief. After first outlining Meade's paper, already published in the *Review of Economic Studies* nine months previously, he describes briefly the discussion on stability that followed Meade's paper. But the most curious aspect of his report is his treatment of the other two papers presented, namely 'contributions to the symposium by R. F. Harrod (Christ Church, Oxford) and Dr J. R. Hicks (Gonville and Caius College, Cambridge), have been published in Econometrica.' Whether the 1936 conference as a whole, and especially the symposium on Keynes, were simply academic exercises, can only be answered by focusing on the symposium itself, the reactions of those who participated and the effect of the IS–LM papers on subsequent developments in teaching and research. It is to the symposium on Keynes's *General Theory* and the IS–LM papers, therefore, that we now turn.[55]

THE SYMPOSIUM

Textual evidence

The symposium on Keynes's *General Theory* opened the conference on Saturday morning, 26 September 1936. Harrod presented his paper first, followed by Hicks and then Meade. Four main themes for discussion arise from the IS–LM papers and their characteristics:

1 the presentation of Harrod's and Hicks's papers;
2 Harrod's comment on Hicks's paper;
3 the discussion on stability; and
4 participants' recollections of and reactions to the papers and the symposium.

With regard to theme 1: while the published versions of Harrod's and Hicks's papers have been placed in comparative perspective above, how they were actually presented at the symposium on Keynes must also be considered. The reasons for this are clear. First, the papers as delivered constituted the respective authors' interpretations of the central message of Keynes's *General Theory*. Secondly, the papers presented were the raw versions of the IS–LM approach before being revised or rewritten for publication, with only one of the respective approaches – the diagram in Hicks's paper – being the object of almost immediate and overwhelming acceptance and recognition, while the similarity between the equational representation in Harrod's and Hicks's papers seems to have been overlooked entirely at the time.

It is indeed fortunate for the history of economic thought that at least one conference participant who attended the symposium on Keynes's *General Theory* took notes. This material has been found in a notebook of Prof. A. J. Brown, who – having then just taken his degree in economics at Oxford – was in the advantageous position of recording what occurred with the enthusiasm and detail of a new member of the economics profession (see figure 1.3).

According to Brown's notes, Harrod first presented the traditional theory of interest in terms of demand and supply equations, using the symbol y for marginal productivity of capital and $y'$ for the interest rate, where, according to Harrod, $y = y'$; he used x for the amount invested per unit time. Harrod stressed that in the traditional theory, income was assumed constant. Harrod then presented an equation of the form

$$x = \phi (y, i)$$

which according to him could also be expressed as

$$i = \psi (x, y)$$

where i indicates income, which he maintained was the multiplier equation. Harrod then asserted that 'Keynes lets y drop out' of this equation. He next presented an equation of the form

$$y' = \chi (m)$$

which he claimed could also be expressed as

$$y' = \chi (m, i)$$

where m is the quantity of money.[56]

Brown's notes on Hicks's paper show that Hicks presented an equation of the form

$$Ix = F (I\ i)$$

where Ix is value of investment, I is income and i is interest rate; and an additional equation of the form

$$M = L (I, i)$$

where M is the given quantity of money. Brown drew the diagram Hicks presented in terms of the intersection of CC and LL curves, with maximum income and minimum interest rate marked off, the quantity of money being given. Again, according to Brown's notes, Hicks made the point that the relative importance of C1C2 (which

Brown noted was the marginal efficiency of capital) and L1L2 'in determining i and I depends where p (their point of intersection) is'. Hicks also stressed, according to Brown's notes, that 'in general, we could put i and I in all three equations . . . Keynes does not put I in 2 [the investment equation].'[57]

In an interview, when asked whether Hicks drew his diagram on the blackboard, Brown replied 'My impression would be yes, but it's possible that it was in the paper . . . we may just have followed what he was saying from the paper, that's very possible. But the IS and LM curves were physically present in some form.' It is important to point out here that the diagram in Brown's conference notes does not appear in the published version of Hicks's paper. Rather, it can be said to be a fusion of figures 2 and 3 that appear in the published paper, or, as Hicks would probably put it, a 'conflation' of these figures. Hicks's CCLL diagram, then, seems to predate the SILL diagram which has come to be accepted conventionally as the original generalized version of Hicks's diagram. The significance of Hicks's 'conflationary approach' to diagrams will be seen in chapter 3.[58]

A photoreproduction of Brown's original notes appears below (figure 1.3). From these, it would seem that the similarity between the equations in the respective papers – equations which are identical in form except for the difference in notation – should have made at least some impression on the participants. According to Arthur Brown, however, it was Hicks's diagram that struck the participants' fancy; so much so that the diagram became the main talking-point, rather than either Harrod's or Meade's equational representation of Keynes's *General Theory*, but more about this later.[59]

What Brown has called 'the sting in the tail' of Harrod's paper, that is, the introduction of a dynamic outlook to what is essentially a non-dynamic framework, was emphasized by Harrod in his comment on Hicks's paper. This′ was recorded by Brown as 'Harrod thinks that not I but dI/dt should be in 2 [Hicks' investment equation]'. Harrod had received earlier encouragement in this regard from Keynes in his letter of 30 August 1936 'I also agree with your hints at the end about future dynamic theory.' Hicks, however, got his own back when he concluded his published paper with a different 'sting in the tail', i.e. when he wrote '*The General Theory of Employment* is a useful book, but it is neither the beginning nor the end of Dynamic Economics.'[60]

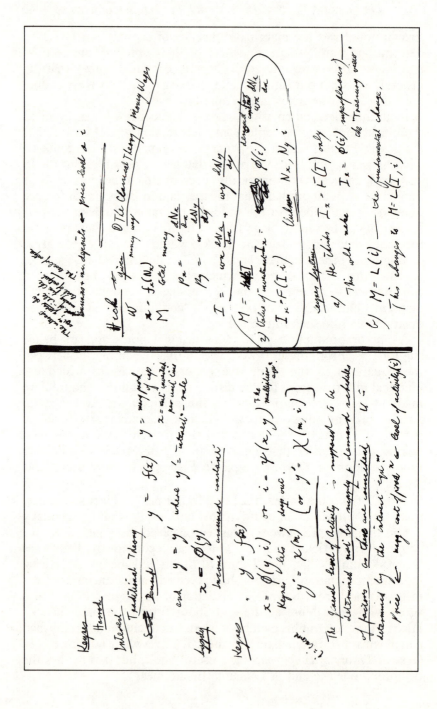

Keynes
Harrod
Interest

Traditional Theory

Demand    $y = f(x)$    $y$ = marg prod

and $y = y'$ where $y'$ = interest-rate
$x$ = act invested per unit Cost

Supply    $x = \phi(y)$
Income amongst saving?

Keynes    $y = f(x)$
$x = \phi(y, i)$   or   $i = \chi(x, y)$  The multiplication eqn
Keynes lets $y$ drop out.
$y = \chi(M, i)$   [or $y' = \chi(M, i)$]

The general level of activity is supposed to be
determined not by supply & demand schedules
of factors   (or these are considered)   $y =$
determined by the interest "eqn"
Price ← marg cost/prod ← level of activity(x)

Hermes + we depends ← price level & $i$

# Hicks → gives   ① The Classical Theory of Money Wages

$W$   money wage
$x = f_1(N_x)$
$M$   total money

$P_x = w \dfrac{\partial N_x}{\partial x}$

$P_y = w \dfrac{\partial N_y}{\partial y}$

$I = w \dfrac{\partial N_x}{\partial x} + w y \dfrac{\partial N_y}{\partial y}$

1) $M = MkT$
2) Value of investment $I_x = \phi(i)$ .   $\dfrac{\partial N_x}{\partial x}$

$I_x = F(I \cdot i)$    Unknown $N_x, N_y, i$

Keynes System

a) He thinks $I_x = F(I)$ only    $I_x = \phi(i)$ superfluous
This will make    the "Treasury" view.

c) $M = L(i)$ — the fundamental change.
This changes to $M = L(I, i)$

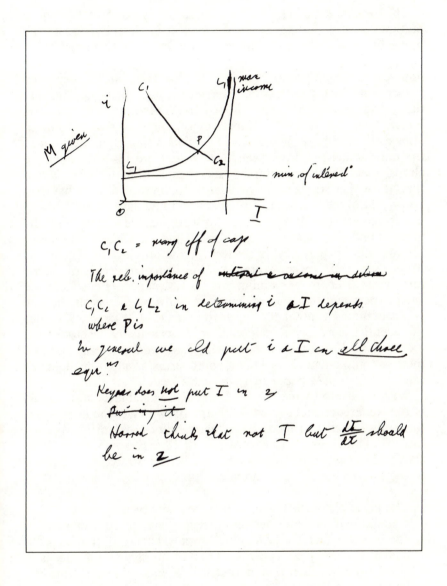

Figure 1.3 Pages from Prof. Arthur J. Brown's notebook, showing notes he made during the symposium on Keynes's *General Theory*, in September 1936

The reason for Hicks's acid remark at the end of his paper becomes clearer perhaps when we look at his introduction to the first edition of *Value and Capital*, published some two years later. Here, Hicks writes 'When I began to work on *Capital*, I had the hope that I should produce an entirely New Dynamic Theory – the theory which many writers had demanded, but which none, at that time, had produced. These hopes have been dashed, for Mr. Keynes has got in first.' Interestingly, there is no mention of Hicks's IS–LM paper in *Value and Capital*, although his account of the development of *Value and Capital* and the IS–LM paper are almost identical. For example, Hicks states in *Value and Capital* that 'the earlier stages of my own work are on record, for what they are worth, in three articles written before I saw the *General Theory*.' The three articles Hicks referred to were his 1933 paper 'Gleichgewicht und Konjunktur' ('Equilibrium and the Trade Cycle'), and his two 1935 papers 'A Suggestion for Simplifying the Theory of Money', and 'Wages and Interest – the Dynamic Problem'. Some forty years later, in 'explaining' his IS–LM paper, Hicks cited the 1935 papers and his 1936 review of the *General Theory* as the key stages in the conceptual development of his IS–LM paper. Whether this identity is simply coincidental or Hicks actually developed the ideas behind *Value and Capital* and IS–LM simultaneously and saw them as complementary is a moot point, since, as noted, he does not refer to his IS–LM paper in *Value and Capital*.[61]

With regard to theme 2 – the discussion on stability in his report of the conference proceedings – Phelps-Brown gives the impression that only Frisch had focused on the stability problem in Meade's case. In Tinbergen's letter to Meade of 18 September 1936 (cited above), however, the stability question was illustrated by reference to the case of market demand and supply:

> The principle of the question may be easily seen in the case of a single market described by a (negatively sloping) demand curve and a (positively sloping) supply curve. If the lag of demand behind price is zero and that of supply behind price is a finite period, then this market will be in stable equilibrium when the slope of the demand curve is greater than that of the supply curve. If, however, supply adapts itself immediately to price and demand shows a finite 'lag' then stability of equilibrium is only present when the slope of the demand curve is less than that of the supply curve.[62]

After reporting Frisch's summary of the discussion, Phelps-Brown gave an illustration of 'supplementary assumptions regarding the behaviour of the system' in order 'to distinguish between a stable and an unstable equilibrium':

> For example, in the well known diagram of supply and demand, if one set of supplementary assumptions is adopted, the equilibrium will be stable or unstable according as
>
> $$D' \gtrless S'$$
>
> and if another set of supplementary assumptions is adopted the equilibrium will be stable or unstable according as
>
> $$D' \lessgtr S'$$
>
> where $D'$ and $S'$ are the derivatives of the functions that express the quantities demanded and supplied respectively as depending on the price.

Since this is almost a verbatim restatement of the point Tinbergen made in his letter to Meade prior to the symposium, it would seem that not only Frisch, but Tinbergen, took part in the discussion that Phelps-Brown reported.[63]

Some thirty-five years after the publication of his paper, Hicks made what is, in my view, the most understated caveat in the history of economic thought. In his 'Recollections and Documents' published in 1973, Hicks recounted – among other things – some of the events leading up to the publication of his IS–LM paper and provided a retrospective critique of both its shortcomings and that of Keynes's *General Theory*. After comparing himself to Bernardo in *Hamlet*, Hicks continued:

> So I think I must first chatter about those old things . . . For there is a good deal about them which has not appeared in print; and some documents about them, which I possess, and which are not without interest. I have tried to reconstruct the story with the aid of those documents, but have not found it easy. Memory is treacherous; I have found dates on some of them which did not square with what I thought I remembered. It seems however to come out as I shall describe.

Hicks then published Keynes's letter to him of 31 March 1937 and stated

> I think I may conclude from this letter (as I have always done) that Keynes accepted the SILL diagram as a fair statement of his position – of the nucleus, that is, of his position. That, in any case, was what it was meant to be – a means of demonstrating the nature of the difference between Keynes and his predecessors – not a statement of what I believed myself.[64]

What Hicks actually believes is given in a most illuminating conclusion: 'For now, at greater distance, we find (I believe) that the *General Theory* loses stature, while the *Treatise*, in spite of its eccentricities, grows. The *General Theory* is a brilliant squeezing of dynamic economics into static habits of thought. The *Treatise* is more genuinely dynamic, and therefore more human.'[65]

The passage quoted above, however, shows that Hicks overlooks the fact that, in *Value and Capital*, he says that 'Mr. Keynes has got in first' as regards the development of 'an entirely New Dynamic Theory'. If a degree of selective memory on the part of Hicks is indeed the case, then in order to obtain a clearer picture of the symposium and its immediate effect upon the economics profession, we must turn to the recollections of the participants themselves and their reactions to the IS–LM papers.

## Recollections and reactions

The half-century 1936–86 brought about fundamental changes on a global scale and for the individual living through this most turbulent period of modern history. With so much having happened, it is not surprising that the 1936 conference and the symposium on Keynes's *General Theory* were more or less forgotten by most of those who deal with the history of economic thought and even by a few people who attended the conference itself. But some participants seem to recall both specific incidents that occurred and their own and others' reactions to the IS–LM papers. Before presenting material collected from interviews and correspondence with surviving participants, one thing must be emphasized. As Hicks noted, 'Memory is treacherous.' It is also, in most cases, selective. Thus, we cannot consider the material presented below as providing a full and detailed account of an event that has not been documented previously, even by those who actually participated in it. The material, however, constitutes the only available supplementary evidence – tenuous though it may be – of the perceptions of the conference and the symposium on Keynes's *General Theory*, of those economists who actually attended.

Of some sixty economists who attended the conference, we were able to contact fifteen surviving participants. Of these, James Meade, George Shackle, David Champernowne and Arthur Brown were interviewed. Other participants provided either written accounts of what they remembered and their general impressions of and reactions to the conference and the IS–LM papers – Phelps-Brown, Hicks, Lachmann, H. Robinson, Bretherton and Clark – or simply did not recall specific details either of the symposium on Keynes or of the entire conference and claimed that they were unable to be of much help – Tinbergen, Hitch, Cohen, Bowley, Makower. In addition, while Kaldor did not attend the meeting – as he was in America at the time – some of his recollections concerning the development of the IS–LM approach throw new light on Hicks's paper and so the relevant material is presented here. Finally, while the recollections of the late Sir Roy Harrod and Prof. Abba Lerner – two personalities who made major contributions to the development of the IS–LM approach and its acceptance by the economics profession – are unavailable, others who attended the symposium – for example Arthur Brown and George Shackle in the case of Harrod, and Ludwig Lachmann in the case of Lerner – seem to recall the reactions of Harrod and Lerner respectively to Hicks's diagram and the symposium on Keynes's *General Theory* as a whole. These reactions – as seen through the eyes of their contemporaries – will also be reported here.

While the symposium on Keynes opened the conference proceedings on Saturday 26 September 1936, participants started to arrive on Friday, 25 September. Champernowne recalled travelling to Oxford with Ursula and John Hicks from Cambridge, as Hicks himself recalls. The conference fee, paid to Henry Phelps-Brown, was 3s 6d, and the IS–LM papers, it would seem, were circulated to participants upon registration according to Arthur Brown, who remembers reading Hicks's and Meade's papers only the night before the symposium. Brown recalls thinking at the time that the former 'took one farther' than Harrod's equation system, which Brown asserts was presented by Charles Hitch in Hilary term, 1936, to students in his revision class in Oxford (see chapter 2).[66]

The symposium on Keynes was, in effect, the plenary session of the conference, and according to those who were there, attendance was most impressive. The speakers were assisted by a blackboard that, in a later session, became the focus of a 'dramatic incident' when, according to Arthur Brown, it collapsed upon Tinbergen's reference to systemic instability when he was presenting his paper, to the amusement of all present. The blackboard played another role – albeit a minor one – in the exchange between Meade and Frisch on stability. According to Meade, after giving his paper, Frisch questioned the stability of his simplified model asking 'is it stable or not? . . . we must consider the stability of the system.' Meade remembers then having what he calls

> a terrific argument with Frisch, with Hicks watching us over his shoulder and giggling at us . . . I said 'these curves, as far as they are curves, all slope the right way'. I'm no mathematician and didn't know much about stability, so I got into a great argument about it . . . Frisch and I were near the blackboard and I said 'now look, if you have a saucer and you put a little ball in it, it will roll down to the bottom and that's stable. And if you turn the saucer upside down and just balance it [the ball] on the top, it's unstable, and if you put it [the ball] on the table like this, it's neutral.' And so I gave Frisch, this great man, this great lecture. And he said, 'it's no good. You must think of a clock with a pendulum swinging you see' . . . and he tried to teach me what stability was actually about. And I said 'that's irrelevant.' And Hicks said 'go on James, go on James, don't give in.' Anyhow, Frisch finally decided that it wasn't worth his while. But Hicks encouraged me. He knew what Frisch was saying but he was having fun and wasn't going to let Frisch knock me out.[67]

Meade's reaction to Harrod's and Hicks's papers is significantly different. In the former case, he had seen the paper before the symposium on Keynes and the material paralleled his own approach. In the latter case, Hicks had indeed pulled something out of a hat – the diagram – although the equations he used may have been 'borrowed' from Harrod's paper and the notation from Meade's. According to Meade, the IS–LM diagram 'did not affect me very much till later. I think it is a very neat and meaningful way of putting the thing . . . it very nicely put the two sides together', but he goes on 'I still feel that we are all saying the same thing. Hicks' is more elegant than mine and Roy's; it is a great teaching device but may oversimplify things.' When asked about Keynes's attitude and Kahn's delayed reaction to IS–LM, Meade replied to the effect that Kahn means Hicks's system is 'too mechanical' and 'too neat', and 'it may very well be that Keynes 1937 paper is his reaction to IS–LM being too mechanical', this, according to Meade, being characteristic of Keynes's 'reaction to any precise mechanical model'. In any event, Meade admits that at the time he was 'not aware of the great importance Keynes was putting on un-certainty'.[68]

Another conference participant was Herbert Robinson, an Oxford contemporary of Arthur Brown and George Shackle, who was a twenty-two-year old doctoral student at the time. Robinson recalls that his own 'reactions at the time and since'

> might be summarized as follows: 1. Keynes succeeded in jolting economists into questioning whether classical economics really reflected reality in a world which seemed to have established an equilibrium with mass unemployment instead of full employment; 2. He succeeded in making us look at the economy as a set of simultaneous equations whose solution could include such an undesirable equilibrium if government fiscal and monetary variables were set at inappropriate levels; 3. The symposium was concerned more with the structure of Keynes' new model of the economy than with his judgment of the nature of the causal relationships postulated. His vast practical experience intimidated primarily academic theor-eticians from questioning this aspect of his work.

Robinson's second point doubtless reflects his acceptance of the contemporary position advocated by Harrod, Hicks and Meade in their IS–LM papers.[69]

Ludwig Lachmann, for his part, recalls not only his reaction to the symposium on Keynes but that of Abba Lerner and others. Because of its importance to the history of economic thought, his recollection of the period is quoted here in full:

> Let me start by sketching my personal background as an economist. I came to the meeting as a bewildered reader of the *General Theory* in order to learn more about it. I found most

people there, some of whom I knew, in the same state. I had been at the London School of Economics since April 1933 and worked under Hayek. Like almost everybody else there I was an 'Austrian'. I knew we were going through a 'bad stretch'. Such giants as Knight and Sraffa had turned against us. I disagreed with Hayek on some points. He admired Pareto, I didn't. (I still don't.) I thought H. failed to pay enough attention to (divergent) expectations.

I had brought from Germany the impression that Keynes was an 'eccentric', and found this confirmed at LSE. I had read GT in February/March 1936 and at first understood very little, but realized Keynes said something of importance about expectations. This roused my sympathy and I wanted to learn more. I found Chapter 12 fascinating. By September I had formed some idea of what GT was about.

My expectations of finding more enlightenment at Oxford were not fulfilled. No doubt it was my fault. I don't recall congratulating Hicks at dinner, but this means little. I knew him from LSE and had been in his Advanced Econs. course in 1934/5, his last year at LSE. He was the most fascinating of my teachers there, the only one willing to discuss futures markets! So I would want to say something courteous and encouraging.

I came away unimpressed by Hicks' paper. Everybody knew Harrod and Meade belonged to the 'inner circle' of Keynesians (we did not as yet call it 'the circus'), but Hicks did not. So we were probably looking for a sophisticated critique which did not come.

I spent a good deal of these September days in the company of Lerner who also was unimpressed. I knew him from LSE. Since he had been converted to the Keynesian faith by Joan Robinson herself he was my mentor in matters Keynesian in those early days. At LSE we all trusted his judgement (in economics, not in politics!)

An episode at Oxford I vividly remember is how Lindhal, talking to a few of us, told us, so far as he understood Keynes, his marg. efficiency of capital was exactly what Wicksell had meant by his natural rate of interest. So, why was he now so fierce on Wicksell and Wicksellians? He spoke with a mixture of sadness and irony.

You have to remember that the economists' world of 1936

was still an 'open' world in which men were used to making up their own minds. There were schools of thought and disputes among them, but there was no orthodoxy with its textbooks. (The few there were were held in low regard.) There was a handful of econometricians, but they tried to persuade their fellow economists, by argument if not by figures.

Nobody I spoke to at Oxford thought of the meeting as a 'new departure'. That a natural dissident like Hicks should unwittingly have spun the thread of a new orthodoxy he has long since come to disdain is indeed an irony of the history of econ. thought!

I came away from Oxford no less bewildered than I had gone there, but also with a more distinct feeling that there was a good deal of interesting things to be found in that Keynesian world which at first glance had struck me as so strange.[70]

Lachmann's 'memories of these autumn days in Oxford' raise a number of very important points about the development of the IS–LM approach and its aftermath. First, Lachmann's disappointment with Hicks's critique confirms the problematic nature of Hicks's paper and its relation to the other IS–LM papers. Secondly, the fact that Lerner was also 'unimpressed' by Hicks's IS–LM representation explains Lerner's efforts to proceed further and develop an even more general approach to Keynes's system (see chapter 3). Thirdly, Lachmann's recollection of Lindhal's discussion of Keynes and Wicksell with some of the conference participants, throws new light on Hicks's comment about the relationship between their respective theories.[71]

In his IS–LM paper, Hicks develops what he claims is a 'generalized *General Theory*'. He then goes on to say that 'when generalized in this way, Mr. Keynes' theory begins to look very like Wicksell's; this is of course hardly surprising.' Hicks here refers to Keynes's account in the *General Theory* of the parallel between his *Treatise* approach to interest and Wicksell's. Hicks continues 'There is indeed one special case where it fits Wicksell's construction absolutely . . . if IS is horizontal, we do have a perfect Wicksellian construction; the investment rate [of interest] becomes Wicksell's natural rate.' Hicks's attempt to reconcile his version of Keynes's *General Theory* approach with Wicksell's probably stems from Lindhal's comment and Hicks's familiarity with Lindhal's views (he had already met Lindhal in London in both 1934 and 1935) and with Myrdal's work, which was duly cited in the published version of his paper. Lindhal's reference to Keynes being 'fierce on Wicksell and the Wicksellians' refers to the attack that starts on the very page of the *General Theory* that Hicks cites in support of his identification of the parallel elements in the two approaches. Hicks's position here cannot be explained except by recalling his positive attitude towards the *Treatise*, and his negative one towards the *General Theory*, which he recounted thirty-five years after his IS–LM paper was published.[72]

Finally, Lachmann recalls that 'Nobody I spoke to at Oxford thought of the meeting as a "new departure" . . . I came away from Oxford no less bewildered than I had gone there.' This would suggest that participants either recognized the identical nature of the IS–LM papers presented at the symposium on Keynes (some – mostly from Oxford – had known of Harrod's equations) or realized that the equations in the papers were similar in nature to Keynes's 1933–4 lectures. What was 'new' and became the talking-point among participants after the symposium, according to George Shackle and Arthur Brown, was 'the diagram'. Before reporting their accounts of Harrod's activities at the meeting, his reaction to the attention given to the diagram and their own views of IS–LM let us turn briefly to Kaldor's recollection of a discussion he had with Hicks in Cambridge after his return from America, and which took place between the September 1936 meeting and the subsequent publication of Hicks's paper in April 1937.[73]

In the first note to his published IS–LM paper, Hicks wrote that it was 'based on a paper . . . read at the Oxford meeting . . . and which called forth an interesting discussion. It has been modified subsequently, partly in the light of that discussion, and partly as a result of further discussion in Cambridge'. Hicks, however, does not mention with whom he discussed his paper, and it has remained a moot point, since Hicks was not part of the Cambridge branch of the 'inner circle of Keynesians', as Lachmann put it. The person Hicks discussed his paper with in Cambridge belonged to the group of economists assembled by Robbins and Hayek at the LSE (Hicks was a former member) and was none other than Nicholas Kaldor, at least according to Kaldor himself. In an interview, Kaldor, asked when he first saw the IS–LM diagram, remembered coming to Cambridge sometime after his return from America and being shown the diagram by Hicks. Since he had not attended the Oxford conference the diagram was totally new to him. Kaldor recalled his meeting with Hicks in Cambridge and his initial reaction to the diagram:

> I stayed there a weekend and he showed me this diagram and I was duly impressed by it . . . because it separates the monetary side and the real side very neatly . . . Hicks didn't put it forward as containing a new idea. He didn't put it forward as a new theory at all but simply as a way of representing Keynes's *General Theory*; a way that is under-standable.

It is important to note that Kaldor was among the first to apply the IS–LM diagram in economic analysis: he used it to represent Keynes's approach in refuting Pigou's arguments against Keynes in the December 1937 issue of the *Economic Journal* (see chapter 3). At this point let us turn to the recollections of Shackle and Arthur Brown about Harrod's activities at the Oxford conference and his reaction to the 'diagram'.[74]

In his book *The Years of High Theory*, Shackle refers to an incident involving Harrod, which occurred after the symposium on Keynes but which has never been dealt with in detail. According to Shackle's published account 'After his paper, Sir Roy was asked whether, when he used the expression "output is increasing" he meant "output has been increasing" or "output is expected to increase".' But Shackle continues that Harrod 'was thinking in terms of physical mechanics, "dynamics" in the sense of forces bearing on a particle and would at that time have nothing to do with ex-ante and ex-post. Physical analogies could still channel the thought of a brilliantly originative mind.'[75]

In an interview, Shackle provided both the background to and context of the Harrod incident. According to Shackle:

> Harrod had just written a book on the trade cycle . . . and after his talk was explaining his growth theory, which he already had in mind in an embryonic form . . . this occurred after the lecture when we were in a little group in a little room informally seated . . . some standing, some seated. And he used these words 'suppose output is growing' and immediately someone said to him 'do you mean that output has been growing or that it is going to grow?'. And Harrod immediately said 'I mean output is growing'. He wouldn't accept the need

for an ex-ante, ex-post distinction at that moment at any rate
. . . he was trying to explain his growth theory . . . and he
rejected the question and he went on . . . Harrod certainly
wasn't a man who wished to demolish the structure of
economics as a systematic orderly body of knowledge . . . he
went in for a simple condensation of ideas. I think Keynes's
work was a great release for Harrod . . . Hicks had an exact
mind and a great skill and ingenuity in building a model and in
putting it together like a watch. Harrod, I think was the more
rudimentary . . . a man with a mind capable of bolder leaps as
it were. My belief is that Harrod seized on the *General Theory*
and he found it stimulating and suggestive and he wrote *The
Trade Cycle* on the basis of it. Harrod did Keynes a great
service because he showed how these ideas could be made into
a new dynamic theory. Harrod came to the conference with a
little green leaflet about his book *The Trade Cycle*, and *The
Trade Cycle* was already out . . . and he was full of it of course
and I dare say that he really didn't think that there was any
sharp dividing line between the *General Theory* and his trade
cycle book . . . and there wasn't, because he really did use
some of those ideas . . . Harrod was explaining what you
could call his growth theory or his trade cycle theory . . .
they're really the same thing . . . I think it is fair to say that
Harrod had come to the meeting to try and expound and
present his growth and trade cycle theory.[76]

Arthur Brown's recollections support Shackle's view of the
rationale of Harrod's activities at the conference and go even
further, providing us with some insight into Harrod's reaction to
the success of 'the diagram'. When asked if he thought that Harrod
may have been upset that Hicks's diagram was so successful, to the
detriment of *The Trade Cycle*, Brown replied:

I'm sure . . . I'm sure he was. I mean the word went round
. . . Charley Hitch remarked that Harrod was peeved that
nobody in Oxford appeared to be reading his great book on the
trade cycle. This must have been in the Autumn of '36, I
suppose, because I think the book came out about September
or thereabouts . . . I wasn't aware of a great splash made by
*The Trade Cycle* in Oxford, whereas the Hicksian IS–LM
thing had made a considerable splash.

Brown continued:

> It . . . became part of the ordinary discourse about Keynes in
> the circle in which I was moving, which was the [Oxford]
> Institute of Statistics, that is to say, Marschak and Marian
> Bowley and Hitch and Bretherton . . . it was accepted as
> containing as much of the *General Theory* as we chose to
> absorb at that time . . . there was an awful lot to absorb in the
> *General Theory*.

Brown added:

> I think . . . he was sad because the book . . . *The Trade Cycle*
> didn't make a bigger splash . . . But we knew where Harrod
> was going and he got there in 1939 in . . . 'Essay in Dynamic
> Theory' . . . Indeed he regarded himself as having gotten
> there in the trade cycle book . . . which was schematized to a
> higher degree in the 'Essay' in 1939. Of course that was his
> turn to make a splash.

Brown concluded 'This is where his mind was . . . he'd done with
the *General Theory* . . . here was his book which should have been
as much regarded as the *General Theory* . . . and people should have
been discussing that . . . instead of Hicks's . . . he was clearly well
on the way to his dynamic system then and went further in the next
two years.'[77]

Finally, let us turn to the views expressed by Shackle and Brown
about their reactions to IS–LM then and now. In an interview
Shackle commented:

> I should say that IS–LM is essentially a general equilibrium
> construction and I always have felt that general equilibrium
> was something that had nothing to do with time. It was an
> abstraction in an atemporal world so to speak. I can't say that
> Hicks ignored time because in his idea of the production
> function in *Value and Capital* – I went to the lectures that he
> gave on this – he supposed that the businessman could put in
> his input at an earlier date or a later date and get his output at
> an earlier or a later date and what he did would depend on the
> rate of interest, but that is a different matter altogether, that is
> logical time. What I think about IS–LM is that it is essentially

an equilibrium construction and if it is an equilibrium construction you haven't got full information until you have explained how the equilibrium comes about; and if you bring in time immediately you've got to say how does the man get the knowledge; how does he find out; how do the partners get themselves into equilibrium. Equilibrium is an abstraction, it is quite timeless, it has nothing to do with time at all. IS–LM is a very elegant and ingenious construction, and I still think it is a valuable thing. I mean you can teach students to understand what IS–LM is all about and then you can say 'Now think of all the difficulties and what it doesn't explain and the questions you have to ask about it and if you think of all the difficulties with IS–LM you get to the *General Theory'*. Well, I think that IS–LM is an equilibrium construction and begs all the questions that general equilibrium does beg. I think that IS–LM is a work of art. It's beautiful and it's ingenious and it's a grand idea and although I think it has all the disadvantages and shortcomings of general equilibrium as a basis for discussion, I do think that it's a brilliant piece of work. When it was produced I think IS–LM was an eye-opener to people but only in its first steps. Diagrams can make things look too simple.[78]

Arthur Brown was also 'impressed' by IS–LM when he first came across it:

It impressed me when I first read the article [before the conference] and it impressed me because it doesn't just do what Meade and Harrod both do, that is to say, present an equation system which they regard as containing the gist of the *General Theory*. He starts with this four-equation system, and he condenses this into the two curves with which we are familiar. This had, I think, a considerable influence on one's ability to understand what was going on. I mean, four equations are quite a lot for the unaided human mind to see the gist of all at once . . . Harrod got the thing down to a four-equation system. The thing that Hicks did was just to dress it up a bit further with the diagrams. When I came to Leeds [from Oxford] one of the first things I did was to make a solid diagram in a box in three dimensions, with interest, income, investment or savings, to put in the four functions, which intersected in two pairs, which produced an IS curve and an LM curve; and I used this as a teaching aid in my first two years. I just took it for granted that this was the sort of thing that Hicks had done in his mind, and he produced something which enabled you to play around with the thing a good deal more. Whereas Harrod and Meade, for instance, had been content to say, here are these four equations, a simple enough system, which give the gist of the new macroeconomics in the sort of way in which the classical equations give the gist of classical economics. Hicks's presentation was of superior neatness. It is more general than the *General Theory*. The *General Theory* is a very complex book and Keynes was a very complex person. You get in the correspondence with Harrod a certain amount of resistance to attempts to simplify the *General Theory* to a point where it's an easily absorbed piece of doctrine. IS–LM was the principal thing that did make it an easily absorbed piece of doctrine ultimately for the world at large and primarily for the economics profession.[79]

As Brown has put it, 'Hicks did a Marshall', but more about this in chapter 3. Let us now turn to the difference between the approaches of Harrod and Hicks to IS–LM and the divergence between Harrod and the Cambridge members of the General Theory group – especially Joan Robinson.

### The Keynesian revolution, conceptual change in economics and IS–LM: Harrod, Hicks and Robinson

In light of the above material on the papers by Harrod and Hicks, we may ask: why didn't Harrod produce the IS–LM diagram himself? This is one of the unresolved questions in the IS–LM enigma if three facts are taken into account: first, that he had developed and circulated his version of the IS–LM equations at about the time of the *General Theory*'s publication in February 1936 (see chapter 2); second, that in his IS–LM paper the comparative statics are analogous to the IS–LM diagram (see chapter 3); and third, that Harrod was the originator of the only diagram to appear in Keynes's *General Theory*. In addition, Harrod himself provides a further variation on the theme of diagrams as tools in economics when, some twenty-five years later, in his 1951 correspondence with Hawtrey on Keynes's *General Theory*, he stresses the importance of the diagram he contributed to Keynes's book (see chapter 4). In order to assess Harrod's position, in relation to Hicks's and the IS–LM diagram, and with respect to the Cambridge members of the General Theory group – especially Joan Robinson – we must consider the variant and divergent views of the Keynesian revolution and conceptual change in economics held by these individuals respectively.[80]

Robinson's view is that the publication of Keynes's *General Theory* constituted a Kuhnian-type scientific revolution emanating from a ' "crisis" in the development of a scientific discipline' and a paradigm shift amongst a 'scientific community' in the Kuhnian sense. But she provides a caveat to the application of the Kuhnian approach to conceptual change in economics when she writes 'so far as the content of the subject is concerned, it is inappropriate to compare economics' with physics, chemistry and biology since 'we cannot command the methods that have led to their success – precise observation of exact recurrences or controlled experiment – and we have no body of agreed and reliable results such as theirs to offer to the world.' Furthermore:

> The Keynesian revolution had many features in common with the scientific revolutions that Kuhn describes, but the subsequent development of the subject was not at all like that of any natural science when a shift of paradigm has occurred. In economics, new ideas are treated, in theological style, as heresies and as far as possible kept out of schools by drilling students in the habit of repeating the old dogmas, so as to prevent established orthodoxy from being undermined.

At this point I should say that Robinson's – and Kahn's – critique of Hicks as the originator of the IS–LM approach is somewhat misdirected. Not only can the IS–LM approach be said to have originated in the General Theory group as we have shown, but it was also accepted as Keynes's central message by two of its members – Harrod and Meade. Moreover, the IS–LM approach was the way a number of the leading exponents of Keynes outside the General Theory group – Reddaway and Champernowne, for example – saw Keynes's central message in 1936 (see chapter 2).[81]

Hicks's position is more difficult to pin down in retrospect. This is because he changed his view of the relationship between economics and other fields of inquiry and thereby the nature of conceptual change in economics over the period 1935–85, while not basically changing his view of Keynes's *General Theory* over the same period. For example, in a paper he gave in London at a symposium on economic theory and the social sciences in 1935, Hicks placed economics between psychology on the one hand, and sociology on the other, dependent upon both for providing cogent solutions to many of the key problems facing the economist. Hicks advocated the development of what he called 'substantial economics' to complement what he termed 'formal economics – the technique which economists have invented to deal with their subject matter'. In Hicks's view 'a complete science of substantial economics could not be content with reference back to the "data" ', which he identified as 'psychological, institutional, or technical'; Hicks claimed that 'it must investigate the data themselves.' In other words, economics alone cannot provide answers to its most pressing questions, for, as Hicks concluded 'if those questions are to be answered, it will only be by a simultaneous attack from several social sciences together. Of that there is little sign at present, nor in these days of specialization, very much prospect. So, in the meantime, you must forgive the economists if they treat the world to a good deal of amateur sociology.'[82]

Hicks's view when the *General Theory* was published, the interpretation he gave it in the form of his version of IS–LM, and the development of the ideas he expressed later in *Value and Capital*, was of economics as a 'soft science'. However, his implicit object was to push economics towards more general theories. When he was writing his IS–LM paper, or, as he puts it, was trying to 'produce it out of a hat', a diagram may have seemed to him more effective than a purely equational approach in getting his view of the central message of the *General Theory* across. Indeed, he had only to think of the example of Marshall's diagram and the Weber–Fechner curve, which impressed him greatly – but more about the possible origins and alternate derivations of the diagram in chapter 3.[83]

Some forty years later, in his paper 'Revolutions in Economics', Hicks shifted his position somewhat to view economics as what could be called a 'semi-soft science', advocating what he termed 'generalization' as a method of theory building. While accepting the fact that the Keynesian approach constituted a type of conceptual revolution in economics, he did not, however, view it as a Kuhnian-type 'scientific revolution'. Moreover, he made the point that there could be no Kuhnian-type 'scientific revolutions' in economics because of the intrinsic nature of economics itself. Hicks, however, never changed his opinion of the *General Theory* from his original review of it in the *Economic Journal* in June 1936, to his most recent references to it. For example, in both the original review and in his IS–LM paper he took Keynes to task over the 'general nature' of the *General Theory*, while in the 1976 paper mentioned above, he states 'Keynes' theory is . . . not a general theory; it is a superbly effective theory, which gains power by what it leaves out.'[84]

Recently Hicks has moved towards viewing economics as a 'semi-hard science'. For example, in his book *Causality in Economics* (1979), he places it 'between science and history', while in his 1983 paper 'Is Economics a Science?', he takes the position that conceptual change in economics proceeds via the application of scientific and quasi-scientific method and explanation, i.e. the development and testing of weak predictions and propositions; this because economics is not an experimental science.[85]

Harrod's views of the relation of Keynes's *General Theory* to pre-existing economic knowledge, the object of economic inquiry, and the nature of conceptual change in economics, always remained consistent. In contrast to Robinson's view, Harrod never took the Keynesian revolution to be of the Kuhnian type, continually professing an evolutionary position. Furthermore, in contrast to Hicks, at the time of his IS–LM paper and afterwards, Harrod took an equational approach to economics, in both his interpretation of Keynes's *General Theory* and his approach to growth, advocating the development of what he called fundamental equations and relations in economics. For example, in his IS–LM paper, Harrod writes 'in my judgement Mr. Keynes has not affected a revolution in fundamental economic theory but a readjustment and a shift of emphasis.' Harrod goes on to describe his object of developing 'dynamic theory' in which 'dynamic principles' would 'come to be as precisely defined and as rigidly demonstrable as the static theory' and which 'will embody new terms in its fundamental equations, rates of growth, acceleration, deceleration, etc. If development proceeds on these lines, there will be a close parallel between the statics and dynamics of economics and mechanics'.[86]

In his presidential address to Section F of the British Association published in September 1938, Harrod returned to this theme, stating that the development of dynamic economics can only be achieved 'effectively if the laws governing increase are as precisely formulated as the static laws. We need a system of fundamental equations using simplifying assumptions – cf. the frictionless surface etc. – in which rates of increase will themselves figure as unknown terms'. Harrod recognized, however, the limitations of economics in terms of 'the impossibility of the crucial experiment' and the fact that in economics 'it is extremely difficult to test hypotheses by the collected data of observation. The operation of the plurality of causes is too widely pervasive. Thus numerous hypotheses are framed, and never submitted to decisive test, so that each man retains his own opinion still.' Harrod continued, 'I do not wish to press these considerations hard, but only sufficiently to upset the complacency of dogmatic upholders of one exclusive method.' He concluded, however, by saying 'only in one way can the academic man change the shape of things, and that is by projecting new knowledge into the arena . . . His specific contribution is the enlargement of knowledge, and particularly of the knowledge of general laws.'[87]

For Harrod, then, Hicks's IS–LM diagram was no more than a 'mechanical toy' or 'swiss watch', an inferior approach to Keynes's *General Theory*. In contrast, Harrod advocated the equational approach to the *General Theory* and economics as a whole, which, being similar to that of physics, was for him both superior and preferable. This is manifest, as shown, in his IS–LM paper, his 'scope and method' paper and in his subsequent work on growth.[88]

This is not surprising, since his model was taken from Keynes's 'fundamental equations' as published in Keynes's *A Treatise on Money* (1930). Harrod gives a retrospective view of the importance of the *Treatise* and its effect on the development of his approach to both the *General Theory* and growth in his book *Money* (1969). There, Harrod also repeats the contention he made over thirty years earlier in his IS–LM paper, about the nature of Keynes's 'revolution', when he states, with regard to Keynes's theory of interest, 'the classical theory is not only not inconsistent with Keynes' theory, but is even an essential part of it, if one interprets the latter in a rational manner and is not put off by some exaggerated observations by Keynes.' In Harrod's view, 'a patient and sensible interpretation of Keynes' thought shows that it is perfectly capable of being accommodated to the classical theory of interest' and indeed that is exactly what Harrod did when, in

Oxford's Hilary term of 1936, he circulated his version of the IS–LM equations (see chapter 2).[89]

But the question remains, were there earlier or parallel attempts to accommodate or reconcile Keynes's 'fundamental equations' and subsequent *General Theory* approach with what was held to be the 'classical theory' at the time? In the course of research on the history of the IS–LM concept we have uncovered a number of them, and it is to these that we now turn.[90]

# 2

# IS–LM: antecedents and variants, 1934–8

## Maurice Allen's marginalia on the quantity theory, c. 1934

Keynes's attempts to break with the classical view of economic theory did not begin with the development of his *General Theory*, nor did the efforts to reconcile his views with that of the classical scheme start with the IS–LM approaches of Harrod, Hicks and Meade. *A Treatise on Money*, published in 1930, was essentially Keynes's alternative to the quantity theory and resulted in a critical response from the adherents of the orthodox theory led by Hayek. The gap between the orthodox position and Keynes's new approach as offered in his *Treatise* would provide an intellectual challenge to one who was influenced by the idea that the development of economics was an evolutionary, rather than a revolutionary process. This was the view held by Harrod, who led the group of young Oxford dons which later became what he called the Trade Cycle group. This group consisted of Charles Hitch, Redvers Opie, Lindsay Fraser, James Meade and Maurice Allen. And it is Maurice Allen's attempt to reconcile Keynes's fundamental equations of *A Treatise on Money* and the orthodox theory, that we will now discuss.[1]

The importance of Allen's effort can best be seen by reference to Harrod's retrospective evaluation of the *Treatise* in his book *Money* (1969). Here, Harrod states:

There are two reasons for reverting to the *Treatise on Money*, in addition to the general one that it is far richer in content relating to monetary thought and practice than the *General Theory* . . . It is . . . impossible to have an understanding of Keynes in depth, if one has not read the *Treatise*. The first of the two special reasons for reverting to the *Treatise* is that the equations . . . set out in a very clear way the distinction between cost inflation and demand inflation. Of the two forces set out as determining the price level, the first represents the ratio of wage increases to productivity increases and the second represents what in the *General Theory* is called aggregate demand . . . The second special reason arises from the treatment of investment and saving. The validity of the expression representing aggregate demand depends on a special definition of income, which Keynes abandoned in the *General Theory* . . . Another virtue of this [*Treatise*] approach is that it draws a strong distinction between personal and normal company saving on the one hand, and, on the other, company saving, or dis-saving, relatively to the norm, that occurs as a result of the inflationary or deflationary process. This dichotomy of saving into two fundamental kinds is lost from view in the *General Theory*; but it is a distinction of the utmost importance for the understanding of money matters both in cycle theory and in growth theory.

Harrod goes on to say that Keynes's fundamental equations

specify determinants of the price level, which contain no reference to the quantity of money . . . but since the quantity equation [$MV = PT$] must be true, it must be supposed that V has accommodating changes, when P changes under the influence of the forces specified out of line with any change in M/T. The accommodating changes in V are explained by Keynes' theory of liquidity preference, which occurs in the *Treatise* as well as in the *General Theory*. The idea of the possibility, as postulated by Keynes, of accommodating changes in V, i.e. when there are no changes in the schedules representing the desires of individuals to hold money, is entirely contrary to the spirit of the quantity theory.

It was just this split that Allen attempted to reconcile in his approach.[2]
Allen began by developing a period version of orthodox quantity

theory. By calling K 'the period of circulation of money' and M 'the stock of money, then the daily money stream is M/K. The price level, where T is the physical volume of daily output, is M/KT'. He then stated 'if a daily change, $\alpha$, in the amount of money [where $\alpha$ may be $>$ or $<$ 0] occurs for K days, then in the (k + 1)th day the stock of money has risen to $M + K\alpha$. If prices have risen in proportion to the increase in money

$$P_{k+1}/P_1 = M_{k+1}/M_1 \quad = \frac{M + K\alpha}{M}$$

$$\therefore P_{k+1} = \frac{M + K\alpha}{M} \cdot \frac{M}{KT} = \frac{\dfrac{M + \alpha}{K}}{T} \;.$$

He then dealt with implications of this variant of the quantity theory. In his view:

The simplest assumption which gives this solution is to hold that in each of K days the public has witheld from expenditure an amount $\alpha$ as if they had sought to restore the real value of the monetary stock to its 'normal level', KT, spreading the 'lacking' [see below] so required over K days. This assumption could be put briefly in the form that the public only spend the receipts from the sale of their output K days after get [*sic*] these receipts – i.e. that they hold their income for just K days before spending – If, on the other hand, they had also spent in any day N any abnormal value of their output in the previous day (N–1) – i.e. if they had held their 'profits' only one day, or if they spend the value of their current output, then the price level by day K + 1 would have risen by

$$\frac{M + K^2\alpha}{M}$$

which is greater than

$$\frac{M_{k+1}}{M}$$

unless K = 1 – i.e. unless people perform 'lacking' or dislacking', spend less or more than the value of their current output – when their income alters, the change in income or prices is out of proportion to the change in the amount of money.

He then discussed 'the quantity theory of money in terms of the theoretical apparatus of supply and demand'. He stated that 'if the rigid quantity theory is to be upheld . . . The elasticity of demand for money is unity. Only then, when output is given, do prices change with the quantity of money – when the inflation has settled down.' He continued:

> Further, the definition of the demand for money must be such that, when the quantity of money is given, any fall in money incomes per period is just equal to a corresponding increase in the demand for money during the same period. The only definition I see that satisfies these conditions is that the extent of an individual's demand for money is indicated by the number of days for which he holds income.

Allen then defined income 'as the receipts from the sale of output and the interest from investments', and 'K days holding of income is defined as the holding of the actual income of day I until day K before spending it in day K + I.' Furthermore 'this definition of the demand for money can be expanded to the usual division of the demand for money into three parts – money held against income by private individuals, money held against business transactions by firms, and money held as saving in the ordinary use of that term.'

At this point Allen turned to the question of whether his period variant of quantity theory could be reconciled with Keynes's 'fundamental equations'. Because of its importance for the history of economic thought, the relevant sections (4–6) of Allen's manuscript are reproduced below:

> §4. Armed with these definitions, one can turn to Mr. Keynes' formulae, and discover if they are compatible with this version of the orthodox theory. One difficulty arises at the outset. These definitions apply to the actual incomes and transactions of the individuals and firms concerned; Mr. Keynes' formulae to 'normal income'. He objects to the view that actual income, E + Q, can be substituted for E in the formulae, on the grounds that it is then necessary to hold that savings and the

value of investment are equal. Using his symbols, we have the formulae:

(i) Total income, $E + Q$, is equal to the receipts from the sale of output, $PR + I$

(ii) Normal income is spent on consumption and saving

$$E = PR + S$$

whence $Q = I - S$. It would appear that if we were to say (that it is) total income, $E + Q$, which is spent on consumption and saving, i.e.

$$E + Q = PR + S$$

then $S = I$. But this difficulty can be overcome by using 'atomic periods'. The total income of day 1, $E_1 + Q_1$ (where subscripts refer to the day) is equal to the value of output in that day $P_1 R_1 + I_1$. Secondly, the total income of day 1 is spent on consumption and saving in day 2,

$$E_1 + Q_1 = P_2 R_2 + S_2$$

So we can say

$$E_1 + Q_1 = P_2 R_2 + S_2$$
$$E_2 + Q_2 = P_2 R_2 + I_2$$

Now

$$E_1 \equiv E_2$$

by its definition as normal income, $\therefore$.

$$Q_2 - Q_1 = I_2 - S_2$$

The increase in profits on day 2 is equal to the difference between saving and the value of investment on that day. To include in income the profits already made does not imply that savings and the value of investment will equate on the day in which that income is spent. I shall assume therefore that in these formulae we can substitute for E, at the beginning of any period with which we are dealing, the actual income which may well include profits that people have just acquired at that time and regard any Q that appear later as changes in profits after that base period.

When saving occurs, the makers of consumption goods incur losses, and can either (a) maintain, or (b) reduce their output. If they follow course (a) then they may either

(i)  finance their losses by cutting down their own expenditures, either in consumption, or in saving;
(ii) sell securities they hold in reserve

§5. But savings which escape diversion into the channels of government securities and decumulated securities do not necessarily reach capital industry as income:

(i)  if new industrial securities are sold, then money will be held against these transactions. These receipts from these sales will be held by capital entrepreneurs and since the securities are not their output (any more than were decumulated securities) the receipts are not income. But this can be income if we make an exception to our definition of income [except in so far as stock exchange dealers hold larger balances against their greater transactions]. Nor, of course does this question arise if the investment is directly made by the savers.
(ii) Money may be absorbed by savings deposits. Here Mr. Keynes analysis weakens if the conditions of demand for bank deposits as against securities applies. Let H be the volume of bank deposits used for savings purposes, r the bank deposit rate, y the yield of industrial securities or selling value. then

$$H = \Phi \, (y/r)$$

such that

$$\delta \, \Phi/\delta \, y < 0; \; \delta \, \Phi/\delta \, r > 0$$

The conditions of demand are expressed by $|\Phi|$. Clearly when new savings appear, y tends to fall as the prices of securities are raised; $|\Phi|$, depending in part on the behaviour of y; in part on the prices of goods; and in part on the initial amount of savings to be invested, and already invested or hoarded, may changed appreciably; r may be affected indirectly.

But Mr. Keynes' general conclusion is unimpeachable. It is not safe to assume, even in the absence of any change in $|\Phi|$, that new savings will go, directly or indirectly, into savings deposits, either wholly or in part. But it should generally be possible to ensure that they do so by manipulation or r, – unless the interconnections between $\Phi$, and r are considerable.

§6. These conclusions can be put in a symbolical form akin to that employed by Mr. Keynes.

Let $E_1$ stand for the actual income of day 1. It is comprised of normal income, and perhaps, some profits made in that period, i.e.

$$E_1 = P_1 R_1 + I_1$$

– and I assume that people have then no non-income receipts. Further I assume that these quantities have been constant for the last K days [K defined as in §1. This avoids considerable unwieldiness in formulae]. Then

$$E_{0-k} = E_1$$

Let $E_2 + Q_2$ stand for the actual income of day 2, defined so that

$$E_1 \equiv E_2$$

and therefore $Q_2$ stands for the (change in) profits in day 2. Let $W_2$ stand for the total receipts of day 2; it equals $E_2 + Q_2$ + non-income receipts, which we limit to the dole, and receipts from decumulating securities. Let decumulation be D; the unemployment benefit B, and taxes T. Then:–

$$E_1 = P_2 R_2 + S_2 + T_2. \quad [\text{For } E_1 = E_{0-k}]$$
$$E_2 + Q_2 = P_2 R_2 + I_2.$$
$$Q_2 = I_2 - (S_2 + T_2).$$
$$W_2 = P_2 R_2 + I_2 + D_2 + B_2$$

If there is no change in the quantity of money, and if the money absorbed by (a) Savings Deposits (b) Income Deposits [i.e. that part of E, or more precisely $E_{0-k}$ which is simply left in the income deposit] (c) Business deposits, other than those held against the dealings $D_2$ by the sellers of the securities; be represented by $H_2$ then

$$S_2 = D_2 + H_2 + (B_2 - T_2) + I_2.$$
$$Q_2 = - [D_2 + H_2 + B_2].$$

More generally, if we say an amount of money X is created in day 2, and spent on consumption, investment, budget deficit, etc. then

$$Q_2 = X_2 - [D_2 + H_2 + B_2]$$

i.e. the losses of day 2 are equal to the amount of money normally expended which is diverted on that day from the purchase of output to new transactions. This seems to me both in harmony with the above version of orthodox theory and (fundamentally?) with Mr. Keynes' formulae.

Allen concluded that while the orthodox quantity theory and Keynes's 'fundamental equations' could be reconciled, there still existed an 'impasse' between the positions of Keynes and Hayek, based upon whether what he called 'the effective stream of money' is kept constant or not. In the former case, according to Allen's interpretation of Keynes, 'money may yet be diverted from the purchase of output, so that incomes, prices, and employment fall, and depression may ensue.' In the latter case, according to Allen's interpretation of Hayek's position 'If the effective stream of money is not kept constant, but instead gross savings [S] are made equal to the value of investment then inflation must result.'

In any event, Allen had shown that Keynes's *Treatise* results could be reconciled with orthodox quantity theory. It now remained for Harrod to reconcile Keynes's *General Theory* results with traditional theory, but more about this in the last section of this chapter.

## Reddaway's simultaneous equations and the Walras–Lange connection (1938)

### *Reddaway's review of the* General Theory

In June 1936, two important reviews of Keynes's *General Theory* were published, one by Hicks in the *Economic Journal*, and the other by Reddaway in the *Economic Record*. Hicks's review contains no indication whatsoever of his subsequent IS–LM approach to Keynes's *General Theory*. In contrast, Reddaway's review provides an equational representation of his view of Keynes's central message, which closely parallels the IS–LM equation system of Harrod, Hicks and Meade. Reddaway was in Australia at the time, and had not been in contact with either his Cambridge contemporaries, for example Champernowne, or those at Oxford, who were also using the IS–LM perspective in their interpretations of the *General Theory*. Interestingly, Keynes wrote to Reddaway, in a letter dated 17 August 1936 'I enjoyed your review of my book in the Economic Record and thought it very well done.' How then, did Reddaway arrive at his equational representation of Keynes's *General Theory*? To answer this question we must first turn to his review, and follow with Reddaway's recollections of how he developed his approach and his attitude towards the IS–LM diagram and its diffusion in pre-war Cambridge.

Reddaway starts his review by comparing Keynes's *General Theory* with the *Treatise*, and then summarizes

Mr. Keynes' new analysis . . . as follows. We visualize a series of levels of employment. As we go up the scale the community's real income increases. Its psychology is such that consumption will increase with increased income, but by a smaller amount; the exact relationship is given by a function which Mr. Keynes calls 'the propensity to consume' . . . given the propensity to consume, the level of employment is determined by the amount of current investment, for it must give that level of income out of which the community will do this amount of saving. It remains, therefore, to find out what determines the amount of current investment. This, according to Mr. Keynes, depends on the relation between 'the schedule of the marginal efficiency of capital' and the rate of interest.

Reddaway continues, however, 'to state precisely how the schedule of the marginal efficiency of capital is to be constructed is almost impossible – there are many complications and mutual interactions.' In a note to this passage, Reddaway writes:

Thus the schedule is greatly affected by the level of employment, because this reacts on confidence. Investment should perhaps be represented as a function of income (Y) and the rate of interest (r) rather than of r alone. This appears to involve circular reasoning, because we started by saying that income depends on investment. But, as shown later [when Reddaway presents the equations] this is not a valid objection, the factors mutually determining one another.

Finally, he asserts that 'we are then left to find what determines the rate of interest.'[3]

At this point, Reddaway introduces his first equational relation

$$M = M_1 + M_2 = L_1 (Y) + L_2 (r)$$

where he defines M as 'the total amount of money available . . . determined by monetary policy'; Y as the level of income; r as the interest rate; $M_1$ as the amount of money people will want to hold 'on current account'; $M_2$ as the 'amount of cash people will want to hold on capital account'; $L_1$ as the 'current account' liquidity function; $L_2$ as the 'capital account' liquidity function.

According to Reddaway:

Now, if we know Y, the level of income, we can deduce $M_1$ and hence $M_2$; and we can then say that the rate of interest must be such that people will want to hold this amount of money on capital account rather than transfer to bonds. But the object of finding the rate of interest is to deduce the amount of investment and hence the level of income. Are we then reasoning in a circle? The answer is no, we are merely faced with the inevitable difficulty of trying to describe a system where the four variables mutually determine one another.

Reddaway then presents his equation system or 'four propositions' as

$$S = f (Y) \text{ (Equation 1)}$$
$$I = h (Y, r) \text{ (Equation 2)}$$
$$I = S \text{ (Equation 3)}$$
$$M = L_1 (Y) + L_2 (r) \text{ (Equation 4)}$$

where 'I stands for investment, S for Saving, Y for income and r for the rate of interest.' The form used here for equation 2 derives from his footnote to the initial form of this equation

$$I = g (r)$$

where Reddaway says 'if we accept the argument of the previous footnote [cited above], this should be written:

$$I = h (Y, r).'$$

This form also appeared in his 1963 discussion of the review, entitled 'Keynesian Analysis and a Managed Economy'.[4]

Reddaway then explains the reason for presenting his equations in what he calls 'a sort of mathematical shorthand'. He writes 'These are set down here to show that we have really got enough relationships.' He then proceeds, however, 'Mr. Keynes, quite rightly in my opinion, deprecates the spurious air of exactness introduced by too much mathematics . . . But in his endeavour to describe the system without this sort of shorthand he has tended to obscure the fact that the determination is mutual.'[5]

In an interview with Reddaway fifty years after the publication of his review, he gave an account of the development of his equational approach to Keynes's *General Theory*. He began:

The story from my point of view is very simple. I arrived in Australia in March 1936. In Melbourne, there were a number of economists who were very interested in Keynes. I'd got a copy of Keynes's book, and there was a sort of economics club called the 'Shillings', and I gave a paper about it, and it prompted two or three more. And although I was only twenty-three, I was picked on by the editor of the *Economic Record* as the person who obviously ought to do the review of Keynes. The date which I delivered the review of Keynes is in my diaries, the 7 May [1936], which is very revealing in a way, that it didn't take a very long time to do. My recollection is that I was given a copy by Keynes and took it with me and read it on the boat.

When asked to what degree he was influenced by Keynes in his view of the *General Theory*, Reddaway replied 'I went to Keynes for supervisions and bits of ideas leaked out, but they were pretty thin. From that point of view, I got my General Theory from the copy of the *General Theory* which Keynes gave to me.' Reddaway then gave his version of why he presented a mutually determined system. He said:

That's pretty simple, though in a way a bit difficult to make exact; it was fifty years ago. But I told you I was giving papers to the 'Shillings' club and I wanted to portray the essence of the Keynes system and that is fairly apparent in the review, that you visualize a number of possible levels of employment with investment in the first place being given and it's a closed system. You had to have a high enough level or low enough level – from whichever way you looked at it – to get the savings to match the investment. So that was the heart of things. Then you had the rate of interest coming from liquidity preference and I found myself – when I tried to make it, I suppose, vaguely mathematical in that form – that I was going round; and particularly if I said that the amount of money depended on the level of income that you have to go round there. And so I wanted to make sure that the thing was the right number of equations for the right number of unknowns and so I scribbled this thing down.

Reddaway continued:

I suppose – this is a bit of an effort at reconstruction – that I took the view that liquidity preference you had to think of as being in two parts. That one bit of liquidity preference was wanted for doing the ordinary day-to-day business and was a function of Y. That's why my equation divides it into two parts.

When asked why he didn't use a 'classical-type' savings function, i.e. introducing interest into his equation 1, Reddaway replied 'Thinking back to this I wouldn't have the slightest objection to complicating the mutual determination by giving some role to the rate of interest as influencing saving.' Reddaway then gave his view of what determines investment in Keynes's *General Theory* system:

Investment in places in Keynes is very much dependent on the rate of interest only but in others it is enormously determined by animal spirits and the level of the national income and God knows what, so I simply felt that if one were taking the book as a whole you really needed to make investment be a function of both. The assumption that it was just a function of the rate of interest – I think I probably had this in mind at the time – was a guide to the people concerned with monetary policy, that they would have a power to influence the rate of interest and that they would regard the rate of interest as affecting investment and they wouldn't be worried about anything else. Whether it would operate entirely by keeping income constant and just moving down a schedule or whether income would come in or not. You see, one of the things I say in the appendix [to 'Keynesian Analysis and a Managed Economy (1963)] is the extreme static nature of the *General Theory*, and Keynes was in my view moderately inconsistent. The letter from Keynes [cited above] was primarily his reply to some comments I had sent him and one of the points was that the level of income affected investment, and he's really accepting that in there. He said 'of course', more or less . . . I mean Keynes was just writing to me; if he disagreed with that I think he would have said so. I suppose so far as I thought I was introducing anything a bit different from Keynes it was in putting that the quantity of money was made up of two parts. Because it seemed to me to be that people might vary their holding of money on account of the rate of interest.

Reddaway then summed up the object of his paper:

What is the causal link? Does it all go from investment to this, to that, to the other; or do you have to come back? I think my mutual determination was equation 4, that you had to go back to income. It almost becomes a caricature that the monetary authorities determine the quantity of money, the quantity of money determines the rate of interest, the rate of interest determines investment, investment determines income, because you have to get it at the level where income will equal saving and that line of causation isn't good enough, there's more mutuality than that. And that's what I was aiming at, mutuality.

In 1937, a year after his review, Reddaway published an article elaborating Keynes's position on the question of 'special obstacles to full employment in a wealthy community'. Keynes, however, when editing Reddaway's draft of an article of that title published in the *Economic Journal* in June 1937, deleted Reddaway's reference to increasing investment opportunities with increasing income. According to Reddaway 'When I wrote it, it included a reaction from the economy becoming wealthier on the level of investment, and Keynes sent me the proofs of the article which he had trimmed, and he trimmed out this reaction.'

When asked about the relation between his equations and IS–LM, Reddaway acknowledged that they were, in fact, parallel approaches. Interestingly, this was noted first by Lange in 1938. Reddaway went on to say:

> I'd never thought of my equations and IS–LM being essentially the same thing until you raised it with me. Never. In fact, I came back from Australia and found people using IS–LM and found it a very artificial sort of device. I think it is because it is trying to get all the business of at least four equations into one diagram and if you get used to thinking that way, fine, but it's overloading the thing. I mean, I feel quite happy to say here are four equations; if you want to see an expository method of looking at the solution of them you can draw the thing with Y and r and say there is a line for these combinations which will enable you to have I = S which it has to be, and you can say there's a relationship between liquidity preference and the quantity of money and these have to be equal, so you get another line, therefore only this combination will satisfy both as an equilibrium condition. But I produced these for the very limited purpose of showing that there were the right number of unknowns, I think my review said that, and also that this was an approximation; that other things came in as well. If you were ignoring them then you could just use this but you musn't interpret the world in these terms. When I came back, I found that people were being taught in terms of IS–LM. I suppose that I regarded IS–LM as an over-clever device for trying to cram too much into one diagram but I never thought that it was virtually a graphication of the four equations which I had produced – each of which seemed to me to be readily intelligible – and gave you the idea of mutual determination and I didn't try to show the mutual determination on a graph. I never drew IS–LM.

Reddaway then made a most interesting point regarding the diffusion of IS–LM in pre-war Cambridge. When asked when he had first encountered IS–LM upon returning to Cambridge, he replied:

> I met it, I suppose, in students' supervision essays. I would guess that I did meet IS–LM more or less in 1938–9, the time I was in Cambridge before the war. Students would not have got it from *Econometrica*. They could have got it from the lecturers

who were lecturing on monetary theory in 1937–8 and 1938–9. Students' essays reflect lectures rather than reading. John Hicks was here, even if he wasn't lecturing on theory, he might well have put this in. You may well find that the way the thing filtered into Cambridge students would be from his lectures.

Finally, Reddaway recalled the atmosphere in Cambridge in 1936 – from a student's point of view:

Ideas certainly got around. My sister did economics for her final year and she graduated in [June] 1936 after the *General Theory* had come out. I remember receiving a letter from her in Australia in which she said it was really funny to see people arguing about Keynes's *General Theory*. She said that it was frightfully difficult preparing for the exams and the perpetual arguments that were going on about Keynes's *General Theory*, probably in the Marshall Society meetings, but there was a sufficiently lively debate on what it all meant essentially by April–May of 1936 in Cambridge; things would have been promulgated very fast and things would be fertile for the type of thing Hicks did.[6]

### The Walras–Lange connection (1938)

In the February 1938 issue of *Economica*, Oskar Lange's article 'The Rate of Interest and the Optimum Propensity to Consume' appeared. This paper not only represented Keynes's system in IS–LM terms but also linked the IS-LM approach to 'the Walrasian or Paretian system of equations of general economic equilibrium'. Lange's opening paragraph stated 'In this paper I propose first to elucidate the way in which liquidity preference co-operates with the marginal efficiency of investment and with the propensity to consume in determining the value of interest and to point out how both the traditional and Mr. Keynes's theory are but special cases of a more general theory.' Lange continued 'the economic relations by which the rate of interest is determined can be represented by a system of four equations.' In a note to this, Lange stated that:

a similar system of equations has been given for the first time by Reddaway . . . While writing this there has come to my notice a forthcoming paper of Dr. Hicks . . . in the meanwhile published in *Econometrica*, which treats the subject in a similar and very elegant way. The form chosen in my paper seems, however, more adapted for the study of the problems it is concerned with. Cf. also Harrod . . . *Econometrica*, January 1937.

Lange's note indicates that he started his paper sometime after Reddaway's review, finishing it only after seeing both Hicks's and Harrod's papers. Lange nevertheless recognized the parallels between Reddaway's equational system and the IS–LM approach on the one hand, and the similarities between Harrod's and Hicks's equation systems on the other.[7]

The equation system Lange presented is as follows:

$$M = L\,(i,\ Y)\ \text{(Equation 1)}$$
$$C = \phi\,(Y,\ i)\ \text{(Equation 2)}$$
$$I = F\,(i,\ C)\ \text{(Equation 3)}$$
$$Y \equiv C + I\ \text{(Equation 4)}$$

where M is the amount of money held by individuals or real value of cash balances; Y is total real income; i is the rate of interest; C is the total expenditure on consumption per unit of time; and I is investment per unit of time. According to Lange, M, Y, C and I are measured in wage units: 'if the amount of money M (in wage units) is given, these four equations determine the four unknowns i, C, I and Y. Alternatively, i may be regarded as given (for instance, fixed by the banking system) and M as determined by our system of equations.' As we can see, Lange's equation system closely resembles the IS–LM approach, with income entering the investment equation via the function for consumption expenditure. This is because, according to Lange:

Investment per unit of time depends – not only on the rate of interest but on the expenditure on consumption [a function of income and interest]. For the demand for investment goods is derived from the demand for consumer's goods. The smaller the expenditure on consumption the smaller is the demand for consumers goods and consequently the lower is the rate of net return on investment.[8]

Keynes's view of Lange's approach is interesting, to say the least. In the course of a debate with Robertson in the *Economic Journal* in June 1938, Keynes wrote:

> In this connection Mr. Robertson refers with approval to an article by Dr. Lange which follows very closely and accurately my line of thought. The analysis which I gave in my *General Theory of Employment* is the same as the 'general theory' explained by Dr. Lange on p. 18 of this article, except that my analysis is not based (as I think his is in that passage) on the assumption that the quantity of money is constant.[9]

In the passage Keynes referred to, Lange 'assumed that the demand for liquidity is a decreasing function of the rate of interest and an increasing function of total income' as he expressed in equation 1. Lange interpreted Keynes's approach to liquidity in similar terms, but when it came to the determination of interest, they diverge, with Keynes's approach, according to Lange, being a special case in which 'the amount of money determines the rate of interest independently of the level of total income.' Thus, he concluded 'both the Keynesian and the traditional theory of interest are but two limiting cases of what may be regarded to be the general theory of interest.'[10]

According to Lange 'it is a feature of great historical interest that the essentials of this general theory are contained already in the work of Walras.' Lange then placed his proposed equation system in the context of both Walras's *Eléménts d'économie politique pure* and *Théorie de la monnaie*, and identified the liquidity preference function as having 'been indicated clearly by Walras', although Walras failed, in his view, to show if it 'depends also on the level of real income'. In any event, Lange said 'our remaining three equations are also contained in the system of Walras [albeit using propensity to save instead of to consume] . . . By introducing the prices of all commodities he brings income indirectly into the equation expressing the propensity to save. His equation thus corresponds to our equation 2.' Lange then showed the Walrasian counterpart to his proposed investment function and to the investment-saving identity via its correspondence, in his view, 'to the sum of the budget equations in the Walrasian system'.[11]

Lange finally presented his version of the IS–LM diagram based upon an indifference approach, calling his variant of IS 'isoinvestment curves' and his variant of LM 'the isoliquidity curve'. When he combined the diagrams by superimposing them, he obtained a unique solution for determining what he called the optimum propensity to consume and save respectively.[12]

Interestingly, some forty years later, Hicks also attributed the development of his IS–LM approach to Walras, claiming that 'the idea of the IS–LM diagram came to me as a result of the work I had been doing on three-way exchange conceived in Walrasian manner.' At first, Hicks's argument closely parallels Lange's position regarding the Walrasian basis for his IS–LM approach, but Hicks then rationalized and justified his initial statement that 'I had already found a way of representing three-way exchange on a two-dimensional diagram (to appear in due course in chapter 5 of *Value and Capital*) – so it was natural for me to think that a similar device could be used for the Keynes theory.' Hicks's account of the origin of his IS–LM diagram will be discussed in chapter 3, while his 'explanation' of the development of his IS–LM approach will be dealt with in more detail in chapter 5. Suffice it to say that by presenting his IS–LM approach as analogous to Walras's general equilibrium representation of the economy, Hicks reconfirmed both his predilection – and possibly that of most of the economics profession at the time the IS–LM papers were presented – for determinacy, symmetry and above all certainty. This was noted by Shackle, especially in his comment on Hicks's 'explanation':

'In this "explanation" Sir John still does not seem to me to acknowledge the central point: the elemental core of Keynes' conception of economic society is uncertain expectation, and uncertain expectation is wholly incompatible and in conflict with the notion of equilibrium.'[13]

### Champernowne's equations and diagrams

In June 1936 – the same month that Reddaway's review of Keynes's *General Theory* appeared in the *Economic Record* – Champernowne published a paper in the *Review of Economic Studies*, entitled 'Unemployment, Basic and Monetary: The Classical Analysis and the Keynesian'. In both an interview and in correspondence, Champernowne recalled submitting the paper for publication 'some time before the publication of the *General Theory*'. He acknowledges the equations and diagrams that appeared in his paper as implying

IS–LM, but was also aware, in the past, of this as what he called a 'familiar result'. According to Champernowne, it is possible that Hicks saw the paper before it was published and may even have edited it. In any event, Champernowne claimed that Hicks, as joint editor of *Review of Economic Studies*, had at least a passing acquaintance with the article. Champernowne's paper, then, may be one of the possible links in the puzzle of the origins of IS–LM, and deserves detailed examination in the context of the author's own view of the purpose and structure of the paper.[14]

In recent correspondence, Champernowne first recalled that the article 'was based on Keynes' lectures and supervisions: this means that I was still only in my second year as an undergraduate reading Economics during most of the time I was writing it . . . reading Part II Economics from Oct. 1933 to June 1935'. After reflection, Champernowne wrote:

On further consideration of the origins of my paper I have vague recollections of an earlier duplicated version of it and this suggests to me that copies of that were circulated to the members of the Oxford–Cambridge seminar, or possibly a purely Cambridge seminar (an offshoot of the Marshall Society, but for third-year undergraduate research students and one or two dons).[15]

According to Champernowne the purpose of his paper was to construct a 'more general system' wherein both Keynes's and the classical systems were 'special cases' of a more general approach. After describing the nature and characteristics of the classical system he outlines it in equational form, and then does the same for 'the system suggested' in his view, 'in "the General Theory of Employment" '. Champernowne adds, however, that the six equations he uses to represent what he calls the Keynesian system 'describe only that part of the Keynesian analysis which deals with the most significant direct effect; in order to take account of the other indirect effects which are discussed in the analysis, but on which less stress is laid, we should have to enlarge the equations . . . and we should have to make them more comprehensive'. Champernowne acknowledges that an IS–LM-type equational system can be derived from his approach: 'since my article gives a pretty general formulation of the Keynesian treatment . . . it is certainly true that by choosing which variables to postulate independent of which others, one can derive IS–LM from the equations.'[16]

Champernowne then provide a series of diagrams to represent the 'classical scheme' and 'the Keynesian scheme', but bases the diagrams used to represent 'the Keynesian analysis' upon his 'enlarged' equational system. This may be seen by comparing the equations he uses to describe the 'Keynesian system' with the equations he uses for both the 'Keynesian analysis' in the diagrams and in the text to represent 'the Keynesian scheme'. On the basis of this he is able, in turn, to 'apply the Keynesian technique to the problem . . . of determining the effect of an increase in thriftiness . . . in the case where the supply of money . . . is fixed'. In other words, Champernowne based his diagrams of 'the Keynesian scheme' on IS–LM-type equations.[17]

According to Champernowne, the first part of his article was basically 'a discussion of what moves the curves about', since 'the curves move around all the time'. The system is always in a 'mist', and affected by 'general nervousness . . . the state of news . . . and expectations of changes in price level'. But Champernowne also considers that both the classical system and his version of the 'Keynesian analysis', i.e. an IS–LM-type equation system can give similar results in specific cases. Champernowne claims that it is not his purpose

> to suggest that the Keynesian analysis is merely an elaboration of the classical analysis. The purpose is to show just how much artificiality must be introduced into the conditions assumed in order that the Keynesian technique should lead to the same results as the classical technique: it is to bring out the point that the Keynesian analysis differs from the classical analysis in the fact that it picks out for emphasis different economic forces such as the stickiness of money-wages, which are evidently extremely important in the short run.[18]

He adds that there is a ' "real" tendency' when dealing with labour supply:

> The 'real supply curve of labour' may be a useful concept for estimating the trend of employment and real wages, of the rate of interest and of saving. If there is such a real tendency, then, when considering such trends, the real wage may be more

significant than the money wage in determining the trend level of unemployment. The Keynesian technique is then likely to yield the same results as the classical technique and it may be simpler to consider the classic analysis direct.

Champernowne continues however:

This method will be of no avail if outlets for investment are so scarce or if the employers are so nervous of any increase in the supply of money that they hoard, and it is impossible to lower the rate of interest sufficiently to cause sufficient investment to keep prices and money wages from falling. For in this case the monetary authority will not be able to prevent a constantly falling cost of living and there will necessarily be monetary unemployment constantly. It will be quite inappropriate to make use of the classical analysis in such a case.[19]

When asked about the similarities between his equational–diagrammatic approach and Hicks's, Champernowne replied:

It seems to me that Hicks and I were interested in rather different problems. I was aiming to elucidate the relation of Keynes's new model with the Marshall–Pigou–Robertson type of model and to provide mnemonics for those wishing to use the Keynes model for investigating the likely effects of particular shifts of 'the state of the news' in the sense of changes which would alter some of the functions underlying some or all of the curves used as mnemonics. Hicks was, I believe, more concerned with enabling those who found sets of simultaneous equations indigestible to digest instead a diagram which he obtained by eliminating one or two variables from the set of simultaneous equations. My emphasis was on the factors Q and Q′ [the state of the news, general nervousness and price expectations] whose changes would shift the curves, and on the need to consider probable indirect effects of the shift in one curve on the positions (and of course also the shapes) of the other curves. My emphasis was also on the scope for judgement in selecting which variables to ignore when considering each one of the three demand and three supply functions represented by the six curves. Hicks's emphasis was on the explanation of the simple model obtained by one particular set of such choices and judgements.

Asked whether Hicks's IS–LM diagram could be derived from his own set of diagrams, Champernowne replied initially:

> I have to confess failure to convince myself that Hicks's curves can properly be derived directly from my curves. Before explaining my difficulties let me quote two dogmas about diagrams and in particular scissors-diagrams: (a) a diagram is a luxury, not a necessity (C. V. Durell); (b) the meaning of either curve in a scissors-diagram only emerges when the other curve is shifted by some change in the conditions. The danger is that these will shift both of the curves, and the moral is that the only significant point of the diagram is the intersection point . . . one cannot obtain Hicks's diagram from my two diagrams without being very precise about which are indepen-dent variables within the functions which the various diagrams illustrate. Any strict derivation has to be written out in terms of the functions and the variables: the translation into an explanation in terms of diagrams would have to be rather clumsy and involve the exact consequence of one or more of the curves moving.

Upon reflection, however, Champernowne reconsidered, and wrote to the effect that his two diagrams [d and e, p. 213 of his paper] would not be a sufficient basis, but, he also said 'As I am sure you realize, one needs the appropriate equations as well, since the two diagrams do not contain all the information in the 4 equations, nor even enough of that information to enable the IS–LM diagram to be plotted . . . I think diagrams are very dangerous without a thorough check using the equations without the diagrams.'

Whether or not an IS–LM-type diagram can actually be derived from Champernowne's equations and diagrams is discussed in detail in chapter 3, where Hicks's view of the matter is also presented. As Champernowne says, considering Marshall's influence on his generation 'any mathematician could, any teacher of economics would represent' a system of IS–LM type equations 'by diagrams'.[20]

### Harrod's equational system and the Trade Cycle group

Taking his lead from Keynes's success in channelling the collective creative energy and enthusiasm of the young economists who helped him in the development of the *General Theory*, Harrod also gathered around him in Oxford a group of young dons to act as a sounding-board for his ideas and provide constructive criticism of his attempt to develop a new theory of the trade cycle based on Keynes's approach. Harrod had started to work on problems of the trade cycle and the theory of distribution as early as 1924–6 after his return from Cambridge, where he spent the Michaelmas 1922 and Lent 1923 terms being tutored in economics by Keynes before taking up his teaching post at Christ Church. While the Oxford group is not as well known as its earlier Cambridge counterpart, it met – though not on a regular basis – and discussed Harrod's work on the *Trade Cycle*. Moreover, members of the group read the chapters of the *Trade Cycle* as it was being written, and the entire book in draft format, and Harrod corresponded with them on their various points of criticism. In addition the structure of what Harrod called the Trade Cycle group resembled the earlier group that formed around Keynes. In the Oxford version, however, Harrod led the group, while Charles Hitch took on the role of intermediary between Harrod and the junior members of the Sub-faculty of Economics and college lecturers who were in the group and those economists at the Oxford Institute who were interested in what Harrod was doing.[21]

It is highly probable that Harrod started to think in terms of his version of the IS–LM equations as early as August–September 1935 when, after an exchange of letters with Keynes, Harrod realized that Keynes had agreed implicitly with his view of the relationship between interest and saving and the multiplier. But, as he was mostly occupied with the development of his extension of Keynes's ideas in the form of the *Trade Cycle*, his IS–LM equations only made their appearance in Oxford about a month after the publication of Keynes's *General Theory*. In his paper 'A Worm's-eye View of the Keynesian Revolution', Arthur Brown gave a brief version of what happened in Oxford at about the time of the publication of the *General Theory*. Brown wrote that he had tried to read Keynes's book:

I cannot remember how far I got – certainly not to the end of
the book – before word came to us, I think in a revision
seminar which Charles Hitch was running, that Harrod had
spoken. What he was reported to have said was an augmented
version of the now famous passage in his correspondence with
Keynes in the previous summer, by which he had established
his claim to have understood what Keynes was really trying to
say . . . the augmentation consisted of a similar account of the
'classical' system, of which Keynes might not have approved,
but which appeared later in Harrod's 'Keynes and Traditional
Theory'.[22]

When interviewed and asked to elaborate on Harrod's approach,
Brown recounted what happened in detail:

I'm quite sure that an equation system purporting to represent
the skeleton of the *General Theory* attributed to Harrod, was
being passed around Oxford within the month after the
publication of the *General Theory* [in Hilary term, 1936]. What
I took to be the nature of the *General Theory* became clear
when I first learnt of the Harrod equations, the four equations
which I took to be its underlying structure.

Asked if the equations in Hicks's IS–LM paper at the 1936
conference reminded him at once of Harrod's equations, Brown
replied

Oh yes . . . Oh yes. We knew they were the same equations.
I'd seen the Harrod equations and no doubt other people in
Oxford had seen the Harrod equations some time before they
had seen the Hicks paper. The majority of people at the
conference had probably seen them at the same time and this
would no doubt make a difference. But in any case, it was
fairly clear to everybody that they were basically the same
equations. It was clear to those who had a preview of Harrod
that the equations Hicks's used as a starting point were old
friends. They were the Harrod equations and what he was just
doing was playing with them a bit, and the playing with them
was the new thing that was exiciting and helpful. I think
Charley Hitch also probably realized they were the same
equations; it's the essential material from which [the] IS–LM

[diagram] is a mathematician's short step. It's not Hicks–
Hansen but Harrod–Hicks IS–LM. My assessment of Harrod
rose in the course of thinking back. Hicks was a mathematician
and this is what made the difference really, I think. I think
that Harrod is not the mathematician of the party, but his
great contributions have all been of mathematical kind in an
odd sort of way, right from marginal revenue onwards. They
are things that are mathematically very simple but profound,
like the growth equation. Harrod liked to see things in a rather
mechanistic way. I think that the further step that Hicks took
of condensing the thing into two functions was important. He
has the IS curve and the LM curve and the solution of the
system, but Harrod did it in words. Having a picture is very
important, since a picture is worth a thousand words. Hicks
did a Marshall. The human mind is very receptive once it's got
past its first year in university, it's very receptive of the idea of
two curves intersecting. Anything more complicated is much
harder to take in, and he got it down to two curves, that's why
Hicks hogged the attention from then on.[23]

When asked whether Harrod may have been upset, having
realized that he was not being given credit as one of the originators
of the IS–LM approach, Brown answered 'I think possibly, this is
conjecture, but it seems plausible.' Was 'Mr. Keynes and Traditional Theory' Harrod's 'last word' on the *General Theory*? Brown
replied 'I think it is his final word on the *General Theory*.' This is
not necessarily due, however, to the lack of recognition of Harrod's
IS–LM approach and the attention paid to Hicks's diagram.
It seems, rather, that at the time of the 1936 conference and
afterwards, Harrod was occupied with developing his approach to
growth and the transition from the ideas underlying his *Trade
Cycle* to his 'Essay in Dynamic Theory'. Indeed, as Brown
relates:

His first exposition of his dynamics in 1939 to the undergraduate economic society made a terrific impact, more than
*Keynes and Traditional Theory*, but they are difficult to
compare because the gist of the former leaked out and
was spread via the grapevine. The actual impact of Roy
expounding a thing himself to a meeting was something
different and that particular sort of impact was made on the

audience I was in when he gave his dynamic thing sometime around the beginning of '39.[24]

Harrod's 'Trade Cycle group' continued after the publication of his book in 1936 and probably assisted him in making the transition from the *Trade Cycle* to 'Essay in Dynamic Theory' over the next two or three years. In fact, Marschak, who had given a seminar in Oxford on business cycle theory, even provided Harrod with a detailed point-by-point critique of his approach to growth, going so far as to draw the time profile of the four growth rates Harrod proposed in his 'Essay'. And Keynes set Harrod straight on the nature of warranted growth. The question put by Matthews to Harrod twenty-five years after the publication of his 'Essay', and Harrod's reply, again point to the fact that Harrod's mind was hardly on the *General Theory* by the time 'Mr. Keynes and Traditional Theory' was published in January 1937.[25]

In January 1964, Matthews wrote to Harrod:

In your book on the trade cycle, published immediately after the General Theory you introduced, as everyone knows, the notion of a cycle model based on the acceleration principle and the multiplier. In 1939 you gave the theory an entirely different twist by using much the same ingredients as the basis of a theory of growth. What we were wondering was what led you to transfer your thinking onto this second track?[26]

Matthews asked Harrod this after having talked to Richard Goodwin about Tinbergen's review of Harrod's *Trade Cycle*. Goodwin maintained that he had informed Harrod about Tinbergen's review after having read it in the original German in the May 1937 issue of *Weltwirtschaftliches Archiv*. Goodwin asserted that he told Harrod that Tinbergen claimed in his review: 'Harrod's theory implied not a cycle but growth (or decay) because it was not possible endogenously to obtain sustained oscillations from the first order linear differential equation implied by the accelerator plus multiplier.' According to Goodwin, 'Harrod only said, "I'll look into it" and never referred to it again – but published his dynamics essay two years later in 1939.' Goodwin adds 'Many years afterwards R.C.O. Matthews asked Harrod if he remembered the conversation; he said he had no recollection of it.'[27]

In fact, Harrod replied to Matthews in two letters in January 1964. In his first letter, dated 7 January, Harrod wrote:

I do not recall seeing the Tinbergen review. And I am quite sure that it had no influence to turning my thoughts in the direction of a growth theory.

It was natural that they should take that turn. For some time I had become convinced that certain problems could be solved only by considering the concomitant movements of variables in a phase of steady growth. What brought this forcibly to my mind were the inconclusive, but very sharp controversies between Hayek and Keynes about the theory of bank credit, and there is evidence of this in my Econometrica article of 1934 (August) about the expansion of credit in an advancing economy (re-published in my 'Economic Essays'). This is not concerned with the Keynesian analysis of saving and investment, but does analyse certain monetary problems in terms of a growing economy. I went on thinking about what more could be done by that type of approach.

I think that the use of the expression 'dynamic determinants' in the Trade Cycle shows that I was feeling my way towards a growth theory that should complement a static theory.

In my Trade Cycle I say of Keynes: 'Mr. Keynes does not formally set out the proper method of dynamic analysis. This method should proceed by asking the following question. What is the rate of growth which, if maintained, will leave the parties content to continue behaving in a way consistent with it?' (p. 150). This surely gives the kernel of thought in my later Essay.

I have similar remarks at the close of my essay on Keynes and the Traditional Theory. This was delivered to the Econometric Society in the summer of 1936 [*sic*], which was presumably before Tinbergen's review. This is to establish my claim that my mind was working independently on these lines. The essay was published in Econometrica of January 1937. Keynes approved of it as an interpretation of him, and I do not recall his saying anything about the dynamic section . . . the so-called Harrod–Domar equation came into my mind suddenly, just like that! I remember brooding on it over and over again, thinking that there must be a snag in something seemingly so simple. This was in the spring of 1938 (my

thoughts in 1937 had been largely occupied with getting
engaged and married!). I worked up the E. J. article during
the Long Vac. of 1938.

Upon further reflection in his second letter, dated 8 January
1964, Harrod continued:

Another point has just occurred to me, with reference to the
subject of my last letter. Tinbergen was himself present when
I gave my address to the Econometric Society in Sept. 1936.
Goodwin doesn't know the date of T's review or where he saw
it? It is most unlikely that it was out by September. It
therefore occurs to me that it was I who suggested to T that
my thought had a closer relation to growth theory than to
trade cycle theory, rather than the other way round. The plea
for a dynamic theory is very clearly stated in this address.[28]

Both Goodwin and Harrod, however, seem to have been affected
by Hicks's adage that 'memory is treacherous', Harrod simply
forgetting Keynes's letter to him of 30 August 1936 about his IS–
LM paper, in which Keynes said 'I like your paper . . . I also agree
with your hints at the end about future dynamic theory.' In any
event, Goodwin's version of his – and implicitly Tinbergen's –
contribution to the development of Harrod's 1939 essay on
dynamics notwithstanding, it is clear that Harrod was involved in
discussing problems arising from the *Trade Cycle* with his group, as
is evident in a letter to Meade dated 7 February 1937. Indeed,
Harrod went on to publish another statement of his approach to
growth within the framework of his review of Lundberg's *Studies in
the Theory of Economic Expansion* in August 1937.[29]

Perhaps the penultimate expression of Harrod's view on dynamics
is to be seen in his review of Hicks's *Value and Capital* published
in the June 1939 issue of the *Economic Journal*. There Harrod took
Hicks to task for claiming 'to have laid the foundations of a
dynamic theory' when in Harrod's view Hicks's 'analysis remains
essentially static.' Moreover, Harrod argued that Hicks used the
term dynamic in a very limiting sense, which could even misdirect
attention from his own broader approach. In Harrod's view,
Hicks's definition of dynamics

as the part of economic theory in which 'every quantity must
be dated' . . . is not the best use to which we may put the word

dynamic . . . we may soon be able to develop an economic dynamics, the foundations of which are not to be found in this volume . . . I believe that some foundation stones of this new theory are already in place [Harrod's essay of March 1939] and that there is some danger that the other [Hicks] usage may deflect attention from this important work.'

But it is still Hicks's name that is associated most directly with IS–LM, although whether this has been or is appreciated by Hicks is another matter, as we shall see.[30]

# 3

# The IS–LMization of Keynes's *General Theory*: equations and diagrams

### Hicks did a Marshall – alternative derivations of the IS–LM diagram

So far our account has been straightforward, as far as IS–LM-type equations are concerned. But a question remains about the possible origins of the IS–LM diagram, an expositional tool which it is doubtful one could 'produce out of a hat'. Two possibilities emerge. Either Hicks developed the diagram himself, without the influence of other concurrent approaches, or he may have been influenced by the work of others and synthesized their approaches with his own. The most probable sources, in either case, for the IS–LM diagram are: Harrod's functions and his *General Theory* diagram, Champernowne's equations and diagrams and Hicks's own analytical method, manifest later in *Value and Capital*.

### *Harrod's functions and* General Theory *diagram*

According to Hicks's letter of 6 September 1936, he had seen Harrod's IS–LM paper before starting to write his own. Moreover, having reviewed Keynes's *General Theory*, Hicks had already seen Harrod's diagram there. In his paper, Harrod has critical elements in the form of equations, unknowns and functional relationships, which he calls $\phi$, $\psi$ and $\chi$ respectively. As Harrod writes:

> We . . . have three equations to determine the value of three unknowns, level of income, volume of saving [= volume of

investment) and rate of interest (= marginal productivity of capital) . . . Thus, if the schedules expressing the marginal productivity of capital, the propensity to consume, and liquidity preference are known and the total quantity of money in the system is known also, the amount of investment, the level of income, and the rate of interest may readily be determined

via his functional relationships. Harrod then executes a series of what he calls 'exercises' using his approach. These exercises illustrate clearly what happens to his system when changes in, for example 'the total amount of money available' or 'rewards to prime factors' occur.[1]

If Harrod's functions are mapped onto his *General Theory* diagram, one obtains a diagram which closely resembles the IS–LM diagram. But to do this, one must first redraw Harrod's diagram taking into account the multiplier, in order to obtain Income on the vertical axis, and then reverse the axes. Whether or not Hicks derived his IS–LM diagram in this manner is a moot point. The parallels between Hicks's diagram and the outcome of mapping Harrod's functions onto his *General Theory* diagram is simply the result of their identical equational representations of Keynes's *General Theory*.[2]

### Champernowne's equations and diagrams

It may have been Champernowne's paper that set Hicks thinking in terms of a combined equational–diagrammatic representation of Keynes's *General Theory*, although in a recent letter Hicks wrote:

What is common between my paper and his seems to be no more than what any intelligent person could have got from a careful reading of the General Theory. What is in mine, but not in his, is the conflation of what appears in his version as several diagrams, on to a single diagram–for good, or for evil, or perhaps for both!

His caveat notwithstanding, the point Hicks makes about 'conflation' indicates that his IS–LM diagram could be derived from Champernowne's equations and diagrams.[3]

In light of Champernowne's comments cited above, we must

utilize both his equations and diagrams. Then we can 'conflate' his diagrams in the following manner. First, let us consider Champernowne's diagram on the supply and demand for money. In this case, the Md curve, Md $(r, \ldots N_0)$ is drawn up with a level of N, $N_0$, assumed. Then let us assume a higher level of N, $N_1$, which necessitates the plotting of another Md curve, Md $(r, \ldots N_1)$ which, for any value of r, brings about an increase in the demand for money. If a standard comparative statics exercise is done, this generates a resulting set of $(r, N)$ pairs that can be plotted accordingly. This, however, only follows if Champernowne's equations are utilized, where the level of income, i.e. N, is taken as being one of the determinants of the demand for (or supply of) money, rather than simply functions of, for example, the form Ms $(r)$ and Md $(r, Q')$.

The IS schedule can be derived from Champernowne's diagram relating to the supply of and demand for saving. Again, given Champernowne's equations we specify the demand for saving curve in his diagram as Sd $(\ldots, r_0)$ and the supply of saving as Ss $(\ldots, r_0)$. Then let us assume that a shift in the demand schedule occurs with increasing interest rate Sd $(\ldots, r_1)$. The effect upon N is to lower it from $N_0$ to $N_1$. This can be mapped onto a diagram with axes of N and r; these exercises are illustrated in figure 3.1. If the supply of savings is positively related to the rate of interest, the employment effect of an increase in the rate of interest would be even larger. Moreover, the exercise Champernowne does in his paper on the effect of an increase in thriftiness can be replicated using the 'conflation' of his diagrams.

According to Champernowne, some time after the publication of his paper he had contact with both Lerner and Kalecki, speaking about his views of Keynes's system with both of them and even discussing diagrammatical representations of Keynes with Lerner. And it was Lerner who was to develop the diagrammatic interpretations of Keynes's system even further, but more about this below. In any event, whether or not Hicks did the comparative statics exercises outlined above is also a moot point. The fact is, as Hicks himself has essentially admitted, they can be done, since Champernowne's diagrams can be 'conflated' into his. Hicks, however, claims that his diagram originated in a different way, and it is to his account that we now turn.[4]

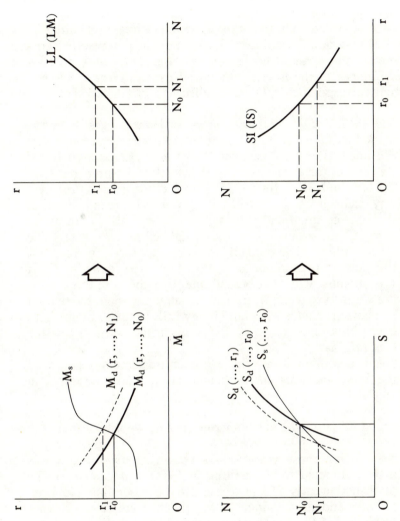

**Figure 3.1** Derivation of SI and LL curves from Champernowne's diagrams

*Hicks's diagram and the application of*
Value and Capital *methods*

As already emphasized, Hicks never claimed to have originated the
IS–LM equations. On the other hand, he claims originality for his
IS–LM diagram. According to Hicks, the diagram results from the
application of methods he developed in the course of writing *Value
and Capital*, to the interpretation of Keynes's *General Theory*. In
recent correspondence, Hicks recalled:

> The IS–LM *diagram* [Hick's emphasis] was suggested by the
> work I had already done on three-way exchange, though that
> did not appear until Chapter V of *Value and Capital*. But it
> was one of the earlier parts of that book to be prepared.
>     I left the LSE in June 1935; I am pretty sure that the three-
> way exchange diagram had been given in lectures (several of
> the LSE group attended those lectures, but also, I am pretty
> sure, Champernowne) at the LSE before that date. The
> Hicks–Allen article on demand theory appeared in early '34;
> the work in preparation of it must have been done in '33. It
> was obvious, with that behind one, that the next thing to be
> done was to re-work Walrasian exchange theory in the light of
> it. I am sure that is what I did in my LSE lectures. I must have
> been thinking in terms of 3–way exchange before I saw the
> *General Theory*.
>     It is possibly relevant that a French translation of a draft of
> the *Value and Capital* Mathematical Appendix appeared in
> 1937.[5]

In an additional letter, Hicks wrote that he would insist

> that during those years (34–38 inclusive) my thought was
> mainly directed to the writing of *Value and Capital* (to be
> published in early '39); anything else was a side-line. Not even
> an independent side-line; the *two* [Hicks's emphasis] Keynes
> papers of '36 and the Hawtrey paper of '39 . . . were, from my
> point of view, just applications of *Value and Capital* methods
> . . . During the 2½ years between the Oxford Conference and
> the publication of *Value and Capital*, IS–LM was in the public
> domain; but I was not following it up.

Hicks continues:

> I don't suppose that IS–LM appeared in my Cambridge
> lectures, which were based on the as yet unpublished *Value
> and Capital*; my Cambridge audience must have found them
> hard to take. The reason why it did not appear is that the
> heavy emphasis on the long-term rate of interest, in the
> *General Theory* (followed by IS–LM) was not in my line. My
> theory of interest (in *Value and Capital*) was a theory of the
> structure of interest rates. That brought me nearer to Hawtrey
> than to Keynes.[6]

In the letters cited above, Hicks makes a number of statements
which deserve further elaboration and investigation. First, Hicks's
emphasis on originating the IS–LM *diagram* – a repeat of his 1980
statement 'that the idea of the IS–LM diagram came to me as a
result of the work I had been doing on 3-way exchange' – is
important. Indeed, in light of his earlier statements about his
contribution to the development of the IS–LM approach – in *The
Crisis in Keynesian Economics* (1974) and 'The Formation of an
Economist' and *Causality in Economics*, both published in 1979 –
this represents a major revision of his claim to having originated the
IS–LM interpretation of Keynes's *General Theory*, even though in
these works he never actually claimed to have originated the IS–LM
equations, as emphasized above.[7]

In *The Crisis in Keynesian Economics* Hicks did say that his IS–
LM paper was, in effect, a revision of his June 1936 review of
Keynes's *General Theory*:

> I had little time to write that review; so I was not (and am not)
> very satisfied with it. Only a few months later I felt that I must
> do it again. The result was the paper 'Mr Keynes and the
> Classics' with the SILL diagram that has got into so many
> textbooks. To many students, I fear, it is Keynes' theory. But
> it was never intended as more than a representation of what
> appeared to be a central part of the Keynes theory. As such I
> think it is still defensible (it would appear that Keynes himself
> accepted it as such).

Hicks adds:

> But I have never regarded it as complete in itself. In fact, only
> two years later, in *Value and Capital* (1939), I myself put
> forward what is surely a very different formulation. This also
> has had much effect; the version of Keynes that is put forward
> in many modern writings (especially, perhaps those descended
> from Patinkin) look to me more like the *Value and Capital*
> formulation than like Keynes' own.

Finally, Hicks maintains that 'In my Mr. Keynes and the
Classics . . . I similarly reduced Keynes' 3 relations to two, taking
the multiplier with the Marginal Efficiency of Capital to form the SI
curve.'[8]

In 'The Formation of an Economist' Hicks asserted that 'the IS–
LM version of Keynes' theory, which I myself produced, but which
has never been highly regarded by orthodox Keynesians, did not
help me', while in his *Causality in Economics*, published in the same
year, he stated:

> For the textbook formalization I must myself take some
> responsibility; for IS–LM first saw the light in a paper of my
> own . . . I have, however continually repeated that I
> considered myself to be doing no more in that paper than
> arranging what then appeared to be a central part of Keynes'
> teaching, for expository purposes. I am sure that if I had not
> done it, and done it in that way, someone else would have
> done it very soon after [*sic*].[9]

Secondly, both his application of *Value and Capital* methods to
what he calls 'the Hawtrey paper of '39' and his assertion that he
was 'nearer to Hawtrey than to Keynes', are problematic, for
Hawtrey agreed with neither. Moreover, Hawtrey's 1939 review of
*Value and Capital* was critical, to say the least, and prompted an
exchange with Hicks which focused on the fundamental differences between them, at least as far as Hawtrey was concerned.
Finally, Hicks himself wrote that he could not agree with
Hawtrey regarding Keynes, preferring Keynes's 'arithmetic' to his
'rhetoric'.[10]

Thus, while one can accept Hicks's contention that he may have
moved 'nearer to Hawtrey than to Keynes', Hawtrey would not

have thought that his views were at all close to Hicks's. Now, Hicks also raises the point in his recent correspondence about his lectures at Cambridge being based on *Value and Capital* rather than IS–LM. However, this is not consistent with his earlier (1979) published account of having 'lectured on IS–LM almost every year from 1938 onwards'.[11]

In any case, to return to the issue of the origins of the SILL (IS–LM) diagram, there cannot be any doubt as to Hicks's originality, for the diagram appears only in his IS–LM paper. However, the question remains as to whether the diagram is simply the outcome of Hicks's effort at two-dimensional representation of an analogue of three-way exchange, or the result of his synthesis of existing equational and diagrammatic approaches via what he called his *Value and Capital* methods.

According to his letter to Meade of 6 September 1936, Hicks did not start to write his own IS–LM paper until he saw what Harrod had to say. This does not mean, however, that Hicks had not thought about a diagrammatic representation of Keynes's *General Theory* prior to seeing both Harrod's and Meade's papers. Indeed, as he has stated, he may have been thinking more or less about this while developing the methods later presented in *Value and Capital*. But it was probably Champernowne's paper that catalysed Hicks's thought to a combined equational–diagrammatic representation of his interpretation of Keynes's *General Theory*.[12]

However, as Champernowne has noted, one cannot derive the SILL (IS–LM) diagram from his diagrams without reference to his equations. Given Champernowne's more general equations, Hicks would have had to specify IS–LM-type equations and then do the comparative statics exercises of Champernowne's diagrams illustrated above.[13]

But, according to Hicks, he did not do this. He claims to have done a *gedanken*-experiment which involved representing a three-way exchange problem in two dimensions, i.e. mapping a set of three simultaneous equations onto a two-dimensional diagram. I contend, therefore, that after seeing Harrod's paper, things fell into place for Hicks, and he was indeed able to do the thought-experiment he describes in his 1980 'explanation' of IS–LM; in effect synthesizing the equational–diagrammatic approaches of Harrod and Champernowne via his own *Value and Capital* methods and arriving at his IS–LM diagram accordingly. In any case, the IS–LM diagram soon became one of the most widely used expositional tools of those engaged in disseminating Keynes's *General Theory*, for example Kaldor and Lerner.[14]

## IS–LM, Lerner and Kaldor

### *Lerner and Keynesian diagrammatics (1937–51)*

In the same month that Hicks's article appeared in *Econometrica*, Lerner read a paper to the Manchester Statistical Society entitled 'Capital, Investment and Interest', in which he dealt with what he called the 'social signficance' of investment via emphasis on the concepts of the marginal productivity and efficiency of capital. Lerner presents the schedule of the marginal efficiency of investment, but then states 'Mr. Keynes calls this the marginal efficiency of capital – probably because any point on it represents a situation in which not only the (social) marginal efficiency of investment but also the (private) marginal productivity of capital is equal to the rate of interest, and he has failed clearly to distinguish between these two concepts.' Lerner then develops a three-dimensional figure to illustrate the relationships between rate of interest, net investment and quantity of capital on which schedules of the marginal efficiency of investment and marginal productivity of capital are drawn.[15]

Between his summary of Keynes's *General Theory* in the October 1936 issue of *International Labour Review* and his *Essays in Economic Analysis* (1953), a significant proportion of Lerner's published work contained various diagrammatic representations of his interpretation of Keynes's *General Theory* approach. These ranged from his SI, M and L curves in his June 1938 paper 'Alternative Formulations of the Theory of Interest' in the *Economic Journal* to the 'LIS' curve – as Hansen called it – presented in Lerner's *Economics of Employment* published in 1951. In light of Lachmann's recollection that Lerner was not impressed by Hicks's IS–LM paper, Lerner's recourse to his own diagrammatic approach is not surprising. What is surprising, however, is that Lerner would want to generalize Hicks's approach to Keynes's *General Theory* via his own diagrammatic interpretation of what he took to be Keynes's central message.[16]

For example, in 'Alternative Formulations of the Theory of Interest', Lerner constructs what he calls an SI curve. This is obtained

as soon as it is recognized that saving must equal investment
. . . For each scale of investment there is a corresponding level
of income. This is determined by the propensity to consume.
For each level of income, there is a corresponding supply
schedule of saving (with respect to the rate of interest) . . .
Thus for any particular rate of interest there is a particular
scale of investment . . . and a particular supply schedule of
saving showing how much would be saved at different rates of
interest if income were at the level corresponding to the
particular rate of interest, so that the two curves will have this
point in common . . . The only legitimate point on the supply
curve of saving is the one which falls on the investment curve
and shows that at that particular rate of interest the amount
saved will be equal to the amount invested. The locus of such
legitimate points for different rates of interest must coincide
with the I curve, making it an SI curve.

Lerner continues 'Dr. Hicks seems to have been successful in
keeping all of these in what seems to me to be a right perspective.
Essentially he has put in a more mathematical manner [*sic*] what I
have endeavoured to show in my curves.'[17]
Some eighteen months later, in his November 1939 paper 'Ex-
ante Analysis and Wage Theory', Lerner again applied diagrammatics presenting his interpretation of the major differences
between Pigovian and Keynesian analyses of the effect of a money-
wage cut upon employment when viewed in 'ex-ante/ex-post'
terms. Lerner then illustrates the 'trap' into which Pigou falls,

attributing the increase in employment to the wage cut rather
than to the reduction of the rate of interest, which alone is
essential – the wage cut being merely one way of bringing
about the reduction in the rate of interest. Or, one might say,
the wage cut has the described effects only through the
reduction in the rate of interest.[18]

It is here that Lerner sets out explicitly – and in diagrammatic
form – the nature of the relationships in what amounts to his
interpretation of the Keynesian system. Lerner presents what he
calls 'a simplified system of interdependent relationships' in which
i, the interest rate, has a direct effect upon A, which is 'the value of
assets other than money'. This in turn directly affects L, which he

calls 'the demand for money to hold'. According to Lerner, 'i also affects I, the scale of investment and C (Y), the propensity to consume. I and C (Y) determine Y, income, and Y also affects L'; all these having, in his view, an 'indirect' effect on L. L, when taken together with monetary policy, 'determines the rate of interest'.[19]

Lerner describes Pigou's case, in which

> I is taken as fixed (at zero), so that this branch of the 'indirect-effect' drops out of the scheme. A wage-cut has the effect of cutting L in the same proportion for given values of A and Y in terms of wage units. This reduces i and increases A, but whether the reduction in i increases or diminishes Y will depend on whether it increases or diminishes C (Y).

Here Lerner cites Kaldor's earlier critique of Pigou's approach – which, as we shall see, was based on IS–LM – but then takes Pigou to task for continuing to use his 'faulty method' in the 'revised account of the argument' that appeared in Pigou's 'Money Wages in Relation to Unemployment' in March 1938. In order to refute Pigou here, Lerner uses Kaldor's mathematical approach, which – with the help of Lange – shows both Pigou's method and conclusions to be fraught with 'dangers', the latter not necessarily even giving consistent results. This Lerner achieves by adopting an IS–LM-type savings function of the form

$$S = F (r, Y).[20]$$

In *The Economics of Control* (1944), Lerner returned to the three-dimensional diagrammatics of his 1937 paper and his distinction between what he calls the marginal efficiency of investment – what Keynes termed the marginal efficiency of capital – and the schedule of the marginal efficiency of investment, which Keynes called the schedule of the marginal efficiency of capital. He then defined 'the marginal productivity of capital' as 'the marginal efficiency of investment when the rate of net investment is zero'. But, in retrospect, Lerner decided that this came too close to the Austrian approach advocated, for example, by Knight. A decade later Lerner revised his view, in his 1953 paper 'On the Marginal Productivity of Capital and the Marginal Efficiency of Investment': 'I am not so sure whether it was a good thing for the understanding and development of economic theory. It might be better to write off completely our investment in this phrase and to speak only of the marginal efficiency of investment.' Nonetheless, he still applied diagrammatics, drawing the marginal efficiency of investment as 'a declining function of the rate of interest'.[21]

The penultimate stage in Lerner's development of Keynesian 'diagrammatics' appears in his *Economics of Employment* (1951). Here he constructs a diagram which aims to illustrate how the schedules of marginal efficiency of capital, consumption and liquidity preference, when taken in conjunction with money supply, determine interest rate. According to this diagram, the interest rate is determined by the intersection of the money supply curve and what Hansen has called Lerner's 'new "sophisticated" curve', which he labels 'LIS'. According to Hansen, Lerner's LIS curve aims to illustrate the 'rather complicated business' of 'how the total demand for money, including both the transactions demand and the asset demand, is affected by changes in income which correspond to changes in the rate of investment (account being taken of the multiplier) consistent with changes in the rate of interest'.[22]

Hansen continues:

The LIS curve is a peculiar hybrid. Visible behind it is the family of liquidity preference schedules; and concealed behind it are the investment–demand function and the consumption function. Thus the LIS curve represents an effort to subsume all three functions into one curve. This is all right so long as no one forgets all three functions. But there is a danger that someone will forget the concealed functions and begin to call the LIS curve a liquidity preference curve. If anyone makes this mistake, he is likely next to make the fatal error of saying that the rate of interest is determined wholly by liquidity preference and the supply of money, and even to assert that the marginal efficiency schedule and the savings function (or conversely the consumption function) have nothing to do with the rate of interest [*sic*].

Hansen then asserts that Lerner has fallen into the 'error' he describes: 'that so lucid a writer as Lerner should fall into this error illustrates well the danger of using a formulation which does not explicitly make use of all the functions involved in the IS and LM method of analysis. The Hicksian method makes it impossible to lose sight of all four determinants – the three functions and the money supply.'[23]

Whether or not Lerner would agree with Hansen is a moot point. Suffice it to say, that it was Lerner's 'diagrammatic' approach that brought Robertson to the recognition of 'two curves of marginal productivity which had previously been used by economists in seeking to explain the level of interest rates'. These were the marginal productivity of capital and what Robertson called 'the marginal productivty of investible funds', which Lerner preferred to call 'the marginal efficiency of investment'.[24]

Some thirty-five years after the appearance of 'Ex-ante Analysis and Wage Theory', Lerner spoke of 'the multifold confusions of thought arising from the ambiguities in the concept of "saving" or "savings" '. According to Lerner 'this blessed word and symbol exuded thick fogs of mystical mischief' which affected even Keynes. 'The virulence of the S-engendered confusions is demonstrated by its ability to infect even Keynes himself, although perhaps only when he was overworked and very tired.' Lerner then recalls that in a meeting at the Federal Reserve in Washington in 1944, Keynes expressed concern lest, after the war, an excess of saving might result in depression and stagnation.

> I suggested that any such depression could be prevented by increasing disposable income (e.g. by deficit financing). Keynes retorted that this would only make matters worse since it would increase the saving. (This led Evsey Domar to whisper to me that Keynes ought to read the *General Theory*).[25]

Lerner, however, had similarly fallen prey to the vicissitudes of 'S', for, as we have seen he adopted an IS–LM-type savings function of the form

$$S = F (r, Y)$$

in his 1939 paper. But this is a far cry from his 1936 *General Theory* summary in which he supposed 'that the amount people save depends only on the size of their income, and that it increases with the size of income.' Perhaps Lerner ought to have read his own initial interpretation of Mr Keynes![26]

## *Kaldor and the application of IS–LM*

Interestingly, Kaldor – who was shown the diagram by Hicks – was among the earliest, if not the first, to apply the IS–LM approach and Hicks's diagram in practice. Only nine months after it appeared in print, Kaldor applied 'the type of diagram used by Dr. Hicks' in his refutation 'Prof. Pigou on Money Wages in Relation to Unemployment' published in the *Economic Journal* in December 1937.[27]

Kaldor starts his critique by focusing on 'the critical function, on which . . . Pigou's demonstration depended . . . the old fashioned savings-function in disguise'. According to him 'It is now, however, fairly generally agreed, at any rate since the publication of Mr. Keynes' *General Theory*, that savings cannot be regarded as a function of the interest rate alone.' Kaldor says 'it is interesting to note that the assumption that savings are largely a function of real income has not been questioned by any of Mr. Keynes' critics. Yet, in the present writer's view it is this assumption, more than any other, which is responsible for the "revolutionary" innovations of Mr. Keynes' system.' Kaldor adds 'if we want to be inclusive, we ought to say that savings depend on the rate of interest, the size of real income and its distribution.'[28]

Kaldor maintains that Pigou's argument is incorrect since 'both savings and investment depend on the rate of interest and on the level of real output.' On this basis, Kaldor asserts

> there is no way in which a change in money wages could affect either the savings function or the investment function. It cannot alter therefore the level of real output which secures equality between savings and investment at a given rate of interest . . . if the rate of interest is given, the equilibrium level is also given, irrespective of the level of money wages.[29]

At this point, Kaldor claims that 'this proposition could be best illustrated by the type of diagram' Hicks used in his IS–LM paper, and then does a comparative statics exercise using the IS–LM diagram. According to him:

> A reduction in money wages cannot affect the position of the IS curve, but it will shift the LL curve to the right, for, by reducing the size of 'working balances' at a given level of real

income, it enhances the size of 'idle balances' and thus reduces the interest rate consistent with that level of output. Its effect therefore is exactly the same as that of an increase in the quantity of money or a reduction in liquidity preference. It is, in fact, nothing more than an alternative way of increasing the quantity of money in terms of wage units.[30]

As noted above, Hicks had shown Kaldor the IS–LM diagram sometime between its presentation in September 1936 and its publication in April 1937. In a recent interview with the author, Kaldor restated his view of IS–LM in general – taking issue with Kahn's condemnation of it – and recalled his 1937 paper, revising somewhat his view of IS–LM because of the problematic nature of the investment function it implies.[31]

Asked how he viewed IS–LM when Hicks first showed it to him, and how he presented it at the time, Kaldor replied:

I thought it was rather clever . . . Hicks presented it to me as a representation of Keynes and that was the whole point. At the time, there were endless arguments about Keynes, on what he was really saying. Moreover, it was a sort of representation of Keynes that would lead one to suppose that his theory isn't so novel as it pretends to be because all the elements in the diagram are good old neo-classical stuff so to speak . . . Investment and saving are both functions of income and the rate of interest. That way you have a whole set of IS curves each for different levels of income. Equally the LM curve might have the same shape even if there were no liquidity preference. So Keynes' idea that the demand for money varies with the rate of interest is not an integral part of the LM curve because the LM curve could simply be a supply curve of money for different levels of income and different rates of interest.

Kaldor was then asked if Hicks presented the diagram to him as a Walrasian or general equilibrium type of representation:

No. I don't think so. Hicks lectured on Walras long before. But this wasn't connected with Walras. This was macro-economics and Walras wasn't . . . it was microeconomics: about n industries and n commodities and n prices and so on, and n–1 equations. I mean Walras is all about counting equations and unknowns. So general equilibrium theory has no use for macroeconomics . . . I am very surprised that Hicks ever says that Walras had anything to do with this.

It was then put to Kaldor that according to Hicks, IS–LM evolved from his earlier works through the reduction of three-dimensional into two-dimensional diagrams on the basis of his *Value and Capital* method. Kaldor answered: 'That may be, if you put it that way . . . It's not inconsistent . . . The main point is that he was trying to interpret the *General Theory*, trying to give a representation of the *General Theory*.'

When asked about the savings function in his 1937 paper, especially in so far as it is identical to the savings function in IS–LM, Kaldor replied:

But everybody represented the savings function as being a function of income and interest. I mean Keynes's objection was that they don't take into account that it's a function of income, only that it's a function of interest. If you read my little 1937 paper in answer to Pigou, it is notable because Pigou admitted that he was wrong and Keynes was right after that. Pigou wrote an article in the September [1937] *Economic Journal* in which he was trying to refute Keynes by saying that lowering wages is not the same thing as using the rate of interest or increasing the real quantity of money, but it's a specific change of relative prices and then I replied to this in which I showed that he made a slip . . . I showed that as an equation system his method shows that you can get the Keynesian results from a classical–orthodox approach just as easily. And then much to everybody's suprise – chiefly Robbins's – Pigou replied to me very nicely and said that he now accepts my main point – which is really accepting Keynes's general position – and he withdraws what he said. And that was in the next issue of *Economic Journal* [March 1938].

Pigou's published reply to Kaldor is instructive, for it reveals that he was indeed quite willing to accept Kaldor's argument, which was based on the IS–LM approach, for it brought Kaldor's – and Keynes's – position closer to Pigou's view. Pigou writes 'I have argued that . . . a cut in money wage rates – not carrying with it an expectation of further cuts – must, when equilibrium is re-established, carry with it an increase in employment, regardless of everything else. Mr. Kaldor replied that, besides increasing employment, it must also entail (except in a special case) a fall in the rate of interest.' However, as Kaldor notes in the concluding passage of his paper:

> Pigou's view that a 'money wage cut is not simply a piece of ritual that enables the real cause of employment expansion – a fall in the money rate of interest – to take effect' cannot be upheld. If the above analysis is correct, it is indeed such a piece of ritual; although, if we want to be quite accurate, the increase in the size of idle balances, rather than simply the fall in the money rate of interest, should be regarded as the ultimate cause of employment expansion.[32]

In his 1938 reply Pigou added:

> I have not been able to follow the reasoning of Mr. Keynes' short note, which preceded Mr. Kaldor's. But what is said in the following paragraphs about the interrelations of money-wage-rates, employment and the rate of interest is much closer to his general view [as put by Kaldor's application of the IS–LM interpretation of Keynes] than the argument . . . of my previous article.

Finally, Pigou concludes 'that . . . a cut in money wage rates will lead to a new equilibrium situation in which employment is larger, and the rate of interest lower, than before . . . As Mr. Kaldor has shown, it is possible to extend an algebraic analysis of the type used in the study of our model to conditions nearer real life [i.e. IS–LM]'.[33]

There was, however, an additional dimension to the exchange between Kaldor, Pigou and Keynes. In fact, the exchange was six-sided, also involving Kahn and Robertson – as noted in Keynes's collected works – and even Hicks, a fact which was not known previously. The debate between Keynes and Pigou and the correspondence between Keynes and Kaldor will not be reviewed in detail here, although a number of crucial points concerning this material must be made.[34]

First, Robertson wrote to Keynes on 17 October 1937. Commenting in this letter on Kaldor's paper – which Kaldor had sent him – Robertson mentions the importance of Hicks's IS–LM paper for the debate 'as we approach the real world'. On 19 October, Robertson wrote to Kaldor, saying that while he could not 'make anything of Keynes' note . . . your note . . . sets out the issues so clearly . . . that I hope you will publish it'. On 23 October Kaldor replied to Robertson:

On looking over the E. J. article, I don't think there can be any doubt as to what his [Pigou's] assumptions were, especially since he introduces the variability of the rate of investment separately, in the last section. On the other hand I really do not think it makes much difference to the argument, with which of the short-run models one works, and I think my argument holds just as much for the Keynesian short-run (which you think is the same as the one Pigou is now assuming) as for the original Pigou model. This, however, is not easy to show. I think Hicks' Econometrica article could help one a great deal.

It seems that in the first draft of the paper sent to Keynes and Robertson, the IS–LM approach wasn't used by Kaldor, being added in order to assist his argument.

Secondly, Hicks agreed with Kaldor's main point in a letter to him dated 23 October 1937, and also noted that he was in the process of developing an alternate way of approaching the issue. Thirdly, Pigou accepted the analysis used by Kaldor, in Keynes's words 'much preferring Kaldor's criticism'.

Fourth, Kahn, while highly critical of Pigou and Robertson, also criticized Kaldor's paper in a letter to Keynes dated 22 October 1937, accusing him, along with them, of failing 'to see the fundamental fallacy – which is the determination of the rate of interest by the rate of discount of the future'. Kahn continues to say that although he had 'not seen Kaldor's article . . . I am sure that publication of it will darken counsel. After all we could all of us write replies to Pigou if you wanted them and I do not see why Kaldor should be thus favoured'. To this Keynes replied on 25 October 1937 'I am quite clear that I must print Kaldor's article, and cannot possibly use my editorial discretion to suppress it. In fact, no one else has sent me any comment on Pigou.'[35]

Finally, in letters to Kahn on 29 December 1937 and to Pigou on 3 January 1938, Keynes highlights the ambiguous nature of the 'hybrid' savings function used by Kaldor and of his own attitude towards the IS–LM approach. In his letter to Kahn, he writes that after Pigou's 'retraction' there are 'only two differences of opinion' between their positions. According to Keynes, the first of these arose from Pigou's 'conviction that the theory of the relation between money wages and employment, via the rate of interest, was invented by Kaldor'. The second, and more important one, was that Keynes thought that Pigou maintained his belief 'that a rise in the rate of interest increases aggregate savings' which, in Keynes's view, Pigou persisted in confusing 'with its increasing savings out of a given income', although Keynes says as an afterthought, 'he may have given this up too – I think he must have – I must look at the article again.'[36]

Whether or not Keynes did take another look at Pigou's paper is a moot point. About a week later, however, in a letter to Pigou to acknowledge receipt of his 'retraction', Keynes wrote:

> I am sorry you could not follow my short note. As far as I can see, you now accept all my contentions . . . Kaldor is mainly a restatement of my General Theory with reference to your special assumptions. These special assumptions make it possible, of course, to reduce it to a simpler form without losing anything. On the other hand, it is really the general case one has to consider, and that it seems to me would be very difficult to treat along these lines. I wish very much that you would now, in light of this more recent discussion, read over again Chapter 19 of my book together with its Appendix. This is the source of the theory that the effect of changes in money wages on employment in a closed system is through the rate of interest, though in the general case it can also work in other ways.[37]

Keynes's acknowledgement of Kaldor's paper as having restated his *General Theory* would seem to imply his agreement with Kaldor's application of IS–LM in the debate with Pigou. Keynes, however, true to form, qualifies this by adding that Kaldor was restating the *General Theory* under assumptions that enabled such a 'simple' formulation as Hicks's SILL type of analysis used by Kaldor to be applicable in this case. But, as Keynes notes, whether such an approach would be applicable in what he calls 'the general case' is another matter altogether. And it was the *General Theory* itself which dealt with this aspect of the problem, as Keynes reminded Pigou.

When interviewed some fifty years later, Kaldor was asked about the implications of the savings function he used in his reply to Pigou for the investment function and the potential misrepresentation of Keynes. Kaldor replied:

> Honestly, all these years I didn't realize what all this about IS–LM being a misrepresentation of Keynes was about. I thought that it meant that in the IS–LM diagram you regard investment as a function of current income and not expected income . . . I see now that by writing an IS diagram, we presuppose that the investment demand function is a single valued function of income and the rate of interest. Well, that is nonsensical, because the investment demand function depends on expected income, not on current income; and, although you can say that, broadly, expected income depends on current income, you can't just equate the two, whatever the behaviour of current income is. Variations in current income would affect expected income, but only gradually and with a certain time-lag . . . I see now that in Keynes's theory an important part was played by sudden variations in the MEC which are not explained, certainly not plausibly explained, by current events. So in postulating a relationship that an increase in income causes an increase in investment, we ignore the fact that the actual interrelationship need not be stable . . . sometimes investment reacts strongly to a change in income, and sometimes in a weak way or not at all, depending on expectations and uncertainty; and how one actually distinguishes between these things goodness knows. It's all right to say we can bring it in but the operational significance of that is not at all clear. Where does uncertainty come in? Probably it comes in in the form that the expected rate of profit must always be higher than the rate of interest. Because investment is an uncertain thing, the more uncertain you are, the higher the rate of profit which you have to expect in order to undertake an investment.

Asked how he saw IS–LM at the time and if he saw it as a valid interpretation of Keynes's *General Theory*, Kaldor replied:

> It is a clever exposition. It separates out the monetary factors and the real factors and shows that there must be some constellation of interest and income at which both the monetary factors and the real factors coalesce, so to speak. That was the clever thing about it . . . I took it to be a pedagogic thing that highlights the essential parts of the Keynesian theory in much easier terms for undergraduates who are studying it. It certainly was not a new idea and Hicks didn't present it as something new. I thought that the *General Theory* could be presented in this diagram, and I thought that it could be until I recalled that it can't because regarding investment as a function of income and interest in the same way as savings, does do a bit of violence to Keynes's ideas; he would not regard investment as a function of income but of expected income, when the latter is liable to sudden variations which are not caused by anything else.

Kaldor continued:

> I think you attribute too much importance to IS–LM . . . It was a useful bit of geometry to simplify Keynes and to make students understand what Keynes was trying to say. But, as we now say, the IS part of it was not a stable function . . . What is wrong with the IS–LM diagram is that it regards investment as a single valued function of these two variables, income and interest, whereas this is only true if the structure of expectations is given . . . But this is something which can vary and is very capricious in its variations . . . Up to Keynes one had the feeling that if you increase investment, given involuntary unemployment, that might be inflationary. This is because one did not take into account that an increase in income increases savings. I always regarded that the most important novel feature of Keynes, much more important than liquidity preference, is simply the relationship of savings to income. I still feel that the most important thing in Keynes is the emphasis on the dependence of saving on the level of income – a relationship which nobody ever denied but nobody took into account.

Finally, Kaldor was asked whether he agreed with Kahn's attack on IS–LM in *The Making of Keynes' General Theory* (1984), i.e. that IS–LM had done more harm than good and had confused the development of economic thought. Kaldor replied 'Why? Does he explain it . . . No. I would not agree that it has done more harm than good.'

Kaldor concluded by saying that he still thought of IS–LM as 'illuminating in bringing out clearly and simply the nature of the problem that Keynes had in mind . . . Keynes certainly didn't react to it like Kahn did'.[38]

Kaldor's view of Kahn's position notwithstanding, his own use of IS–LM against Pigou marked only an initial application of the IS–LM interpretation of Keynes's *General Theory*. It was left to others – Alvin Hansen for example – to make IS–LM into the conventionally accepted interpretation of Keynes, i.e. to institutionalize IS–LM as 'Keynesian economics'.

## Hansen and the institutionalization of IS–LM

In October 1936, Alvin Hansen's review of Keynes's *General Theory* appeared in the *Journal of Political Economy*. Hansen called his critique. 'Mr. Keynes on Underemployment Equilibrium' and concluded it with:

> The book under review is not a landmark in the sense that it lays a foundation for a 'new economics'. It warns us once again, in a provocative manner, of the danger of reasoning based on assumptions which no longer fit the facts of economic life . . . The book is more a symptom of economic trends than a foundation stone upon which a science can be built.[39]

Hansen's review was reproduced in his *Full Recovery or Stagnation* (1938), but he seems to have fundamentally changed his view of Keynes's *General Theory* between the review's 1936 and 1938 versions. In the latter, Hansen deleted the passage cited above from his concluding remarks. Moreover, he edited out major sections of his earlier version critical of Keynes's approach, adding only one section regarding the marginal efficiency of capital, although taking issue with Keynes in this case.[40]

For example, Hansen deleted his critique of Keynes on the propensity to consume, its measurement and possible fluctuations. Hansen claimed in his 1936 version that such 'difficulties and obscurities arise from Keynes' failure to give exact definitions and to employ them consistently.' Furthermore, when Hansen added the passage on the relationship between the marginal efficiency of capital and the production costs of investment goods, he adopted an alternative criticism of Keynes's position. In addition, in his later version he deleted or edited a number of passages that attacked Keynes's view on methods of establishing full employment. Finally, he altered fundamentally the tone of his conclusion by completely removing the critical sentences cited above. The 1938 version ends with the statement 'Out of discussion and research will come bit by bit an improved theoretical apparatus . . . and a more accurate appreciation of social psychology . . . and of the precise character of the economic environment in which humans act as individuals and in groups.'[41]

What brought Hansen to change his mind about Keynes's *General Theory* can only be explained by his interpretation of Keynes via 'an improved theoretical apparatus' which, in his case, is probably the IS–LM approach. Indeed, between the publication of his revised review of Keynes and his *Monetary Theory and Fiscal Policy* 1949, Hansen focused increasingly on what brought him to accept the *General Theory*, i.e. the IS–LM interpretation. As Hansen puts it in his preface to that book:

> In my *Business Cycle Theory* (1927) . . . I stressed the role of real or non-monetary factors – somewhat against the stream of Anglo-American thinking in the 1920's. This point of view also pervaded my *Economic Stabilization in an Unbalanced World* (1932), *Full Recovery or Stagnation?* (1938), *Fiscal Policy and Business Cycles* (1941), *America's Role in the World Economy* (1945), and *Economic Policy and Full Employment* (1947). All these books devoted only a limited space to money and monetary theory. The present work, however, is devoted mainly to the subject of money and it gives a much fuller discussion of the role of money than I have presented in any of my earlier writings.[42]

Hansen interprets Keynes through what is essentially the 'looking-glass' of Hicks's 1937 paper. This is evident in the initial note to his chapter 'Income and the rate of interest': 'The analysis given in this chapter is based on Keynes' *General Theory*; but heavy reliance is placed upon the brilliant work of J. R. Hicks in his "Mr. Keynes and the Classics".' Hansen then outlines an equation system and presents what he calls the LM schedule, which is a crucial development in the evolution of the IS–LM approach. The important thing to understand here is that the introduction of Hansen's LM schedule does not just constitute a minor change in terminology. Rather, it marks the beginning of the institutionaliz-ation and conventional acceptance of Hicks's SILL diagram for the purposes of both interpreting and representing Keynes's *General Theory*.[43]

Up to this point, except for some notable exceptions, for example Kaldor (1937) – and Modigliani (1944), who will be dealt with below – discussion of Keynes's *General Theory* was conducted more or less in terms of the 45-degree line and 'Keynesian cross', with Hicks's SILL diagram being only 'a suggested interpretation'. Indeed, in his earlier Keynesian-type works, this is how Hansen dealt with Keynes's *General Theory*. From Hansen's *Monetary Theory and Fiscal Policy*, however, his IS–LM schedules became the standard interpretation and representation of Keynes's *General Theory* and what has been called 'the core of modern macro-economics'.[44]

Hansen's equation system, which he describes as 'a difficult and complicated course with many ramifications and interrelations', is set out below:

$$I = I \text{ (i) (Equation 1)}$$
$$C = C \text{ (Y) (Equation 2)}$$
$$L = L \text{ (i, Y) (Equation 3)}$$
$$M = L \text{ (Equation 4)}$$
$$Y = I + C \text{ (Y) (Equation 5)}$$

According to Hansen 'the various functions' are in 'real terms', while equation 4 'means that $M = L$ in the equilibrium sense'.[45]

Perhaps his attitude towards the nature of Keynes's system overall is indicative of what lies behind Hansen's thinking – and especially his reference to the Keynes–Robertson connection established by accepting his IS–LM world-view. In his book Hansen writes about 'taking a broad view of the Keynesian theory of the determination of income and the rate of interest'. In particular, he notes 'considering the Keynesian system as a whole without concentrating too narrowly on certain passages in the *General Theory*, there is much more agreement between Robertson and Keynes than appears on the surface.'[46]

Whether or not Keynes would concur with Hansen on his view of the degree of agreement between his *General Theory* approach and that of Robertson is difficult to say. Robertson would probably have agreed that having accepted and presented IS–LM as the central message of Keynes's *General Theory*, Hansen was moving closer to his world-view than to Keynes's, as Robertson remarked to Meade – upon reading Meade's IS–LM paper – over a decade previously.[47]

Hansen's articles in the Harris volume on Keynes, *The New Economics* (1948), shed some light on Hansen's advocacy of the IS–LM approach. In his paper 'The *General Theory*', Hansen writes:

> It would be a mistake, I think, to make too sharp a dividing line between pre-Keynesian and Keynesian economics . . . It is further true, I believe, that economic research has tackled new problems and is better equipped with tools of analysis by reason of the work of Keynes. Moreover, a correct appraisal of Keynes's work cannot be made by confining attention to the contents of the General Theory.

Additionally, in his paper 'Keynes on Economic Policy', Hansen states:

> An examination of recent and current literature will disclose that there has come into general use, since 1936, a considerable list of new technical terms, new concepts, and a new theoretical apparatus. With few exceptions . . . writers on monetary, business-cycle and general theory now use as a matter of course these new concepts and tools of analysis. In this sense friend and foe alike have become Keynesians . . . and just as a new theoretical language has come into being, so also we have come to speak a new language in terms of practical policy.

In both papers, Hansen advocates the combination of Keynesian and Robertsonian approaches which he had tried earlier in his *Fiscal Policy and Business Cycles* (1941). The 'new language' Hansen speaks of became IS–LM, which he subsequently presented as the language of what he saw as 'Keynesian economics' in *A Guide to Keynes* (1953).[48]

Hansen's representation of Keynes's *General Theory* by means of IS–LM schedules in *A Guide to Keynes* is a prime example of the use of diagrams as tools to convey interpretations of the central message of a theory for expository and especially pedagogic purposes. Hansen presented IS–LM as an amalgam of Keynesian–Pigovian–Robertsonian and Swedish approaches to savings and investment on the one hand, and liquidity preference and money supply on the other. When the composite schedules intersect, the equilibrium level of income and interest rate is given since they are 'determined together at the point of intersection'.[49]

Hansen claims that the determinate interest theory of 'the Keynesian analysis' when 'looked at as a whole' is based on the investment, saving (or consumption) and liquidity preference functions and the quantity of money. 'But', he continues,

> Keynes never brought all the elements together in a comprehensive manner to formulate expressly an integrated interest theory. He failed to point out specifically that liquidity preference plus the quantity of money can give us not the rate of interest but only an LM curve. It was left for Hicks to utilize the Keynesian tools in a method of presentation which makes it impossible to forget the whole picture.[50]

According to Hansen, 'Keynes saw clearly . . . that the classical (or neo–classical) formulation gives us no interest theory but only the IS curve, and in effect he stated it in these terms.' Hansen adds 'having understood the first half of the story, Keynes did not, however, see that his own interest theory was equally indeterminate. He flatly asserts that the "liquidity preference" and the "quantity of money" between them tell us "what the rate of interest is".' 'But', Hansen maintains

> this is not true, since there is a liquidity preference curve for each income level. Until we know the income level, we cannot know what the rate of interest is. What we can learn from the family of liquidity preference curves and the quantity of money taken together is the LM curve, but this alone cannot determine the rate of interest.[51]

Hansen concludes his argument by taking Keynes to task over the fundamental structure of the *General Theory* system. He cites Keynes as saying 'that saving and investment are "determinates of the system, not the determinants".' Hansen continues:

Now this is of course true. But in the very next sentence he includes the rate of interest as a determinant of the system along with the propensity to consume and the schedule of the MEC. But this is just what is wrong. The rate of interest is, in fact, along with the level of income, a determinate and not a determinant of the system. The determinants are the three functions (1) the saving (or conversely the consumption) function, (2) the investment demand function and (3) the liquidity preference function, plus (4) the quantity of money. Given these Keynesian functions and the money supply, the rate of interest and the level of income are mutually determined.[52]

In his evaluation of chapter 14 of the *General Theory*, Hansen also focuses on the nature of Keynes's savings function, arguing that it is of the hybrid form, i.e.

$$S = S\,(i, Y)$$

and also reiterates his view of Keynes's 'error' in specifying the factors determining interest when evaluating chapter 16. According to Hansen, in this chapter

Keynes appears to argue that an increase in the propensity to save cannot affect the rate of interest. This is wrong and illustrates the fact that he often (perhaps usually) thought that the rate of interest can adequately be explained wholly by liquidity preference and the quantity of money. This . . . is wrong because we never know which liquidity preference schedule is applicable unless we already know the level of income. If he had learned to think of the problem in terms of Hicks's IS and LM curves, he would have never asked 'Why, the quantity of money being unchanged, a fresh act of saving should diminish the sum which it is desired to keep in liquid form at the existing rate of interest'. The implied answer which he expected to elicit from the reader is wrong.[53]

To sum up, what characterizes Hansen's aproach to IS–LM – in contrast to Hicks's – is his view that it is not 'a suggested interpretation' but the only possible way of interpreting and representing Keynes's *General Theory*. In effect, Hansen forces Keynes's variegated and chameleonic theory into an IS–LM mould. It is not surprising, therefore, that the 'neo-classical synthesis' succeeded, having such fertile ground to fall upon. And it is to Modigliani's use of the IS–LM approach to attain this synthesis that we now turn.

### Timlin, Modigliani and the synthetic approach

Some two decades after publishing his paper 'Liquidity Preference and the Theory of Interest of Money' (1944), Modigliani surveyed the developments in monetary and macroeconomic theory that had occurred, 'since the early forties, when the process of digesting the *General Theory* and integrating it with the earlier streams of thinking had been more or less completed'. The two outstanding examples of how the *General Theory* was 'digested' and 'integrated' with previously held economic doctrine are Modigliani's classic and often-cited paper of 1944, and Mabel Timlin's *Keynesian Economics* (first published in 1942 and reprinted in 1948), which seems to have been overlooked – as well as Lange's 1938 paper – by the new generation of Keynesian–Walrasians (see chapter 5).[54]

Timlin gives the aim of her study in no uncertain terms: 'No attempt will be made to restate Mr. Keynes' own analysis directly . . . It is expected rather to synthesize with the work as it stands in Mr. Keynes' own publications such ideas of other authors as appear relevant to the content of the system and useful in making its properties apparent.' Timlin then presents her version of Lange's 1938 equation system which she calls 'the Keynes–Lange system':

$$i = L \ (M, \ Y) \ \text{(Equation 1)}$$
$$C = \phi \ (Y, \ i) \ \text{(Equation 2)}$$
$$I = F \ (i, \ C) \ \text{(Equation 3)}$$
$$Y = I + C \ \text{(Equation 4)}$$
$$[Y = S + C] \ \text{[Equation 4a]}$$

where i = rate of interest; L, $\phi$ , F are what Timlin calls liquidity, multiplier and investment functions; M = quantity of money; C, I,

S, Y are the levels (or rates) of consumption, investment, saving and income respectively.[55]

According to Timlin, 'the most important of the objects in setting' her proposed system 'out at this stage is to make clear the interdependent [and simultaneous] character of its elements.' Timlin defends her interpretation of the *General Theory* with:

> It is to be noticed that on page 245 . . . Mr. Keynes describes the rate of interest as one of the independent variables of the system. On page 246, however, he describes the rate of interest as dependent 'partly on the state of liquidity-preference (i.e. on the liquidity function) and partly on the quantity of money measured in terms of wage-units'. Equation (1) above conforms to this description . . . It is to be noted that Mr. Keynes's own formulation puts the quantity of money in the position of the dependent variable, just as Dr. Lange's does. See *General Theory*, p. 199.[56]

Timlin concludes the defence of her interpretation by pointing 'to Mr. Keynes' approval of Dr. Lange's "general system" as an analysis of his own', referring to Keynes's comment on Lange in the *Economic Journal* of 1938 (cited in chapter 2). Interestingly, Timlin makes no use of the IS–LM diagram. Rather, she developed a diagrammatic representation of the 'Keynes–Lange system' which, according to her, was adequate to illustrate 'the system of the shifting equilibrium which lies at the heart of Keynesian theory'. Timlin's diagrammatic interpretation of 'the character of the Keynesian system', however, never received wide attention or, for that matter, acceptance by the economics profession, for Hicks's diagram had come to 'rule the roost'.[57]

Modigliani, while noting Timlin's work, based his 1944 paper on a combination of the original Lange and 'Hicks' equations and Hicks's SILL diagram. As Timlin did, he stated his objective at the outset:

> To reconsider critically some of the most important old and recent theories of the rate of interest and money and to formulate, eventually, a more general theory that will take into account the vital contributions of each analysis a well as the part played by different basic hypotheses . . . from this analysis will gradually emerge our general theory of the rate of interest and money.[58]

Modigliani's generalized equations are:

$$M = L \ (r, \ Y) \ \text{(Equation 1)}$$
$$I = I \ (r, \ Y) \ \text{(Equation 2)}$$
$$S = s \ (r, \ Y) \ \text{(Equation 3)}$$
$$S = I \ \text{(Equation 4)}$$
$$Y \equiv PX \ \text{(Equation 5)}$$
$$X = X \ (N) \ \text{(Equation 6)}$$
$$W = X' \ (N) \ P \ \text{(Equation 7)}$$
$$C \equiv Y - I \ \text{(Equation 8)}$$

where according to him Y is money income, M is the quantity of money, which he takes as given, r is the interest rate; S and I, saving and investment, both in money terms; P is the price level; N is aggregate employment; W is the money-wage rate; X is 'an index of physical output'. Finally, C is consumption in money terms.[59]

Modigliani notes that in the system given above there are eight unknowns and seven equations, relation 8 being an identity, so he provides an additional equation for the supply of labour which is related to the wage rate. He then gives two alternative forms for this equation, one for what he calls 'the classical system' and one for 'the Keynesian system'. In addition, he provides a variant for equation 1, which he terms 'the crudest quantity-of-money theory', which is of the form $M = kY$. He then says 'it is very interesting to see what part is played under these conditions by equations (2) and (3), the saving and investment equations that have been so much stressed by all the Keynesians [*sic*].' On the alternate version of equation 1 which determines income, according to Modigliani, equation 2 turns into an 'orthodox' type 'supply of saving schedule', i.e. saving being determined by the interest rate. Similarly, equation 3 turns into a 'demand-for-saving schedule'. When represented diagrammatically in Marshallian form, the intersection of the schedules, which is the equilibrium point, gives the level of the interest rate. Modigliani then presents two alternative models to his interpretation of the Keynesian system, one based on the quantity theory of money, the other being what he calls his 'general theory of the rate of interest and money', comprising the basis for what was later termed the 'neo-classical synthesis'. According to Modigliani, in the latter 'the suppliers of labor as well as the suppliers of all other commodities are supposed to behave "rationally".' As he puts it, 'under "static" assumptions and "flexible wages", the rate of interest and the level of employment do not depend on the quantity of money.' Rather, in this case 'the rate of interest is determined by all the equations of a Walrasian system except the supply of and demand for money equation', although 'in the first approximation of partial equilibrium analysis, the determination of the rate of interest must be associated with . . . the saving and investment schedules.' Modigliani illustrates his alternatives – both the 'crude quantity theory' and his more 'general' approach – by reference to the SILL diagram.[60]

In re-evaluating his 1944 model, Modigliani takes it 'as a representation of where monetary economists thought money stood in relation to the economy at about that period'. He went on to compare it with what he called his 'mid-fifties model' which is, in his words, 'a general equilibrium framework'. Modigliani then states 'most of the differences between the 1944 and the mid-fifties model are matters of elegance, clarity, and minor improvements', except for his correction of an error in homogeneity assumptions. Thus, while Modigliani says that the mid-fifties model can be characterized by its 'explicit reliance on a general equilibrium framework', and notes that he did not have 'the benefit of this crutch' in his earlier version, his 1944 model still has an implicit general equilibrium formulation based on a combination of Lange's equations and Hicks's diagram. Moreover, it is doubtful that without the benefit of the latter 'crutch', i.e. Hicks's SILL diagram, he would have arrived at his 1944 model at all. In other words, it was the IS–LM approach that enabled Modigliani, as Lucas has put it to, take his 'pioneering step toward a "neo-classical synthesis".'[61]

The Hicks diagram, in its variant forms, CCLL, SILL, or IS–LM, however, is not unique in its attempt – and some may say its ability – to convey the central message of a theory that had previously been expressed only in literary, or, at most, in mathematical, i.e. equational form. Indeed, Arthur Brown's description of Hicks having 'done a Marshall' is apt in two respects: first, by his use of diagrammatic in conjunction with equational representation of what he took to be the key concepts in Keynes's theory; and secondly, by recognition for having originated a diagram that subsequently took on an existence separate from the verbal or equational approach from which it was derived, the diagram's originator not having developed either the verbal or equational approach himself. Marshall's acknowledgement of Cournot's contribution to his own approach, however, was not a matter of citation for the sake of the history of economic thought. Rather, without Cournot's work, Marshall could not have developed his equational–diagrammatic approach. In other words, as Champernowne has noted, in order to draw a diagram like the IS–LM diagram 'one needs the appropriate equations as well.'[62]

# 4

# Harrod and Hawtrey, 1936–7 and 1951–2: variations on the theme

### Harrod and Hawtrey on Keynes's *General Theory* and Harrod's *Trade Cycle*, 1936–7

A year after the appearance of the *General Theory*, Hawtrey's *Capital and Employment* was published. In it, Hawtrey outlined both his own economic world-view and gave detailed critiques of Hayek's, Pigou's, Douglas's, Keynes's, and Harrod's views respectively. According to Hawtrey, Keynes, Hayek and Harrod had read the chapters dealing with their work and assisted him 'with their comments' on 'the interpretations' he had 'placed upon their views'.[1]

Harrod was supposed to review Hawtrey's book; 'only a shortish review unhappily for the Listener', as he put it in a letter to Hawtrey on 26 February 1937. Only a week later, in a letter dated 4 March, Harrod told Hawtrey that he had been asked not to write the review, since he would be, in effect, reviewing a book criticizing his own work. This letter, however, deals with much more than the 'embarrassment' felt by *The Listener* upon asking Harrod to review, in essence, his own book, even though Harrod informed the magazine that he 'hadn't been feeling any embarrassment at all, since the part about' his book 'was confined to one chapter not closely related to the rest', and thus, while appreciating their point, he 'regretted their decision'.

In any event, Harrod was quite complimentary overall about *Capital and Employment* in his letter to Hawtrey of 4 March 1937: 'I may say that I found your book most fascinating reading, quite extraordinarily clear and in many respects convincing. I liked the passages on Hayek and Douglas very much but do not agree with all you say about JMK, but I expect he is standing up for himself.' Harrod then detailed the points on which he disagreed and agreed with Hawtrey's treatment of Keynes's approach, of his own views, and of the relationship between the positions expressed in the *General Theory* and the *Trade Cycle*.

One of the most interesting issues Harrod raised in his letter was the problem of 'public works'. While Hawtrey gave it a 'qualified blessing' (in Harrod's words), Harrod took issue with Hawtrey's view that 'anything that Governments can do in the direction of expenditure is pitifully small.'

> Your point . . . seems unfair when you say that the amounts involved are 'pitifully small' (small compared with the extra supply of nuts a manufacturer could lay in because the rate of interest had fallen?). Pitifully small certainly when you consider the defining of purchasing power when a great slump is under weigh [*sic*]. But not necessarily too small perhaps if undertaken before the slump has gathered strength, and not small at all, I submit, compared with the extra holding of working capital which you would stimulate by banking policy.

In this letter Harrod also took Hawtrey to task for misrepresenting his – and Keynes's – view of the cause of 'trade depressions'. In *Capital and Employment* Hawtrey had written 'they both alike trace trade depressions to a deficiency of demand arising from absorption of cash'; Harrod being 'rather amused to read' this interpretation.

> You give an excellent account of my monetary theory and I have no complaint. But that particular sentence should be interpreted by the reader with an eye upon the author. I do not trace trade depressions to an absorption of cash! This is your view. I don't deny that an absorption of cash occurs. But I claim that to be the consequence of the depression, which is itself traced to the interaction of the relation and the multiplier. I say I was amused because precisely the same type of, dare I call it, egocentricity occurs in a review of my book by Robertson in the Canadian Journal. Having explained how the boom is going forward he says at this point Mr. Harrod supposes an increase of hoarding to occur, as tho' I (and not DHR) regarded that as a significant matter!

The causal forces seem to me to arise out of the nature of investment and saving; the consequence is a decrease in the velocity of circulation which has to be explained. My explanation is that in consequence of forces connected with real investment making for depression, money is shifted over from active circulation to capital account (I notice that you independently give a similar explanation of the absorption of cash by traders). It can only get back into active circulation if something occurs to stimulate trade. What is that something? It can only be those forces already discussed on the preceding pages. It may be that the long rate will fall and provide some stimulus; but I repeat that there is no reason to suppose that it must fall sufficiently to send all the money back. This is the crucial point on which Keynes' analysis of liquidity preference, though I agree in thinking it in many respects unsatisfactory and incomplete, seems to me a real contribution, needing further development.[2]

Two problems emerge from this letter. First, take Harrod's attitude towards Robertson's review of the *Trade Cycle*. Note that while Robertson did focus upon 'a process of hoarding' setting in 'after an advance', he added:

And in face of which monetary policy may be relatively powerless. For the level of the long-term rate of interest at any moment depends partly on what its level is expected to be over a fairly long future, so that its movements are not nimble enough to solve the problems set to it both by the behaviour of the principle of acceleration and by fluctuation in the rate of invention.

This, however, is exactly how Harrod criticized Keynes:

Mr. Keynes builds high hopes on the clever manipulation of the long-term rate by banking policy . . . To be sceptical about this is not to be sceptical about his theory of the determination of long-term rates. It only entails the view that his liquidity preference schedule is in certain circumstances extremely elastic . . . Thus it seems improbable that banking policy, however inspired and well informed, could secure a sufficient fluctuation in long-term interest rates to ensure a steady advance.[3]

Secondly, take Harrod's view of Keynes's concept of liquidity preference 'I agree in thinking it in many respects unsatisfactory and incomplete'. Which aspects, and how did Harrod get around the 'shortcomings' in Keynes's approach, for example in his IS–LM paper, which had appeared in print only two months before? A careful reading of Harrod's IS–LM paper is required, focusing on his attitude towards Keynes's notion of liquidity preference, in order to answer the latter question. As for the former, it will be necessary to refer to Harrod's 'examination' of Keynes's concept of liquidity preference in his book *Money* (1969).[4]

An indication of what underlies Harrod's interpretation of liquidity preference can be seen in the equation for interest rate determination in his IS–LM paper and his explanation for inserting income into it. Even though his equation differs somewhat from Keynes's approach, he takes the latter to task:

> What right has Keynes to gut the monetary equation . . .? Has, then, the banking policy no power . . .? Yes, certainly it has. The fact is that the power residing in the monetary equations has already been used up in Keynes' system in the liquidity preference equation and it cannot therefore exert any direct influence . . . To make it do so would be to use its determining influence twice over. In fact in Keynes' system all the old pieces reappear, but they appear in different places . . . It might at first be thought that the liquidity preference schedule is a new piece, and that therefore either the new system is over-determined or the traditional writers must have been wrong in supposing that their system was determined. But it is not really a new piece. The old theory presupposed that income velocity of circulation was somehow determined. But precisely how was something of a mystery. Thus the old theory assumed that there was a piece there but did not state exactly what it was. Keynes' innovation may thus be regarded as a precise definition of the old piece.[5]

Some three decades after his IS–LM paper was published Harrod dealt with Keynes's idea of liquidity preference in his treatment of the 'Keynesian revolution' in *Money*. Harrod stated that while he thought a study of Keynes's liquidity preference necessary, his examination was 'not intended as a precise exegesis of Keynes's ideas at the moment when he put them on paper in writing the *General Theory*'. Rather, 'It is more useful to give a broad, and even sometimes critical, treatment, emphasizing those aspects which may be considered durable and continuously useful . . . This is especially appropriate in the case of Keynes, whose own mind was very adaptable; he would not have regarded his own book as a sacred text.'

Harrod continues 'in my opinion Keynes does not give nearly enough weight to the precautionary motive, and is wrong in saying, as he does in one place, that the precautionary motive is not interest sensitive. Thereby he gives far too much work, in relation to the whole system, to the speculative motive.' Harrod cites Viner's argument 'that the funds held for the speculative motive are not large enough to have the great influence that they are made to have in Keynes' system', and continues 'I am inclined to agree with Prof. Viner that the amount of money held for the speculative motive in ordinary times is not very great. I would suggest that, on the contrary, there is at any time a large amount of money held for the precautionary motive.' Harrod concludes by maintaining that 'Keynes makes the amount of money required for the precautionary motive a function of the money value of the national income, like that required for the transactions motive itself, and argues that it is interest insensitive. This is paradoxical.'[6]

Harrod, of course, would have to see Keynes's approach here as paradoxical, since his IS–LM system required an equation for interest determination in which both the quantity of money and the level of income appeared. In order to do this, Harrod altered Keynes's liquidity preference equation but maintained that it did not differ fundamentally from Keynes's approach. As Harrod put it in his IS–LM paper 'In his liquidity preference equation, Keynes includes the demand for money for whatever purpose, and the quantity of money that appears in it is the total quantity of money in the community. Harrod, however, split this 'into two parts, the amount required for active circulation and the residue'. He then defines 'the quantity of money which appears' in his equation interpreting Keynes's liquidity preference 'as that residue, and the demand which the equation expresses as the demand for purposes other than those of active circulation'. Harrod defends his interpretation of Keynes's equation as a 're-definition of terms' that 'is merely an expository device and does not imply any departure from Keynes's essential doctrines [*sic*]'. On this basic, Harrod is able to justify his insertion of income into his 'liquidity preference' based equation of interest determination 'since the amount of money required for active circulation by consumers and traders depends on the level of income'.[7]

By doing this, Harrod reconciled Keynes's liquidity preference and interest theory with that of the classical theory, showing that if his equational approach is accepted 'the classical theory is not only not inconsistent with Keynes's theory, but is even an essential part of it.'[8]

Hawtrey's reply to Harrod's letter, on 24 April 1937, included the issue of public works: 'Not only have I recognized that there are arguments for public works in certain conditions, but I believe that I am the only economist who has ever stated exactly what they are. My fellow economists generally ignore them as completely as they ignore my arguments on the other side.'

Harrod did not reply to Hawtrey's April letter until 1 October 1937, and Hawtrey replied only in December 1937. Among other things, he responded to Harrod's point about 'Tinbergen's failure to find a correlation between the rate of interest and trade fluctuations':

I do not know to what periods or countries he [Tinbergen] applied his analysis. Since rising prices cause a high short-term [rate] and the high short-term rate causes falling prices the absence of any correlation would not in itself be very surprising. But as a matter of experience the effect of rising prices (or expanding demand) in raising the rate and of falling prices (or contracting demand) in lowering the rate so greatly predominates that there is a correlation which requires no mathematical analysis to discover it. A comparison of the table of average rates of discount in Pigou's Industrial Fluctuations . . . with that of unemployment will readily satisfy you . . . In my letter . . . I pointed out that if your theory of the trade cycle were true, the first symptom of a depression would be a fall in the long-term rate of interest.

### Harrod and Hawtrey on Keynes's *General Theory* and the Harrod diagram, 1951

In early 1951, Hawtrey was completing a second edition of *Capital and Employment*, and sent Harrod both the chapter that dealt with Harrod's work up to 1948 and a rewritten chapter on Keynes.

Harrod replied on 17 May 1951, that while he was satisfied with Hawtrey's treatment of his theories – calling it 'a lucid and fair account' – he did not agree at all with his interpretation of Keynes's views:

> In the case of Maynard, on the other hand – odd that it should be him that I have to make a stand about! – I think you do not represent his views correctly. He would not agree that 'if the marginal efficiency of capital were above the conventional rate of interest, the market would have to raise its rate accordingly.' On the contrary, capital only would expand to be at the point at which its m.e. [marginal efficiency] was equal to the conventional rate of interest. If this happened at unemployment, the 'resources' would be forthcoming owing to higher income and saving, if at full employment, there would be inflation, and the resources would be forthcoming thro' price and profit inflation. The sentence before is wrong if by 'it tended to be equal to the m.e. of cap', you mean that it would tend to move towards equality. In the Keynes scheme it is the volume of capital outlay that moves, not the rate of interest; in this case it would expand until the m.e. fell to the conventional rate of interest. I am giving Keynes doctrine, not arguing about it! There are some consequential amendments required in the following pages.[9]

Hawtrey replied on 30 May 1951, taking issue with Harrod's assertion that he had misrepresented Keynes's view. Hawtrey refuted Harrod's statement about the movement of the volume of capital outlay rather than the interest rate: 'the General Theory does not support' this 'unqualified statement'. In his interpretation 'If the quantity of money be supposed to be given, income and the rate of interest are connected by the relation

$$L_1 (Y) + L_2 (r) = M.$$

If k be the multiplier and I investment, $Y = kI$.'
Hawtrey continued:

> I is a function of r in virtue of the relation between marginal efficiency and the rate of interest. Consequently Y is a function of r. The rate of investment is pushed to the point where the marginal efficiency of capital is brought to

approximate equality with the rate of interest . . . The theory of liquidity preference makes the rate of interest and the amount of the idle balances mutually dependent, but it interposes no obstacle in the way of the investment market taking the initiative in raising the rate . . . there will result a decrease in $M_2$, and (if M be supposed fixed) an equal increase of $M_1$. Corresponding to the new $M_1$ there will be an increased income, Y. At the same time, in virtue of the multiplier, there will be increased investment, I, such that $Y = kI$. The rate of interest is determined by the equation

$$L_1 (kI) + L_2 (r) = M.$$

So long as M is given, it is r that must be adapted to I, not I to r. For the relation of I to r is determined by marginal efficiency, and any movement of r which does not accord with that relation must be corrected by the investment market. The proposition that 'it is the volume of capital outlay that moves, not the rate of interest', presupposes that the amount of money is so varied as to determine the rate of interest. Therefore M must no longer be assumed to be constant.

Also:

Keynes was chiefly interested in the case where the rate of interest is below the conventional rate. The speculative motive then limits the inflow of funds into the investment market, and the rate of interest is determined by the function

$$M_2 = L_2 (r)$$

. . . In the case where the rate of interest is above the conventional rate we have little guidance from Keynes as to what happens to $M_2$, but I think it is safe to assume that the amount of money withheld from the investment is not considerable enough to affect the rate of interest materially. If so, the rate is determined substantially by marginal efficiency. If variations in $M_2$ can be neglected, then M determines $M_1$, $M_1$ determines Y, Y determines I, I determines marginal efficiency and marginal efficiency determines r. When you say that capital outlay would expand either by increased employment or by a rise of prices through inflation, you are tacitly assuming that sufficient money is created to enlarge Y.

Hawtrey concluded, 'I need hardly say that the foregoing is governed throughout by assumptions of Keynes's to which I could not subscribe, not only his postulate, but the simplified functions $L_1$ and $L_2$.'

Harrod replied in a letter dated 7 June 1951 and immediately took Hawtrey's argument to task:

> What I feel about it is that you are arguing about the conclusions that Maynard ought to have derived from his own premises (which you do not accept) rather than the conclusions which he did derive from them . . . If there is one thing about his theory about which I am absolutely clear, it is that he held that an increase of investment demand, say a movement to the right of the whole 'marginal efficiency of capital' schedule, did not have a direct effect upon the rate of interest. If the shift to the right caused an increase of activity in real investment and through the multiplier generally, that would entail a greater demand for the transactions motive, leaving less over to satisfy other demands for liquidity and thus, unless banks increase the quantity of money available, raise interest rates. If the increased investment happened to be accompanied by a decline in the liquidity preference, there might be no effect upon the interest rate.

Harrod continued:

> You will understand that my task is to state what Maynard actually held, not whether he was right or wrong! He would be the last person to wish any theory of his own to remain frozen. At the same time, I think that in reference to him one ought to quote the thoughts he actually had. Of course I may be wrong about this, but I did talk so much about it with him in the year or two prior to his illness, and have since perused all the correspondence, notes, etc. that took place at the time of the composition of the General Theory, that I feel I know it pretty well.

A week later, on 15 June, Hawtrey replied and restated his argument:

> Keynes did of course insist that the rate of interest was determined in the first instance by liquidity preference, and

that investment and income had to conform to the rate which the quantity of money brought about. But my contention was that you went too far in attributing to him the view that liquidity preference is 'the sole determinant of the level of the interest rate'. I can quite imagine Keynes using those very words, but, if he had, he would never have intended to rule out the repercussions of marginal efficiency upon the investment market . . . He set out his position in his chapter on the Classical Theory of Interest. According to the diagram on p. 180, a given investment demand-schedule is consistent with various levels of income, and there is no determinate result unless 'from some other source we can say what the rate of interest is'. This other source is 'the state of liquidity preference and the quantity of money' . . . But he did not regard the state of liquidity preference and the quantity of money as by themselves determining the rate of interest. The banks determine the total quantity of money M, but a further process, of which they have no cognisance, is needed to divide M into the parts $M_1$ and $M_2$. The division has to conform to the formula

$$L_1 \, (kI) + L_2 \, (r) = M.$$

Hawtrey continued:

Keynes, confining himself to a static analysis, had little to say about the process by which the appropriate division is reached. But he regarded the adjustment of I to r as taking time . . . Your comment that, on the concluding page of my letter of 30th May, it is the 'full employment rate of interest' that has to be compared with the conventional rate shows that I failed to make my point clear. It is the market rate of interest on which the speculative motive depends. So long as the market rate is below the conventional rate so that people delay placing their money in securities, the idle balances, $M_2$, will accumulate. Keynes believed that to be the decisive factor in determining the rate of interest.

Hawtrey ended with: 'My conclusion is that the unqualified statement that "liquidity preference is the sole determinant of the level of the interest rate" is irreconcilable with Keynes's own analysis.'

Harrod's reply of 19 June 1951 again points to the difference between his interpretation of the relationship between income and interest rate, saving and investment, and liquidity preference and money supply, and Keynes's *General Theory* position. Indeed, it highlights the importance of Harrod's diagram in the development of his version of the IS–LM approach:

> I still feel that you are trying to force matters somewhat. I was myself responsible for the diagram on page 180 which was an attempt to demonstrate to Maynard that his theories were not quite so out of line with the classical position as he supposed. However I do think that he held consistently in the General Theory that the rate of interest was determined by liquidity preference and the quantity of money, and by those only, and that he did not consider that a shift to the right in investment demand schedule would have any direct effect on the rate of interest. We had this point out again and again[10] . . . I still think that what takes you off Keynes' lines is a misunderstanding of his view in regard to the division of M between $M_1$ and $M_2$. The banks determine the volume of M . . . If bank money came into existence by open market operations, Keynes held that none of it in the first instance would go into the $M_1$ circuit; it would all go into the $M_2$ pool. If the effect of the increase in the latter was to cause new investment, and so through the multiplier, new activity, then indeed some of the money would go off into the $M_1$ circuit. How the new money was divided between the $M_2$ pool and the $M_1$ circuit in the final equilibrium would depend on the elasticity of the liquidity preference schedule, the elasticity of the marginal efficiency of capital schedule, the value of the multiplier, and the effect, if any, on the money value of the wage unit.

Harrod continued:

> I am sorry that I was confused about the conventional rate of interest. Here again I come across some difficulty in reading you. You say that if the market rate is below the conventional rate, the idle balances, $M_2$ will accumulate. This is not so. It is the inverse of Keynes's theory of causation. $M_2$ is simply M-$M_1$ . . . The excess of the conventional rate above the market rate would have no effect on the volume of $M_2$. $M_2$, the size of

which is determined by forces which have no direct connection with market and conventional rate, will determine what the relation between them is. If $M_2$ is large in relation to people's normal liquidity preference, then the market rate will tend to sag below the conventional rate, and conversely.

Harrod concluded:

You say that when the market rate is above the conventional rate, $M_2$ is zero, or at any rate negligible. Not necessarily so. This all depends on the elasticity of the liquidity preference schedule. Supposing that $M_2$ is very low because $M-M_1$ is very low, we cannot say how far above the conventional rate the market rate will be. If people are extremely zealous to rebuild their liquidity (which, however, they will not be able to do) the market rate may go very high. If, on the other hand, people do not mind very much about their loss of liquidity, the market rate may stay only slightly above the conventional rate.

Hawtrey acknowledged Harrod's position in his reply of 26 June 1951, which closed the correspondence: 'The principal issue between us seems to be the part which Keynes would attribute to the investment market in determining the rate of interest . . . But the precise manner in which the cash balances of the investment market are classified does not really matter very much. I doubt whether Keynes ever gave any thought to the matter.' Hawtrey concluded:

When Keynes maintained that it was liquidity preference and not marginal efficiency that determined the rate of interest, did he not mean that the banks have the power to determine the rate of interest by creating or extinguishing money? Even if they refrained from exercising the power, and left the amount of money and therefore the rate of interest to chance, the responsibility still rested on them, and they could be deemed to have exercised their power in a blind and negligent way.

Hawtrey's reference to Harrod's *General Theory* diagram and Harrod's comments on the 'correctness' of Keynes's views and his explanation of the diagram's purpose, raise a number of issues which deserve more detailed consideration. For example, in his letters to Hawtrey of 7 and 19 June 1951, Harrod essentially recalls the exchange he had with Keynes more than fifteen years before – published in Keynes's collected works – about Keynes's view of savings and investment compared with his own, which he expressed via his *General Theory* diagram.[11]

The point that Harrod argued 'out again and again' with Keynes – as he put it in his letter to Hawtrey of 19 June 1951 – is evident in the Keynes–Harrod correspondence of August and September 1935. Keynes wrote to Harrod on 27 August 1935, 'My theory is that the rate of interest is the price which brings the demand for liquidity into equilibrium with the amount of liquidity available. It has nothing to do with saving.' Harrod replied in a letter on 30 August:

> You say that 'the rate of interest has nothing to do with saving'. This does seem rather extreme and isn't necessary. You don't need to deny that the rate of interest has some effect on the amount of any given income saved. All this would mean would be that the value of the multiplier is a function of, among other things, the rate of interest.

Harrod then proposes his diagram. Keynes, after having found Harrod's diagram 'both correct and very useful as a help to exposition' decided to 'appropriate it', as he told Harrod in a letter of 10 September 1935. Harrod's diagram (the purpose of which is cited above) thus became the only diagram to appear in the *General Theory*.[12]

But Harrod's diagram is a major step in the development of his IS–LM approach. Hansen seems to have noted this implicitly in his *A Guide to Keynes* (1953). Hansen asserted:

> it is not true that the diagram on p. 180 in the *General Theory* closely approximates Hicks' IS curve . . . since the multiplier must be taken account of in redrawing the whole thing on different axes – one axis being Y, or income, and the other being i, or the rate of interest. The slope of the IS curve will be much flatter than a curve connecting the points of intersection of the family of savings curves with the investment curve in Keynes's diagram.

This is just the point, however, for Harrod had taken the multiplier into account when proposing his diagram, having made it 'a function of, among other things, the rate of interest'. The similarity between Harrod's 'redrawn' diagram and Hicks's notwithstanding, Harrod's diagram enabled him to represent savings as a function of both income and interest, a crucial element in his IS–LM approach.[13]

### Harrod's influence on Hawtrey's revised interpretation of Keynes's *General Theory*, 1952

In the preface to the 1937 edition of *Capital and Employment*, Hawtrey claimed that 'the primary purpose' of his book was 'to show how explanations of trade depression and unemployment now widely accepted have been vitiated by certain false assumptions in regard to the relation of credit regulation to the capital market'. While he criticized the approaches of 'recent economic works' such as Keynes's *General Theory*, he claimed no 'authority other than' his 'own for the interpretations placed upon their views'. Hawtrey's 1937 chapter on Keynes is the longest of his critiques, the others being of Hayek, Pigou, Douglas and Harrod.[14]

In his 1952 edition of *Capital and Employment*, Hawtrey's critique of Keynes's *General Theory* is still the longest, but as he notes in his preface, the earlier 'criticism of Keynes . . . has been largely re-written. That criticism, as it apeared in the first edition, was the outcome of a prolonged correspondence with him, first in 1935 when he was still writing his book, and later when I was writing my criticism of it.' Hawtrey cites Keynes's letter to him of 31 August 1936:

> I am thinking of producing in the course of the next year or so what might be called footnotes to my previous book, dealing with various criticisms and particular points which want carrying further. Of course, in fact, the whole book needs rewriting and re-casting. But I am still not in a sufficiently changed state of mind as yet to be in the position to do that.

As Hawtrey remarks, however, Keynes never got around to completing 'this process of reconstruction'.[15]

In the preface to the 1952 edition Hawtrey adds that while he could have left his critique of Keynes unchanged, 'it seemed much in need of revision', and that he had 'been led to re-write the greater part of the criticism'. Hawtrey continued 'In doing so I have felt that a closer study of what Keynes wrote, and of what is implied in it, was required than during his lifetime, and I have found some corrections necessary in my former presentation of his views.'

What Hawtrey didn't mention in his preface, however, was his extensive correspondence with Harrod on his interpretation of Keynes's *General Theory*. In fact many of the 'corrections' Hawtrey made in his 'former presentation' of Keynes's 'views' were the result of Harrod's comments on Hawtrey's 1952 chapter on Keynes.[16] For example, in his 1937 introduction, Hawtrey takes issue with Keynes's attack on what he calls 'the classical doctrine of interest' via liquidity preference, asserting that 'I do not think Mr. Keynes's claim to have superseded the postulates of the classical theory of interest can be sustained.' In his 1952 version, however, Hawtrey adopts Harrod's view of Keynes's liquidity preference concept when he states that one of Keynes's 'most important contributions to economics has been the introduction of the concept of liquidity into the theory of capital and interest. But the idea has its limitations. It supplements the classical doctrine of interest, but is far from superseding it'.[17]

Hawtrey made an additional 'correction' to his interpretation of Keynes on the basis of his correspondence with Harrod. This can be seen in his revised presentation of the nature of what Keynes called the 'speculative motive' and its relation to liquidity. In his 1937 treatment Hawtrey claimed that 'the inclusion of the "speculative motive", on which the function $L_2 (r)$ is based, under the general heading of "liquidity preference" is rather misleading . . . whatever the applicability of Mr. Keynes's theory of liquidity preference to the long-term rate of interest may be, it cannot offer any explanation at all of the short-term rate.' By the time he returned to this issue in 1952, Hawtrey had changed his view somewhat, so that while repeating his position on 'the applicability of Keynes' theory of the speculative motive' he now maintained that 'at the same time, the short-term rate of interest may quite properly be described as the price of liquidity. While the long-term rate affects $M_2$, the short-term rate affects $M_1$.' This follows from Harrod's claim, in his letter to Hawtrey of 19 June, concerning the factors setting the 'amount of' M that 'goes off into $M_1$' and the problem of rebuilding liquidity in relation to the elasticity of the liquidity preference schedule.[18]

With regard to the first point, as Harrod put it:

> The amount of this [M] that goes off into $M_1$ is determined by (a) the money value of the wage unit, (b) the marginal supply price of goods in general, and (c) the volume of activity. Unlike the quantitative theorists he [Keynes] did not consider that any of these three values were directly affected by the volume of money. The marginal supply prices and the level of activity were both governed by the total of effective demand, which depended upon the propensity to consume and the propensity to invest. The quantity of money would only determine the volume of activity indirectly through the rate of interest.

Hawtrey replied on 26 June:

> In the last paragraph of your letter of 19th June you contest my statement that, when the market rate of interest is above the conventional rate, $M_2$ is zero or negligible. You say that, if M minus $M_1$ is very low, and people are extremely zealous to rebuild their liquidity, the market rate may go very high. But unless M actually falls short of $M_1$, there is no deficiency of liquidity. $M_2$ is zero, but so long as the market rate of interest is judged to be high, there is no ground for withholding surplus cash from the investment market, so zero is its natural level. That is the case which I had in mind when I wrote in my letter of the 30th May, 'M determines $M_1$, $M_1$ determines Y, Y determines I, I determines marginal efficiency, and marginal efficiency determines r'.

### Harrod and Hawtrey on fiscal and monetary policy, 1936–7 and 1951–2

Harrod's influence on Hawtrey's interpretation of Keynes's *General Theory* is also seen in the change in Hawtrey's views on the efficacy of fiscal and monetary policy in the 1937 and 1952 editions of *Capital and Employment*. For example, in the introduction to his 1937 edition, Hawtrey focused mainly upon credit regulation as the major 'instrument of regulation' for 'the avoidance of monetary instability'. He criticized Hayek's proposed 'monetary policy' and maintained that 'the ideal policy would be to stabilize the consumer's income, not keeping it absolutely fixed but adjusting it to the growth of the factors of production in such a way that equilibrium requires the level of wages to remain unchanged.'[19]

Hawtrey's 1937 critique of what he called Keynes's 'remedial proposals' are numerous and will not be recounted in detail here. Suffice it to say, however, that Hawtrey objected to both Keynes's idea of 'communal saving through the agency of the State' and his suggestion of the need for what Hawtrey calls 'investment by the Government', concluding that 'whether Mr. Keynes's purpose is to keep the rate of interest and marginal efficiency high or to keep them low, investment by the Government is superfluous.'[20]

In the introduction to his revised 1952 edition of *Capital and Employment*, Hawtrey still advocated credit policy and the manipulation of bank rate as flexible and powerful tools, but had to admit that both what he called 'budget policy' and monetary policy had come into their own. This is evident from his pessimism about 'the possibility of guarding against monetary instability with all its disastrous consequences . . . If bank rate does not meet the need, what is left? . . . If the banks cannot regulate the borrowing of the traders and consumers effectively, there is still the Government . . . and monetary policy has fallen back on Government action'.[21]

This is indeed a turnaround by Hawtrey from his April 1937 letter to Harrod, in which he stated – in reference to the French attempt to 'stave off the depression in the early stages' by government expenditure – 'in the early stages [of a depression] . . . the procedure by bank rate (and possibly open-market operations) is likely to be adequate, without any support from Government expenditure.'

In his revised chapter on Keynes's *General Theory*, Hawtrey included long sections on 'liquidity preference and monetary policy' and 'the functions $L_1$ and $L_2$' together with a rewritten section on Keynes's 'remedial proposals'. In all three sections the points made by Harrod in his 1951 correspondence with Hawtrey are taken up. In addition, when re-evaluating Keynes's remedial proposals, Hawtrey admits misinterpreting Keynes's notion of 'communal saving', which Keynes presented in a passage dealing with capital scarcity and net saving in conditions in which full employment would possibly come to an end. In Keynes's view, even if such a condition approaches 'it will still be possible for communal saving through the agency of the State to be maintained at a level which will allow the growth of capital up to a point where it ceases to be scarce.' According to Hawtrey ' "communal saving" here is not to be identified with public works as a device for maintaining full employment. It is just the reverse.' Hawtrey notes 'I have to confess that in the first edition of this book I misunderstood this passage. I suppose that if additional saving can only be brought about by additional investment then communal saving must take that form.' Hawtrey continued 'public works constitute active investment by the State, calculated to offset an excess of saving. Communal saving offsets a deficiency of saving.'[22]

More significant, however, are Hawtrey's concluding remarks on Keynes's *General Theory* and what, in his view, were its shortcomings: 'Keynes made many noteworthy contributions to economic science. He introduced the concepts of liquidity preference and a liquidity premium into the theory of the capital market and the rate of interest. He showed that the long-term rate of interest is a "highly psychological" or rather "a highly conventional phenomenon".' 'But', Hawtrey continues, Keynes's 'conclusions, as formulated in the *General Theory*, are subject to narrowing assumptions.' Among these, in Hawtrey's opinion

> is the assumption that the amount of capital outlay reacts directly to the rate of interest, and that, whereas the speculative motive responds to the deviation of the rate of interest from a conventional or fairly safe rate, capital outlay is determined not by the deviation but by the absolute level of the rate. Along with these assumptions, is the fiction that the idle balances, $M_2$, can be separated, from the active balances, $M_1$. And the functions $L_2$ and $L_1$ carry abstraction and simplification beyond what is consistent with any useful practical application.[23]

Some indication of Harrod's attitude towards monetary as compared with fiscal policy may be found in his *Trade Cycle* (1936). As noted above, Harrod took Keynes to task about the latter's view of the efficacy of 'banking policy'. Harrod expanded on this critique in his *Trade Cycle* chapter on 'remedial measures':

> Mr. Keynes in his recent volume has taken a somewhat optimistic view as to the plasticity of the long-term rate under

the influence of monetary policy. If only the banks, by open-market operations, supply the public with a sufficient amount of money, they can reduce the price, which is required to make people sacrifice liquidity and invest in loans, to any level they please. In principle this may be so. But if a very great increase of money is required to reduce the rate of interest by a minute amount, the policy may become impracticable . . . And at this point the monetary recipe can do no more. If the fall in the long-term rate so far secured by open-market operations is insufficient to hold up the recession . . . no further injection of money will prevent the price-level falling.

As for fiscal policy, Harrod supported public works both 'for the reflationary effect of public works' which 'will bring money out of capital accounts into active circulation once more' and because public works are 'a useful mechanism for sustaining prices'.[24]

Thirty years later, in *Money* (1969), Harrod returned to the theme, again favouring fiscal over monetary approaches. For example, when discussing policy measures for 'ironing out the business cycle', Harrod maintained 'It may be thought that both monetary and fiscal measures would come in handy. If only it were possible to get more fiscal flexibility, it might be argued that fiscal policy, as against monetary policy, should be stressed.'[25]

To sum up, in his 1952 edition of *Capital and Employment*, Hawtrey agreed with most of Harrod's arguments and positions manifest in both Harrod's IS–LM paper and the 1937 and 1951 correspondence between them. However, while it cannot be said that Hawtrey ever 'accepted' Keynes's *General Theory* in its entirety, he was still brought to modify somewhat his interpretation of Keynes's views by Harrod's arguments and, in effect, Harrod's IS–LM approach.

# 5

# IS–LM revisited: diagrammatics, rediscoveries, explanations and controversies

## Harrodian dynamics and Hicksian diagrammatics, c. 1950

Between the publication of *Value and Capital* in 1939 and Hansen's transliteration of SILL into IS–LM in 1949, Hicks did not make much use of his diagram. In the article 'La Théorie de Keynes après neuf ans' ('Keynes's theory after nine years'), published in *Revue d'économie politique* in 1945, Hicks – while ostensibly retracting his 1937 conclusion that the *General Theory* was the economic theory of 'depression' – restated his interpretation of Keynes's theory via an IS–LM world-view, when treating the determinants of investment, for example. In this article, however, Hicks did not utilize his diagram.[1]

On his own account, Hicks was catalysed into considering the trade cycle in detail by Harrod's book *Towards a Dynamic Economics* (1948), and presented 'a suggested interpretation' of Harrod's dynamic theory in a review article on Harrod's work in the May 1949 issue of *Economica*. In this, Hicks took the opportunity to reply, in part, both to Harrod's original review of *Value and Capital* and critique in his 1948 book, and gave an interpretation of Harrod's dynamics, which he subsequently developed, expanded and published as *A Contribution to the Theory of the Trade Cycle* (1950). In this book, Hicks 'reintroduced' his diagram, which he thought had not been used enough, set out a variant of his LL curve, which he called the 'L curve', and utilized his SIL diagram to present his ideas on the nature and determinants of the trade cycle. Hicks's review of Harrod's work and especially his 1950 book, are therefore important elements in tracing the IS–LM story.[2]

Hicks began his review article 'Mr. Harrod's Dynamic Theory' by criticizing Harrod's definition of dynamics – as Harrod had Hicks's definition in *Value and Capital* – and taking issue with Harrod's concept of 'warranted growth'. In Hicks's view, 'warranted' growth means 'very little more than that it is a possible path of development'. Moreover, according to Hicks, because of the nature of Harrod's proposed dynamic system 'little use can be made of the theory. It is extraordinarily hard to use it either for the explanation of events, or for the prediction of what is likely to result from changes introduced by policy . . . because he will have no lags, his system explodes out of the time dimension.'[3]

Hicks then attempts to improve on Harrod's theory, 'by some modification of Mr. Harrod's assumptions' in order 'to overcome the deficiency'. Hicks justifies this modification since 'the prize is a great one, for no one can study Mr. Harrod's work at all deeply without feeling that results of really great significance are just round the corner.' At this point, Hicks introduces lags and period analysis into his suggested interpretation of Harrod's theory, and then synthesizes a system of 'lagged Harrod' type equations with what he calls the mechanism 'the mathematical economists . . . seem to have got hold of' in order 'to build up a construction which will combine the merits of each'.[4]

Hicks developed and expanded his interpretation of Harrod's dynamic theory and the trade cycle further, using the SILL diagram in his 1950 book. First he outlined the 'antecedents' that brought him to his analysis of the trade cycle and the utilization of his diagram for this purpose. According to Hicks, his approach was based upon Keynes's *General Theory*, Frisch's macrodynamics theory and especially Harrod's dynamic theory. As Hicks put it in his opening chapter:

I have certain very definite obligations to Mr. Harrod, which I should like to make quite explicit . . . in the course of my work, I was coming to feel an increasing dissatisfaction with the 'macrodynamic' model; but it was not until I read Mr. Harrod's book that I realized what it was that I had overlooked. Then everything began to fall into place . . . I could kick myself for not having seen it before. After all, the essential ideas which I am taking from Mr. Harrod are not new ideas, put forward by him for the first time in 1948; if one had had the eyes to see, one could have seen them nearly a decade ago [1939, 'An Essay in Dynamic Theory'].[5]

In fact, Harrod's 1948 book was a restatement and expansion of both his 1938 'Scope and Method of Economics' paper and his 1939 'Dynamic Theory' paper. For example, in his chapter on 'The Need for a Dynamic Economics', Harrod discusses the important 'dichotomy' between statics and dynamics in economics, which he thought should be 'analogous to the division between Statics and Dynamics in physical science', a theme which he originally raised in his 1938 paper. In this chapter Harrod criticized both Hicks's *Value and Capital* approach to dynamics, and Keynes's *General Theory*. He maintained that Hicks's view of dynamic economics, i.e. the dating of quantities, while 'interesting', was not applicable to dynamics as he saw it: 'in Dynamics as I conceive it, dating is no more necessary that in statics.' He asserted that in 'the formulation and handling of its subject-matter Keynes' *General Theory* is essentially static', and continues 'there is one concept, however, which plays a central role in the *General Theory* which is not static, and that is why the *General Theory* will not be fully satisfactory until it is brought into relation with Dynamics . . . positive saving, which plays such a great role in the *General Theory*, is essentially a dynamic concept. This is fundamental.' Harrod then states that Keynes's theory is essentially a 'General Theory of Equilibrium' rather than 'a theory of general equilibrium'. He concludes, however 'The Keynesian concepts are not enough. And the crying need is for the formulation of dynamic concepts and the enunciation of a minimum set of . . . dynamic principles.'[6]

Hicks's 1950 book gave him the chance to reintroduce IS–LM and expand it to the analysis of the trade cycle. His chapter 'The monetary factor', states:

The ideas which we now want to get out of the Keynes theory emerge very easily if that theory itself is put into a particular form – a form which I myself suggested in an article written a few months after the publication of Keynes's book. I still feel that the diagram which was worked out in that article gives the most convenient summary of the Keynesian theory of Interest and Money which has yet been produced. In itself the diagram is nothing more than an expository device; but since more use can be made of it than has yet been made, it will not be out of place to reintroduce it here.[7]

Hicks then gives an account, of 'the basic generation' of what he calls the 'SI' and 'L' curves. First he assumes constant money wages and that the wage-unit is in money terms. In this case, the marginal efficiency of capital (MEC) schedule would show the inverse relationship between monetized investment and interest. Hicks says that given a level of investment, the multiplier determines equilibrium level of money income so that, also given the interest rate, the level of investment can be read off via the MEC and, in addition, once the investment level has been read off, the consumption function determines the level of money income. Hicks then states 'taking both of these steps together, we can say that with a given MEC schedule and a given consumption function, there is a determinate money income corresponding to each rate of interest.'[8]

Hicks continues:

> If we now construct a diagram with income (Y) on the horizontal axis, and interest (r) on the vertical, the relation between interest and income can be drawn out as a curve, the SI curve . . . This curve can be defined as showing the level of income which keeps equilibrium saving equal to equilibrium investment at each rate of interest. Since a fall in interest increases investment, and an increase in investment increases income, the SI curve can be relied upon to slope downwards from left to right.

Hicks goes on to 'relax' his assumptions, 'a good deal', but without, in his view, affecting the character of the SI curve 'substantially'. The major assumption he relaxes involves the effect of interest on saving, taking 'account of a possible direct effect of the rate of interest on saving'. He continues 'if a fall in the rate of interest affects the volume of saving forthcoming out of a given income, the multiplier becomes a function of the rate of interest. But with a given rate of interest there will still be a determinate multiplier, so that income is still a function of interest as before.'[9]

Hicks then describes the construction of what he calls 'the

liquidity curve (L)', which is based essentially on the assumption that, given the quantity of money and liquidity preference, the interest rate 'is a function of money income (Y)'. According to Hicks 'this relation can be expressed as a curve on the same income–interest diagram' he used to illustrate the SI curve. He concludes 'since interest rises as income increases, this liquidity curve L . . . will slope upwards to the right.' Hicks then deals with the shape of his 'L curve', abandoning the assumption about money supply as being 'given'. On this basis he is able to draw a liquidity curve, L, 'which shows the relation of income and interest, not with a given "supply of money" but with a given monetary system – and the curve will be more or less elastic according as the monetary system is more or less elastic'.[10]

Hicks then outlines the complete SIL diagram. At the point of intersection of the SI and L curves, given the marginal efficiency of capital (MEC) and liquidity preference schedules, the consumption function and monetary system, the interest rate and money income are determined simultaneously. And: 'It is this simultaneous determination . . . which effectively sums up the Keynesian system.'[11]

Having more or less covered the whole of his 1937 presentation, Hicks then maintains 'this is as far as Keynes's argument takes us.' But Hicks now goes further, introducing 'lags' into his SIL system. According to him, two types of lags act upon the SI curve, those arising from the multiplier side and those originating on the MEC side: 'the SI curve does not show an actual position which will be established automatically and immediately as soon as the rate of interest is fixed at some particular level; all it can show is the equilibrium Y corresponding to a given r.' Hicks then deals with the lags affecting the L curve, on the demand side, where changes in income affect it with a lag, and on the supply side, where 'lags in the response of the banking system also effect the curve'.[12]

Hicks asserts that the relationship between his SI and L schedules is identical to that between demand and supply curves, claiming that the SIL analogue over the cycle to the conventional 'cobweb' of demand and supply is 'the savings–investment–liquidity cobweb'. He shows the variants of his proposed SIL cobweb by using the diagram to illustrate both systemic contraction and expansion over the cycle, while in his final chapter on 'the place of the monetary factor', he utilizes his 'L curve' for describing processes in both a closed and open economy.[13]

A number of points arising from Hicks's account of the development of his ideas on the trade cycle and his 1950 version of IS-LM deserve attention. First of all, he starts his account of the 'ancestry' of his approach, by referring to ideas he borrowed from Keynes. In order to develop his ideas on the trade cycle, Hicks took both the mechanism of saving–investment determination and the multiplier, leaving aside Keynes's theory of interest rate determination, which, in Hicks's view, encompasses 'liquidity preference and the interest–investment schedule called the MEC'. According to Hicks 'It is now very commonly accepted, even among the most faithful Keynesians, that the particular way in which the doctrine of the *General Theory* was arranged tends to exaggerate the importance of interest; thus it is fully in accordance with the dominant trend of economic thinking to push this side of Keynes's work a little into the background.' Hicks continues:

> Apart from the change of emphasis, I am broadly prepared to accept the General Theory as a short period theory, and I shall use it in that capacity. But I shall have to emphasize some consequences of Keynes's teaching which he himself did not bring out sufficiently, and I shall have to do some significant reshaping of the foundations so as to fit them for a place in a structure which is different from that for which they are designed.[14]

In view of Hicks's reintroduction of his 1937 diagram to explain processes over the cycle, however, it is not clear whether in the passage cited above Hicks is referring to Keynes's *General Theory per se* or his IS–LM interpretation of it, the foundations of which have to be 'reshaped' to make it 'fit' into his view of the monetary aspects of the cycle.

Secondly, in his account of the derivation of his SILL, or – as he calls his 1950 version – SIL diagram, Hicks makes no mention of either Walrasian-type exchange representation or reduction of a three-dimensional into a two-dimensional diagram via his '*Value and Capital* methods', something which he does in his later accounts of the origins of his 1937 diagram, mentioned previously.[15]

Finally, Hicks attributes his adoption of the 'acceleration principle' to the influence of Frisch's 1933 paper. In fact, he claims to have compounded a ' "macrodynamic" theory . . . out of Keynes and Frisch', which he linked up to Harrod's dynamics to obtain his approach to the trade cycle. The problem here is that neither his 1945 paper – which, according to Hicks's preface was incorporated into his 1950 book – nor his 1949 review of Harrod's 'dynamics', which contained 'the central idea, round which' his argument was built, mention Frisch's 1933 paper. On the other hand, in Hicks's 1945 paper, Harrod's *Trade Cycle* is mentioned, and Hicks also refers to it in his 1950 book, when discussing the cause of the downturn in the cycle.[16]

Thus, the question remains whether Frisch's 'mathematical' approach or Harrod's 'relation' expressed – albeit in verbal form – in Harrod's 1936 book on the trade cycle was the source of Hicks's adoption of the 'acceleration principle'. In light of Hicks's adoption of points from Harrod's *Trade Cycle* in his 1950 book and his mention of it in his 1945 paper, one could conclude that by the time of his 1950 book, Hicks had basically synthesized Harrod's ideas on the trade cycle, IS–LM and dynamic economics with his own views. This was catalysed, as Hicks himself puts it, by Harrod's 1948 book, and brought Hicks from his 1949 review of Harrodian dynamics to his 1950 version of SIL diagrammatics.[17]

Over twenty years later, in his 1974 volume *The Crisis in Keynesian Economics*, Hicks claimed that in his trade cycle book, he attempted to do for Harrod's *'Dynamic Economics . . .* what SILL had done for the *General Theory'*, which was, in his view, to open 'up new vistas beyond those directly contemplated' by Harrod and to 'formalize' Harrod's work. However, Hicks then retracted the earlier defence of his trade cycle volume, both in his 1977 book *Economic Perspectives* and in a 1979 reply to Coddington's survey of Hicks's 'contribution to Keynesian economics'. A similar pattern of justification and explanation, and even to a certain extent retraction, can be seen in Hicks's attitude towards his diagram, especially in the face of the post-Keynesian attack on the IS–LM approach that characterized the decade between 1970 and 1980, as we will see later in this chapter.[18]

### The Clower–Leijonhufvud approach and the rediscovery of the Keynes–Lange system

Some two decades after Modigliani's successful initiation of the neo-classical synthesis using an IS–LM-type framework, Clower and Leijonhufvud started their effort at differentiating 'Keynesian economics' from what they saw as the essence of the 'economics of Keynes'. In Clower's words, their approach was based on an attempt 'to express matters as Keynes might have expressed them had he been less steeped in Marshallian habits of thought'. Indeed, Clower's well-known 1965 paper 'The Keynesian Counter-revolution' is noteworthy in many respects, both for what it includes and for what it leaves out.[19]

Clower begins his paper by pointing to 'the ambivalence of professional economists' to what he calls 'the Keynesian counter-revolution' he claims 'was launched by Hicks in 1937 and now [1965] being carried forward with such vigour by Patinkin and other General Equilibrium theorists'. At the start, Clower's view of the development of economic thought from Hicks's 1937 paper through *Value and Capital* and to Patinkin is problematic, to say the least. Indeed, Hicks himself took issue with Clower's statement, in *The Crisis in Keynesian Economics* (1974). According to Hicks, his 1937 IS–LM interpretation of Keynes is 'surely a very different formulation' from that in *Value and Capital*. In Hicks's view, 'the version of Keynes put forward in many modern writings especially those descended from Patinkin' appeared to him 'more like the *Value and Capital* form than like Keynes's own'. Hicks even notes that 'several of the papers in the Clower readings answer to this description.'[20]

Even more problematic, however, is why Clower makes no mention in his 1965 article of either Lange's 1938 paper or Timlin's 1942 book, the importance of which we have seen. This is difficult to understand because Clower's general approach is foreshadowed in Lange's 1938 paper, in which he presents Keynes's system in terms of that of Walras and in Timlin's development of what she called the Keynes–Lange system. For example, when Clower sets out what he calls the 'post–Keynesian dilemma', he states 'that Keynes himself made tacit use of a more general theory'. This, in Clower's view 'leads to market excess-demand functions which include quantities as well as prices as independent variables and, except in conditions of full employment, the excess-demand functions so defined do not satisfy Walras' Law'. Clower concluded, therefore 'that there has been a fundamental misunderstanding of the formal basis of the Keynesian revolution'. Clower then outlines his interpretation of what he considers the cardinal element underlying Keynes's *General Theory*, which he calls the 'dual decision hypothesis' of household (consumption–saving) behaviour.

This involves reconciling Keynes's *General Theory* with Walras's Law. In Clower's words 'it is worth remarking explicitly that the dual-decision hypothesis does not in any way flout Say's principle . . . It would be more accurate to say that this hypothesis assigns greater force to the principle', where according to Clower 'the distinction drawn . . . between Walras' Law and Say's Law is not relevant . . . from a formal point of view, the two propositions are equivalent.'[21]

Clower's justification for his approach will not be discussed here. According to Clower, however, 'Keynes either had a dual-decision hypothesis [of household behaviour] at the back of his mind, or most of the *General Theory* is theoretical nonsense.' Interestingly, Lange, in his 1938 paper, introduces the income identity

$$(Y \equiv C + I)$$

as 'the sum of the budget equations of the individuals' noting that 'investment or saving decisions can be different.' Lange then distinguishes between Walras's approach – 'the equality of the value of the *capitaux neufs* and the excess of income over consumption', i.e. saving – and that of his own system which, in Lange's view is 'as in the theory of Mr. Keynes' because it 'is an identity'. According to Lange, 'whatever the investment and saving decisions are, the volume of total income always adjusts itself so as to equalize saving and investment actually performed. This is a simple budget relationship, for the individual's incomes are equal to the sum of expenditure on consumption and investment.' Lange claims that his identity 'corresponds to the sum of the budget equations in the Walrasian system' and shows 'how expenditure on consumption and investment determine the total income. When this budget relationship is taken account of, there is no need any more for a separate equation indicating the equilibrium of saving and investment decisions based on some given income, however defined'. Clower's 1965 attempt to link Keynes's system with that of Walras via the dual-decision hypothesis would seem, then, to originate in Lange's 1938 paper and Timlin's subsequent development of the Keynes–Lange system.[22]

In his series of works published between 1967 and 1969, Leijonhufvud is even more explicit than Clower in attempting to base his view of Keynes's theory upon a Walras-type system. Again, however, there is no mention of either Lange's seminal 1938 paper or Timlin's 1942 book on the Keynes–Lange system. Taking his lead, it would seem, from Clower, Leijonhufvud asserts in his 1967 paper, for example, that 'the prototype' for the 'class of models generally used' by 'the majority school – dates back to the famous paper by Hicks'. He claims that 'this standard model appears to me a singularly inadequate vehicle for the interpretation of Keynes' ideas'. Leijonhufvud then identifies 'at least two major factions' that use 'the standard model' and coexist – albeit uneasily – 'within the majority school'. He terms these 'revolutionary orthodoxy' and 'neo-classical resurgence' respectively. In his opinion, however, the Clower approach is the most suitable 'interpretation' of Keynes's *General Theory*.[23]

The Clower–Leijonhufvud approach essentially involves replacing Walras's *'tâtonnement'* by Clower's idea of a 'central "market authority".' In other words, they propose the removal of Walras's 'auctioneer' and its replacement by Clower's notion of an 'automatic bookkeeper' – whose role is to ensure 'information coordination'. As Leijonhufvud puts it:

> To make the transition from Walras' world to Keynes' world, it is thus sufficient to dispense with the assumed *tâtonnement* mechanism. The removal of the auctioneer simply means that the generation of the information needed to co-ordinate economic activities in a large system where decision-making is decentralized will take time and will involve economic costs. No other 'classical' assumptions need to be relinquished.

Leijonhufvud concludes 'The only thing Keynes removed from the foundations of classical theory was the *deus ex machina* – the auctioneer which is assumed to furnish, without charge, all the information needed to obtain the perfect co-operation of the activities of all traders in the present and through the future.' As noted, however, they simply provide a 'central market authority', i.e. what can be called 'the invisible bookkeeper' in its place, thus enabling their version of a synthesis between Keynes's and Walras's approaches.[24]

In an article published a decade after Clower's 'rediscovery' – albeit unattributed – of Lange's approach and Timlin's proposed Keynes–Lange system, Clower and Leijonhufvud took what they called a 'Keynesian perspective' on 'the co-ordination of economic activities'. In this article, they modify the idea of a 'central market authority' – or 'invisible bookkeeper' – to the notion of a 'central supermarket' established by 'social contract'; this complete with a 'central trade coordinator' which, as they put it, 'is the counterpart . . . of the familiar *deus ex machina*, of the . . . auctioneer'. To be brief, they have restated the link that Lange made between Keynes and Walras some thirty years earlier, which was subsequently developed by Timlin more than twenty years prior to Clower's 1965 paper. They have simply turned the Keynes–Lange system into the neo-Walrasian synthesis.[25]

In their presentations, Clower and Leijonhufvud were critical of the IS–LM approach. For example, in his 1967 paper, Leijonhufvud claimed that IS–LM was 'a singularly inadequate vehicle' for interpreting Keynes's *General Theory*. Moreover, in their 1975 paper, Clower and Leijonhufvud claim that the 'standard Keynesian model . . . economists have developed in response to the stimulus' of Keynes's *General Theory*, i.e. 'IS–LM, and all that' not only has a 'capacity for mischief' but, in their view, limits consideration of 'the central question posed by Keynes's assault on received doctrine: is the existing economic system, in any significant sense, self-adjusting?.' According to them 'the standard model hardly allows us even to frame the central question in a manner that would direct research onto a promising track. The comparative statics of IS–LM constructions has a well-demonstrated capacity for converting questions about adjustment performance (or, if you will, stability) into questions about sundry elasticities in the minds of economists.'[26]

Leijonhufvud's 'critique' of IS–LM in 1983, restated in his survey of Hicks's views on 'time and money' – is also problematic, both for what it takes into account and what it ignores. In his paper 'What was the Matter with IS–LM?' and his subsequent survey of Hicks's views, his main point of criticism focuses on the issue of 'sequencing'. According to him, 'IS–LM ignores the sequence of events within the period.' He continues 'Ignoring sequencing becomes a source of trouble in particular in connection with comparative statics uses of the IS–LM model – i.e. the uses that are the stuff which macrotexts have been made of for several decades but which Hicks did not consider in reassessing the model.'[27]

In 'What was the Matter with IS–LM?', Leijonhufvud proposes a model which he calls a 'full information' macroeconomic (FIM) model, to be used in place of (or as a bench-mark against) what he terms 'Hicks's classical model'. For purposes of comparison, however, the FIM model, 'should . . . have a reasonable family resemblance' to IS–LM, according to Leijonhufvud. His proposed FIM model takes into account the sequence of events whereas IS–LM in his view 'can be a cumbersome, inappropriate framework for representing theories that make non-standard assumptions about the knowledge of transactors and, consequently, about the time-phasing of events'. In contrast, his FIM model – in its full information general equilibrium (FIGE) states – ensure that attention will be paid 'to the sequencing of events'. And this 'in order to understand the theoretical reasons why the system is supposed not to be in full information general equilibrium and also in order to understand the interaction of real and monetary phenomena in the system'. His conclusion, therefore, is that 'IS–LM, handled as if it were a static construction, will pay no attention to the sequence of events', while what he calls 'the comparative statics' of IS–LM is 'inferior' to that of his proposed FIM model.[28]

But Leijonhufvud did not pay attention to the fact that his proposed FIM model is similar, if not identical, to the Keynes–Lange system developed by Timlin over forty years earlier. Timlin presented a number of models in the Keynes–Lange system she developed, which she called the 'fundamental' and the 'supplementary' models. The latter were, in her words, 'two model worlds' characterized by variant forms of time-lags. The 'fundamental model' represents 'the world in terms of a series of temporary equilibria, a convention which is implicit in the *General Theory* itself and which has been made explicit and expanded by both Mr. Lerner and Prof. Hicks'. On the other hand, 'in the worlds of the supplementary models, we get a little closer to the real world.' This is because in both 'supplementary' model types, Timlin takes into account what Leijonhufvud called – over four decades later – 'the sequence' of economic events. For example, she describes the time sequence of contractual arrangements between those providing 'the services of the factors of production' and the time sequence relating to contracts made by the entrepreneur 'for the sale of consumption goods and services and of new securities'. She continues 'thus when entrepreneurs make their plans for production . . . they may either underestimate or overestimate demands.' According to Timlin, 'the supplementary models therefore permit conditions of limited disequilibrium'. She concludes that, 'the world in which we live . . . is really a combination' of her proposed 'fundamental' and 'supplementary' models.[29]

To sum up, in my view Clower and Leijonhufvud seem to protest too much about IS–LM as an interpretation of Keynes, since their approach is similar, if not identical, to the Keynes–Lange system. And, as shown above, this system is a variant – albeit one overlooked by most of the economics profession, including Clower and Leijonhufvud themselves – of the IS–LM approach.

### The post-Keynesian attack and Hicks's 'explanations'

While Leijonhufvud was putting the finishing touches to his 1968 book, Hicks was in the process of publishing a collection of papers which he called *Critical Essays in Monetary Theory*. In this volume, his 1937 IS–LM paper was reprinted, together with a revised version of his 1957 *Economic Journal* article 'The Classics again' – originally a review of Patinkin's book *Money, Interest, and Prices*. This was rewritten, since it was originally 'pulled out of shape by the reference to Patinkin'. In both the preface to this volume and in 'The Classics again', Hicks defended IS–LM as a 'suggested' interpretation of Keynes's *General Theory*, but expressed some doubt as to its ability to represent the 'classical' position concomitantly. For example, in the preface to his book, Hicks calls his IS–LM approach 'a potted version of the central argument of the *General Theory*' saying he used it 'in that way in the concluding chapters' of his 'book on the Trade Cycle'. However, he did not think it a good representation of the 'classics'. 'As a diagnosis of the "revolution" it is very unsatisfactory. It is not a bad representation of Keynes; but it does not get his predecessors (the "classics" as he called them) at all right. I have long felt that there was more to be said.'[30]

Hicks took the opportunity to expand on these themes in his revised article, 'The Classics again', claiming that his IS–LM diagram made it possible 'to express the essence of the Keynes theory on a single diagram'. Hicks's account of the construction of his diagram in the revised article deserves to be recalled. According to him, if real income and interest are measured along the axes, the SI curve can be drawn 'based on the MEC schedule and the consumption function' which 'at various rates of interest' connects 'those levels of income at which saving equals investment'. Hicks continues that since investment increases as interest decreases, while income increases with increasing investment, the SI curve slopes downward. The LL curve shows, for each given level of income, the interest rate at which the demand for money is equal to 'a given supply of money'. Hicks claims that since the demand for money increases with income, while it decreases with interest, the LL curve slopes upward. In this case, equilibrium, which 'can easily be shown to be . . . stable' occurs at the intersection of the SI and LL curves. Hicks makes no mention here of deriving the diagram via what he later called his '*Value and Capital* method'; this version of the diagram's derivation is quite similar to his 1950 version.[31]

Hicks asserts that his SILL 'construction', although it 'has a Keynesian tendency . . . contains nothing whatever that is inconsistent with "classical" theory'. He then presents two variants of the SILL diagram: the first representing the 'form of "classical" theory' proposed by Hume and Thornton – which he terms the 'short period form' of the classical theory; the second showing what he called 'the classical long period – full equilibrium theory'. Hicks did admit, however, that 'there is an important respect in which "the first variant" is unsatisfactory. It pays insufficient attention to the element of time.' This caveat notwithstanding, Hicks concluded: 'the two "classical" diagrams' he drew showed that 'there is no fundamental opposition between the Classical model and the Keynes model.'[32]

Whether or not Hicks's *Critical Essays* collection catalysed the post-Keynesian attack on IS–LM is debatable, since critiques of IS–LM as the 'essence' of Keynes's central message had appeared before Hicks's 1967 volume. The period following its publication, however, was characterized by strong assaults on IS–LM, led by Robinson, Davidson, Pasinetti, Minsky, Weintraub and Kahn, while Hicks's defence of his diagram took the tone first of justification, and then of explanation.[33]

Joan Robinson, for example, in *Economic Heresies* (1971), launched a virulent attack on the IS–LM interpretation of Keynes's *General Theory*. It consisted of two major points. The first was that IS–LM is a 'mollifying version of his system of ideas which turned it back once more into a variant of the quantity theory'. This followed from the LM schedule being an increasing function of income, with the IS schedule being a decreasing function of interest, so that there is only one level of income and interest 'at which the curves cut'. According to Robinson, 'this is the equilibrium position corresponding to the given fixed amount of money.' She asserts that 'here we have the quantity theory in its purest form.' Robinson's second point is that 'on this basis was erected a number of fantastical notions . . . the whole complex of ideas was somehow spliced onto a Walrasian version of neo-classical theory and used to bind up the wounds which the great slump had inflicted on *laissez-faire* orthodoxy.' She concludes that Leijonhufvud's 1968 book 'is valuable because he destroys this construction by its own internal contradictions and clears away a good deal of rubbish, while remaining strictly within the framework of monetary theory.'[34]

If accepted, Robinson's first point would explain why Dennis Robertson, for example, as early as 1937, not only recognized that the IS–LM approach was closer to his own world-view than to that of Keynes, but also advised its utilization and accepted its policy implications as recounted above. Robinson's second point and its conclusion, however, is questionable. For, in agreeing with Leijonhufvud, it could be said that she is simply 'doing a Hansen'. But, in this case, instead of replacing the 'L' in 'SILL' by an 'M', to make 'IS–LM', as Hansen did, Robinson is in effect supporting the replacement of IS–LM by its Keynes–Lanage variant, i.e. by an approach which is similar, if not identical.[35]

Davidson took up Weintraub's earlier critique of IS–LM in his 1972 book *Money and the Real World*, proposing what is, according to the post-Keynesian interpretation, a 'purer' version of Keynes's system. The early criticism levelled by the post-Keynesians at the IS–LM interpretation, and especially that of Robinson, put Hicks on the defensive.[36]

Hicks responded initially to the post-Keynesian critics of his diagram by publishing Keynes's letter to him regarding his IS–LM paper in an article 'Recollections and Documents' in 1973. He thus 'got in first' with his own interpretation of Keynes's letter. A year later, in his *The Crisis in Keynesian Economics*, Hicks again justified his diagram, citing Keynes's letter to him as proof that his diagrammatic approach to Keynes's *General Theory* was 'still defensible'.[37]

In the same year that Hicks expounded his view of the problems besetting Keynesian economics, Pasinetti published what was perhaps the most important post-Keynesian critiques of the IS–LM approach. In his 1974 essay on 'The Economics of Effective Demand' in his *Growth and Income Distribution*, Pasinetti presented what he considered the cardinal difference between Keynes's

*General Theory* system and the IS–LM interpretation – which he took as having been originated solely by Hicks. Pasinetti termed Hicks's 'procedure . . . typically un-Keynesian' rather than 'anti-Keynesian' in nature since, in his view, 'Hicks is not after all an extreme anti-Keynesian'. According to Pasinetti, it was Hicks who 'has in fact broken up Keynes' basic chain of arguments. The relations have been turned into a system of simultaneous equations, i.e. precisely into what Keynes did not want them to be'.[38]

In the Keynes centenary volume, *Keynes and Modern World* (1983), Pasinetti returned to this theme. In his opinion:

> The relevant thing to notice is that ever since the *General Theory* was published, the great majority of those who then became known as 'Keynesian' have done everything they possibly could to eliminate any revolutionary aspect from the *General Theory*, to expunge from it, bit by bit, what was in contrast with mainstream economics. The process started, it must be said, in England, with Hicks's . . . famous article, but it was carried out most effectively in the US, where the successful Keynesians have been precisely those who have carried out the task of looking for a reconciliation of the Keynesian concepts with traditional theory . . . the direct pupils of Keynes here have always strongly opposed this trend; they have always determinately insisted on Keynes's irreconcilability with traditional economics, but have not been listened to.

Whether Pasinetti had Harrod, Meade or even Kaldor in mind when writing this is debatable since the first two were members of the General Theory group and Kaldor was amongst Keynes's staunchest defenders, while all three also had leading roles in the early dissemination of the IS–LM approach.[39]

Over the decade between the publication of Robinson's critique of IS–LM in *Economic Heresies* and Hicks's 1980 'explanation' of IS–LM, the post-Keynesian attack focused essentially on what Weintraub called 'Hicksian-Keynesianism'. Minsky, for example, in his 1975 volume on Keynes, was highly critical of both Hicks and IS–LM, while Weintraub restated his views the next year in a critique of Hicks's 'crisis' volume. Robinson also continued her attacks on Hicks's advocacy of IS–LM over the decade, as manifest especially in her collection of essays *What are the Questions?* (1980).

A year before, Hicks published *Causality in Economics* in which he again defended IS–LM, justifying what he regarded as his own derivation of it in terms of 'getting in first', as noted previously.[40]

Hicks's 1980 'explanation' of IS–LM, however, did not seem to satisfy the post-Keynesians, especially Kahn. In his 1984 book recounting his version of the development of the *General Theory*, Kahn made the strongest attack on Hicks up to that date. According to Kahn, Hicks's IS–LM diagram had done serious damage to the development of economic thought, and Keynes did not protest enough when IS–LM first appeared. With the exception of, for example, Robinson's insightful 1971 critique and Pasinetti's 1974 query about the formal validity of IS–LM as the standard representation of Keynes's *General Theory*, the post-Keynesian attack on IS–LM has mostly been similar to Kahn's, i.e. based upon intuitive argument and problematic textual interpretation. The reason for this probably stems from Keynes's own ambivalence with regard to the IS–LM approach and thus it is not surprising that his 'direct pupils', and especially their followers, i.e. the post-Keynesians, have had difficulty in pinning the IS–LM chimera down and focusing their critique accordingly.[41]

### Isomorphism and the IS–LMics of controversy: neo- and post-Keynesians, monetarists and new classical rational expectationists

Samuelson observed, in his comment on Leijonhufvud's paper speculating on Keynes's opinion of the rational expectations approach (see *Keynes and the Modern World*), that there exists 'a complete isomorphism' of the monetarist models expounded by Friedman and Meltzer with those 'written down by Keynesians like Tobin or Modigliani'. However, according to Samuelson, not only is 'the new classical economics . . . a return with a vengeance to the pre-Keynesian verities', but if one believes in it, then one 'can no longer believe in the behaviour equations and relations of the *General Theory*' as expressed by the 'three-equation macro system of the *General Theory* type', i.e. 'the IS–LM curves of the Keynesian system'. Samuelson asserts that 'American Keynesians' like himself should not be complacent in the face of the new classical rational expectationist assault, suggesting that they should be 'reconstructed' and not 'unreconstructed Keynesians'. In this context, Samuelson describes the position represented by what he terms the 'Robinson–Pasinetti–Garegnani' (RPG) position as 'neo-Keynesian'. In my view, however, 'neo-Keynesian' is better used to describe the position taken by the 'American Keynesians', for example Tobin, Modigliani and Samuelson himself, while the term 'post-Keynesian' is more apt for describing the 'RPG' position.[42]

Indeed, Tobin, prefers to be called 'neo-Keynesian', which is the outcome, in his view, of being both a 'Keynesian' and a 'neo-classical'. Tobin also differentiates himself from post-Keynesians who, he thinks, view him as 'a reactionary'. Tobin's position is typical of the neo-Keynesian view of the *General Theory*, especially when he claims that it is basically a system of 'functions, and simultaneous equations', i.e. an IS–LM interpretation. In his Jahnsson lectures volume (*Asset Accumulation and Economic Activity*) – in which he reflected on recent theoretical developments in macroeconomics – Tobin defended the IS–LM approach against its detractors, ranging from the critique of the Walrasian-Keynesians (who simply rediscovered what Timlin called the Keynes–Lange system), through the monetarist challengers of the Keynesian world-view (who argue with the neo-Keynesians in terms of IS–LM), to the new classical rational expectationists, who seem to reject both the Keynesian world-view and the IS–LM analytical tool-kit. As Tobin put it, the theme linking his lectures was 'how theorists do and should model the macroeconomic structures they are trying to describe'. Tobin terms Hicks's 'IS–LM formalization' of 'the Keynesian model . . . the principal analytic apparatus in many macro textbooks, courses, journal articles, policy applications throughout the world'. While acknowledging the validity of some critiques of IS–LM, Tobin adds 'I do not think the apparatus is discredited. I still believe that carefully used and taught, it is a powerful instrument for understanding our economies and the impacts of policies upon them.'[43]

Tobin also recognized the isomorphism between the analytical tool-kit of his neo-Keynesian approach and that of the 'monetarist macroeconomics' of Friedman and Meltzer, when he acknowledged that the new classical rational expectationist assault was directed at both and did not accept the validity of their common technique of analysis, i.e. IS–LM. Indeed, for Tobin the debate between the neo-Keynesians and the 'earlier' monetarists focused 'on the shape of the Hicksian LM curve' and what affects it.[44]

Meltzer proposed an additional interpretation of Keynes and the factors that differentiate the Keynesian and monetarist world-views. In his 1981 article 'Keynes's *General Theory*: A Different perspective', Meltzer developed an eight-equation IS–LM-type system which included what he called 'the missing equation' in Keynes's system. Meltzer then reduced this to a three-equation system that encompassed the conventional equations associated with the IS and LM curves, and an equation for an additional curve, which he called the SS curve. According to Meltzer, this equation and curve represents an aggregate supply function that becomes a fixed relation between aggregate supply and employment when the price level is constant. Meltzer then gave his interpretation of Keynes in terms of this threefold equation–curve system.[45]

Meltzer defended his 'different perspective' of Keynes in 1983 by restating his earlier interpretation. He 'derived IS and LM equations based, in part, on Keynes's response to Hicks' and repeated his advocacy of a supply of aggregate output function in both equational and diagrammatics (SS curve) form in order to complete his interpretation of Keynes's system. Meltzer concluded: 'there are many interpretations of Keynes. Mine differs from others in several ways that I have tried to elaborate. I would be misinterpreted, however, if I failed to repeat my earlier [1981] statement that "no single set of statements is the correct re-statement" of the *General Theory*.'[46]

Meltzer's 'On Keynes and Monetarism' – his contribution to the Keynes centenary volume – appeared the same year (1983). It began 'there are many interpretations of Keynes and many versions of monetarism . . . In my interpretation, the *General Theory* is Keynes's attempt to explain why the economy fluctuates around a stable equilibrium level that is below the level of output that society is capable of producing.' Meltzer then notes the isomorphism between the early monetarist analytical technique (citing the example of Friedman's 1974 general framework) and what he took to be Keynes's, interpreted in terms of IS–LM. Meltzer then interprets the new classical rational expectationist model also in terms of IS–LM, something which Lucas, for example (and others) would probably take issue with, since the new classical rational expectationists would reject the IS–LM approach *pre se* as a valid analytical technique, preferring their own rational expectations approach.[47]

Meltzer concludes that despite the isomorphism in their analytical technique, his interpretation of 'Keynes's theory' is, of course, different from Friedman's – and Meltzer's – monetarist world-view. Furthermore, it also differs from the rational expectationist approach, while there is a high degree of isomorphism between Friedman's world-view and that of the new classical rational expectationists. Finally, according to Meltzer 'Methods in economics have changed in the direction of increased formalism since Keynes's time. Keynes never wrote down an algebraic statement of his theory, although he accepted Hicks's (1937) algebraic restatement with some important, specific qualifications.'[48]

The validity of Meltzer's interpretation and conclusion notwithstanding, his insights can assist us in classifying both 'schools' and 'schoolmen' here. This follows from

1 his recognition of the element of isomorphism between his own IS–LM-type interpretation of Keynes and the analytical technique of the earlier monetarists;
2 his attribution of isomorphism to the relation between Friedman's world-view and that of the new classical rational expectationists; and
3 his opinion that 'the post-Keynesians are the most active group emphasizing expectations as a driving force in the *General Theory*.'

Harcourt has distinguished two analytical approaches amongst the post-Keynesians. The first is indeed based upon long-run expectations, as noted by Meltzer. This approach is taken, for example, by Shackle, Davidson and Kregel (type I post-Keynesians). But, according to Harcourt, there exists another post-Keynesian analytical technique, which I would call 'periodist' (type II post-Keynesians). This category encompasses both those focusing on short-period analysis, for example Robinson and Kalecki, and those exhibiting neo-Ricardian views, for example Garegnani, Bharadwaj, Eatwell, Milgate and Pasinetti, who focus on the long period.[49]

The Meltzer–Harcourt insights enable us to develop a classification framework for dealing with the phenomenon of isomorphism and its relation to the IS–LMics of controversy. First, let us suppose that the possible macroeconomic world-views are of either 'Keynesian' or 'monetarist' variety. Secondly, let us suppose that the possible macroeconomic analytical techniques tool-kits are of either the 'IS–LM', 'expectationist' (short-term/long-term) and 'periodist' (short-run/long-run) varieties. A combination of these possibilities results in the following contingency table 5.1:

**Table 5.1**  Macroeconomic analytical technique

| Macroeconomic world-view | IS–LM | Expectationist | Periodist |
|---|---|---|---|
| Keynesian | A | B | C |
| Monetarist | D | E | F |

Included in category A are the neo-Keynesian approaches of Tobin, Modigliani and Samuelson, and also the Clower–Leijon-hufuvd, i.e Keynes–Lange approach. Category B encompasses the type I post-Keynesian approach of Shackle, Davidson and Kregel, based on the long-term expectational aspects of Keynes's *General Theory*. Category C, encompassing type II post-Keynesians, includes the approaches of Robinson and Kalecki (short-run periodists) and Garegnani, Bharadwaj, Eatwell, Milgate and Pasinetti (long-run periodists). Category D includes the monetarist approaches of Friedman and Meltzer. The new classical rational expectationist approaches of Lucas and Sargent, among others – focusing on short-term rational expectations – are encompassed by category E, while category F includes the approaches advocated by Phelps and the long-run (NARU) monetarists.[50]

Now, two degrees of isomorphism – strong and weak – can be identified in the classification framework outlined above. As both Samuelson and Tobin have noted, there is strong isomorphism of analytical technique between models in categories A and D, while both Meltzer and Lucas have stressed the strong degree of isomorphism that characterizes the world-views of those in categories D, E and F, albeit not sharing analytical technique as far as IS–LM is concerned. In contrast, as Tobin has remarked, there is only a weak degree of isomorphism between the approaches of those in categories A, B and C, since, although they share a 'Keynesian' world-view, their analytical techniques are different.[51]

Interestingly, Leijonhufvud has proposed that there may also exist a weak degree of isomorphism along a diagonal linking categories A and E, at least according to his interpretation of Keynes's view of short-term expectations. In his Keynes centenary paper 'What would Keynes have thought of Rational Expectations?', Leijonhufvud cites a passage from the *General Theory* which, according to his interpretation, shows that 'Keynes' own treatment of short-term expectations should give pause to anyone tempted to attack' the new classical rational expectationist approach 'on the grounds that it assumes too much foresight on the part of agents'. In the passage Leijonhufvud refers to, Keynes stated 'it will often be safe to omit express reference to short-term expectation in view of the fact that in practice . . . there is a large overlap between the effects on employment of the realized sales-proceeds of recent output and those of the sales-proceeds expected from current input.' According to Leijonhufvud 'the omission of "express reference" is achieved, of course, by simply equating expected and realized real income, a procedure subsequently imbedded in the Keynesian cross, in IS–LM, and thus in the entire Keynesian literature. This is "perfect foresight" such as the rational expectations people have not allowed themselves to indulge in!'[52]

Other observers have also commented on what they have taken to be a weak isomorphism between their interpretations of Keynes and the new classical rational expectationist approach, for example Colander and Guthrie, Rutherford, and Torr. Colander and Guthrie maintained that if the 'rational' basis was altered to a 'reasonable' one, then the 'expectations theorists' and Keynes could be said to have a common approach. Rutherford went so far as to claim that not only do there exist parallels between the approaches of Keynes and the new classical expectationist model, but that, 'manifestly, the distinction between Keynes and RE (rational expectations) theorists does not lie in any fundamental differences in defining knowledge.' Rather, what Rutherford sees as 'discrepancies' between the two approaches 'relate almost exclusively . . . to Keynes's stress on the non-homogeneity of economic phenomena over time'. The category of Keynesian approach to which Colander, Guthrie and Rutherford must be referring is not difficult to ascertain, since both Shackle and Davidson would reject any hint of isomorphism between the analytical techniques of categories B and E above, as manifest in Davidson's view of the RE approach (for example 1978, 1980) and Shackle's comment on Rutherford's paper itself.[53]

In light of the material presented above, a number of points may be made about the role of IS–LM in recent controversies in economics. First, while the IS–LM approach has been attacked by the post-Keynesians, it has been defended (and used) by monetarists and neo-Keynesians alike, both in their debates with each other and in their respective interpretations of Keynes. Secondly, the nature and existence of isomorphism between the categories outlined above revolves around the IS–LM approach and the role of (or lack of) various types of expectations in it. Thirdly, while some rational expectations models can be expressed in terms of IS–LM analogues, as Meltzer has done for example, the new classical expectationist approach – while exhibiting a degree of weak isomorphism with the IS–LM treatment of short-term expectations – still rejects IS–LM and what it represents, as a valid analytical technique. And in this there is a degree of weak isomorphism between the new classical expectationist and long-run monetarist positions and both post-Keynesian views of IS–LM because, although they do not share a common analytical technique, they both completely reject the analytical validity of IS–LM. To sum up, the IS-LM approach – while not necessarily the focus of the current controversies in economics – plays an important role in most and is even at the centre of some of them.[54]

# 6

# IS–LM and interpreting
# Mr Keynes: an overview

In the preceding chapters, I have attempted to outline the history of
the IS–LM concept in economics from its inception to the present
day. However, the problems involved in getting the account
straight have been and are numerous, and the history itself has
many sides to it. In this chapter I will try to bring together its many
threads and present a valid and coherent way of dealing with the
issues raised by the IS–LM interpretation of Keynes's *General
Theory*. These issues – and the conclusions to be drawn regarding
them – involve:

i   the nature, origins and development of the IS–LM concept;
ii  the characteristics of the General Theory group and Keynes's
    reaction to IS–LM;
iii the reaction of the economics profession to IS–LM and the
    present position of the IS–LM approach;
iv  the IS–LM case in comparative perspective and its implications
    for the history of economic thought.

## Harrod–Hicks–Meade IS–LM

In his first annual Hicks Lecture delivered at Oxford, Solow
concludes that 'it is remarkable that IS–LM has served us so long
and so well . . . The story speaks well . . . for J. R.'s [Hicks's]
inspiration.' While one would not go as far as Solow and rate IS–
LM with 'Mendel's Laws, the elasticity of demand . . . the wheel'
for example, the origins of the IS–LM approach could still be
compared with that of Keynes's *General Theory*; at least as far as

multiple discovery is concerned. While Patinkin has recently refuted the claims of both 'the Stockholm School' and Kalecki to have originated and developed earlier versions of Keynes's *General Theory* independently, the issues are different for IS–LM and the *General Theory*. For IS–LM the issue is not one of competing claims to independent multiple discovery; far from it, for neither Harrod nor Meade ever claimed to have originated the diagram, nor Hicks the equations. Rather, in the case of IS–LM a sequential cross-fertilization of ideas – or a sequential conceptual synthesis – occurred. Indeed, as Blaug has noted – albeit in another context – 'the IS–LM apparatus is a perfect example of Hicks's unusual ability to synthesize the ideas of other economists.'[1]

Thus, while independent multiple discovery of IS–LM could be implied from Solow's remarks about the identical nature of the equation systems in Hicks's, Harrod's and Meade's papers, textual evidence shows that this is not the case. The IS–LM approach is first the product of the discovery of an equational system by Harrod and Meade, which they took to be representative of Keynes's *General Theory*. Then, based on the Harrod–Meade equational system, came Hicks's crucial discovery of a way to represent this equational system diagrammatically, synthesizing equational and diagrammatic approaches in his now famous 'suggested interpretation' of Keynes's *General Theory*.[2]

The lack of reference to the contributions of Harrod and Meade to the IS–LM concept is not surprising because the existence of a widespread IS–LM approach has never been recognized. Moreover, even Solow did not recognize the important of Harrod's and Meade's contributions to the IS–LM approach relative to Hansen's, and thus did not question the historical accuracy of what has previously been termed 'Hicks–Hansen IS–LM' by virtually all economists and historians of economic thought; that is, if they did not attribute the IS–LM model solely to Hicks.[3]

A brief survey of the literature of the fifty years since the publication of Harrod's, Meade's and Hicks's papers in 1937 should suffice to illustrate these points. First and foremost, Hicks's failure to acknowledge both Harrod's and Meade's papers in his own, gave the initial impression that he discovered the IS–LM approach independently and alone. Thus, while Lange (1938) mentioned Harrod's paper (and also Reddaway's) he overlooked Meade's. Timlin, in her 1942 book, also neglected to mention Harrod and Meade, while Modigliani, the initiator of the 'neo-classical synthesis' in his 1944 paper, attributed his IS–LM approach to Hicks, Lange and Timlin, but also failed to mention Harrod and Meade. Indeed, it took Paul Samuelson – in his 1947 *Foundations of Economic Analysis* – to remind the economics profession that James Meade was also an 'early interpreter' of Keynes's *General Theory*, although this was subsequently overlooked by Klein in both editions of his *The Keynesian Revolution* (1950; 1968). In fact, Klein made no mention of either Harrod's or Meade's papers, and Harrod is not even mentioned in the index to Klein's 1950 edition. Interestingly, in the chapter 'The Keynesian revolution revisited' in the 1968 edition, Klein wrote:

> After the interpretations, in consistent mathematical form, by Hicks and Lange, Keynesian thinking settled along these lines:
>
> $$S\ (r,\ Y) = I\ (r,\ Y);\ M = L\ (r,\ Y)$$
>
> where Y is aggregate money income; r is the interest rate, and M is the nominal stock of cash . . . This is an informative and succinct way of expressing the theory in what I would now like to call a pedagogical model.[4]

Hansen mentions neither Harrod nor Meade in his texts of the late 1940s (1949 for example). With the publication of his 1953 *A Guide to Keynes* – in which he IS–LMized Keynes's *General Theory* but took no notice of either Harrod's or Meade's papers – the course had been set for 'Hicks's model' as manifest in 'Hicks–Hansen IS–LM'. By the late 1950s and early 1960s, critiques like those of Weintraub (1959; 1960) and Horwich (1964) focused specifically on what was called 'Hicks's model' and 'the Hicksian framework'. Horwich – whose survey of the literature on the development of IS–LM was later termed 'scholarly and thorough' by Leijonhufvud (1968) – attributed the discovery of the IS–LM approach to Hicks, citing neither Harrod's nor Meade's papers, but mentioning Lange's. Weintraub (1960) went so far as to state that while Hicks originated the IS–LM curves 'Hansen (1949) has probably taught us most about this approach.'[5]

The mid- and late 1960s saw the Clower–Leijonhufvud assault (1965; 1968; 1969) on the neo-classical synthesis and Hicks–Hansen Keynesianism – based in fact upon Timlin's Keynes–Lange system, as shown above – but again with no reference to Harrod's and

Meade's papers. Winch also attributed the IS–LM approach to Hicks and Hansen in his 1969 volume *Economics and Policy*. It was only George Shackle who – having attended the 1936 Oxford conference and symposium on Keynes – again reminded economists of the existence of Harrod's and Meade's papers in his masterly *The Years of High Theory* (1967), but again his reference was not taken up by the economics profession or by its historians of thought.[6]

In the early and middle 1970s, the post-Keynesians initiated their concerted attack on Hicks and IS–LM, starting with Robinson (1971) and Davidson (1972), and developed by Pasinetti (1974) and Minsky (1975). All of them attribute IS–LM to either Hicks alone or to both Hicks and Hansen, with no mention of either Harrod or Meade, while Minsky, as Klein, does not even mention Harrod in the index to his book on Keynes![7]

The mid- and late 1970s saw the appearance of studies based on primary textual material from Keynes's papers and correspondence with the principals in the development of IS–LM, although Hicks 'got in first' with his 1973 article publishing Keynes's letter to him about IS–LM. Both Moggridge (1976) and Patinkin (1976) utilized Keynes's correspondence in their respective treatments of IS–LM, with Moggridge giving a negative tone to Keynes's remarks on Hicks's paper, although he makes no reference to Harrod's and Meade's papers. Patinkin, also makes no mention of Meade's paper in his 1976 study entitled *Keynes' Monetary Thought*, while Deane, in her 1978 volume *The Evolution of Economic Ideas* cites Moggridge's critique of Hicks's interpretation of Keynes's letter about his IS–LM article, but does not mention either Harrod's or Meade's interpretations of the *General Theory*.[8]

Coddington's 1979 survey 'Hicks's Contribution to Keynesian Economics', seems to have spurred Hicks on to his own reformulation of how he developed the IS–LM diagram, although Coddington also makes no mention of either Harrod's or Meade's papers. In his 1979 'reply' to Coddington, Hicks makes the following most interesting statement, part of which he repeats in his 1980 'explanation of IS–LM':

> It hasn't been generally noticed that the device by which I made my IS–LM diagram is similar to that which I used in *Value and Capital*, Chapter 5, for collapsing a three-way exchange on to a single figure. So it also was a product of my Walrasianism. It is not surprising, in consequence, that those

who were unwilling to think of the price system as an equilibrium of related markets (Dennis Robertson on the one hand, Joan Robinson on the other) did not care for it. Neither, accordingly, was ready to admit, what seems to follow from the IS–LM diagram, that the Keynes theory, and the so-called 'Classical' theory are both of them special cases of something more general . . . I must have lectured on IS–LM almost every year from 1938 onwards; as soon as one incorporated the change in wages that (on the most orthodox Keynes) must follow on the attainment of full employment, one must soon have been driven to that kind of generalization. So when, at this stage, I counted myself a Keynesian, it was an IS–LM Keynesian that I meant.

In light of the problematic aspects of the diagram's derivation presented above, and the evidence of Robertson's positive view of IS–LM, one must simply resort to Hicks's own caveat that 'memory is treacherous'.[9]

The early and mid- 1980s saw the IS–LM approach again being attributed solely to Hicks, or to Hicks and Hansen, by Tobin (1980) and Morgan (1981) for example. Hicks mentions neither Harrod nor Meade in his 1980 'explanation' of IS–LM. Lucas simply followed, in his *Studies in Business Cycle Theory* (1981), 'the classic exegesis' of Hicks's 1937 article, while Meltzer (1981; 1983a; 1983b) based his IS–LM view of Keynes on Hicks's 'standard interpretation' and '1937 algebraic restatement' without reference to either Harrod or Meade. Leijonhufvud also only mentioned Hicks in his Keynes centenary paper (1983), while Pasinetti's reply to Leijonhufvud focused solely on Hicks's 1937 paper, with no mention at all of Harrod and Meade. Klamer (1984) simply repeated the 'conventional wisdom', going so far as to say that the neo-Keynesians 'especially relied on the IS–LM framework, which John Hicks and Alvin Hansen devised as a formal interpretation of Keynes's *General Theory*'. But it was Leijonhufvud's paper 'What was the Matter with IS–LM?' (1983), attacking 'Hicks's classical model' because it 'has served us ill' that catalysed the theme of Solow's first Hicks Lecture in May 1984. While Solow's message was not that Harrod and Meade should also share in any 'blame' for the IS–LM approach, he still did not give them credit for their fundamental contribution to its discovery and development.[10]

To sum up, the contribution of Harrod and Meade to the IS–LM approach – the former originating its equational form, the latter both refining the equations and writing the first textbook based on the IS–LM approach – by far outweighs Hansen's popularization of Hicks's diagram and 'IS–LMization' of Keynes's *General Theory*. In light of the evidence presented above, only one conclusion can be drawn about the originators of the IS–LM approach: the IS–LM interpretation of Keynes's *General Theory* should be termed Harrod–Hicks–Meade IS–LM.[11]

## The General Theory group, Keynes and the IS–LM approach

One of the more puzzling aspects of the IS–LM history is the split in the General Theory group. While some evidence has been provided above, the question remains: was there indeed a distinct difference between the attitudes of members of the General Theory group towards Keynes, the *General Theory* and its diagrammatic or equational representation? Additional evidence of the split in the General Theory group, however, can be seen in previously unpublished correspondence between Harrod, Kahn, Durbin, Robertson, Meade and Kaldor; and in the differences between James Meade's 1936 *Economic Analysis and Policy* and Joan Robinson's 1937 volumes *Essays in the Theory of Employment* and *Introduction to the Theory of Employment*.[12]

The role of Roy Harrod in the development, defence and dissemination of Keynes's *General Theory* is well known. In fact, on 13 November 1934 Kahn wrote to Harrod about the problems involved in getting Keynes's message across, referring to Harrod as someone upon whom Keynes could rely and who would lead those supporting Keynes in the battle to spread his ideas. Harrod, however, did not take on the mantle of 'leader' of Keynes's 'disciples'. Rather, it could be said that he preferred to be an objective, but sympathetic, supporter of Keynes, albeit asserting his own interpretation of Keynes's central message.[13]

Thus, in a letter to Durbin dated 7 February 1936, the same week as Keynes's *General Theory* was published, Harrod wrote:

I quite agree that Keynes would do better for himself by being less far-reaching in his claims. But these geniuses are apt to have prima donnaish temperaments and we should lose . . . if we refused to listen to them on this account. But I confess that I don't think very much of the results of 'a century of scientific thought'. Economics – as you with your scientific training must know quite well – has been much more scholastics than science. And anyhow, it can all be written on the back of a postage stamp, can't it? . . . But, I quite agree, he is very naughty.

In a letter to Harrod some five months later, dated 22 July 1936, Robertson commented on Harrod's attitude towards Keynes's *General Theory*, saying 'Yes, I agree that is the right attitude to take about JMK's book, though it is not easy here [in Cambridge] in face of the whirlwind campaign of proselytisation. My trouble is that while I have a limited sympathy with some of the conclusions, I don't find the concepts helpful.'[14]

Robertson's 1937 letter to Meade commenting on Meade's book *Economic Analysis and Policy* and his IS–LM paper, included an observation on the 'split' in the General Theory group. This was restated in a slightly different form in a letter from Robertson to Kaldor, written from the LSE and dated 16 February 1939, in which Robertson said:

It is evident that if people of the calibre of Hicks, Harrod, yourself (as well as the stricter sect of disciples) have got so much out of the GTE [Keynes's *General Theory*] there must be great merits in it. It is perhaps inevitable that I should have been unduly sensitive to its distortions and exaggerations! Let us hope that in time what is fruitful in it will have been absorbed into the corpus of economic theory and what is not, discarded. Meanwhile, the existence of the book does, I think, create a difficult pedagogical problem.[15]

In fact, both Kaldor and Durbin were faced with the 'pedagogical problem' of Robbins's opposition to using Keynes's *General Theory* at the undergraduate level at the London School of Economics only two years before. In a recent interview with the author, Kaldor recalled:

Robbins was very anti-Keynes all the time and he just didn't know how to refute Keynes. He and Keynes were together on the Economic Advisory Council during MacDonald's government and they got into some sort of row over tariffs. And so Robbins was very emotional about Keynes and very hostile to him . . . Robbins simply told me – once he came to my room – that it [*General Theory*] is a controversial book which is not very suitable for undergraduates . . . if he said it to me I dare say he must have said it to other people too.

Thus, both Durbin and Kaldor first used Keynes's *General Theory* at the graduate level; Durbin in his lectures on 'the modern purchasing power controversy' during the Michaelmas term (October–December) 1936, Kaldor in his lectures on 'the problems of the theory of economic dynamics' during the Lent term (January–February) 1937. Robbins did not use Keynes's *General Theory* in his undergraduate course of lectures on 'general principles of economic analysis' that started in October 1938. Rather, it would seem that he preferred to use Hicks's IS–LM article as a teaching tool in that part of his lectures dealing with what Robbins termed 'dynamics, money and interest'.[16]

There is no mention of Durbin's and Kaldor's use of Hicks's IS–LM article in their lectures at the LSE, in the pre-war catalogues, although Kaldor did utilize IS–LM in supporting Keynes and refuting Pigou, as shown above. Kaldor's use of IS–LM in this context and the support he received from Robertson takes on new meaning when a recent discovery by Pollit is taken into account. Pollit discovered an earlier exchange about Keynes's *General Theory* and 'the effect of cost reduction on employment' between Dobb, Robertson, Hicks and Sraffa that took place during May–June 1937. In this exchange, Robertson reacted to Dobb's argument by referring to Hicks's IS–LM paper: 'As Hicks brings out in his new [Econometrica] article, there is no justification for tying the [money] schedule of marginal efficiency of capital to the wage-rate', while Hicks himself, replying to Dobb, completely agreed with Robertson's views on the role of the interest rate in the wages–employment nexus.[17]

As I have indicated, the split in the General Theory group can also be seen in the differing interpretations of Keynes's *General Theory* taken by James Meade in his textbook *Economic Analysis and Policy* – which originally appeared in 1936 and went into a second edition in 1937 – and that of Joan Robinson, as manifest in her volume of *Essays in the Theory of Employment* and textbook *Introduction to the Theory of Employment*, both published in 1937.

Meade's important book, the object of which was 'to expound the whole corpus of economic theory' for students 'with full use of the more recent developments' was, according to his preface, much influenced by both Keynes's *Treatise* and *General Theory*. In addition, the major part of Meade's book was read in manuscript by Robinson, who suggested 'many material improvements'. In any event, the conceptual model underlying Meade's book was the same as that in his *Review of Economic Studies* paper, as can be seen from the text itself and from Meade's response to Robertson's observations on his book in their 1937 correspondence, to which I referred earlier.[18]

For example, Robertson's letter of 25 April 1937 initially questioned Meade's treatment of the wage–price–interest–employment nexus which Robertson 'had thought of raising' with Meade for 'some time'. In his reply, dated 26 April 1937, Meade answered 'in terms of my article in the Review of Economic Studies' putting 'the whole argument in terms of that article' and its equations. Robertson replied on 9 May 1937 that Meade seemed 'to be abandoning JMK rather than expounding him' as cited above. Meade answered Robertson a week later, on 16 May 1937, and said 'On the question of wages I agree that one must either go step by step or go straight to the new equilibrium and examine it. I believe my method in my book, as in my article in the Review of Economic Studies, is essentially the second.'[19]

Meade continued to deal with Robertson's point about his book 'in terms of my RES article', which is IS–LM, as I have shown; Meade, along with Harrod and Hicks, having originated the IS–LM approach.[20]

Joan Robinson interpreted Keynes's *General Theory* in an entirely different manner in her 1937 *Essays* and *Introduction* to what she called 'the theory of employment'. According to Robinson, her textbook was based on both the *General Theory* and her *Essays*, and its purpose was 'to provide a simplified account of the main principles . . . for students who find they require some help in assimilating . . . Mr. Keynes' *General Theory*'. The conceptual model Robinson outlines in her textbook is, in fact, identical to one which Pasinetti specified in equational form almost four decades later, in his 1974 critique of Hicks's IS–LM.[21]

Interestingly, in her collection of essays published in 1937, Robinson has an essay entitled 'Diagrammatic Illustrations'. In the opening paragraph, Robinson wrote 'An attempt to submit the

*General Theory of Employment* to diagrammatic treatment is subject to grave objections, since few of the concepts concerned can be reduced to precise quantitative terms.' She continues 'A formalized treatment may . . . be of use merely as an alternative method of expressing some of the propositions' she made in the essays that preceded it. Robinson adds 'It will be found necessary to make a number of simplifications in order to reduce them to a form which can be expressed in a two-dimensional scheme.' Nonetheless, Robinson develops a diagram with interest rate and employment as axes, which used both what she called long- and short-period labour 'demand' and 'supply' curves to illustrate various aspects of her interpretation of Keynes's *General Theory*.[22]

Robinson also dealt with the problem of 'determinacy' as compared with 'indeterminacy' in economic theory. In her view, economists exhibit a natural bias 'in favour of determinateness':

> Theoretical economists usually display an extreme anxiety to discover 'determinate' solutions of the problems which they study. Determinacy, for the economist, means that the problem is susceptible to analysis by the methods which he has been brought up to use . . . the first task of the analytical economist is therefore to discover determinate problems on which to work . . . if the problems in the real world are not determinate in the economist's sense, predictions about events in the real world cannot be made by means of economic analysis, and economics can never become a science.

She continues:

> To discover too much 'indeterminacy' in the real world would . . . deprive the economist of self-respect, if not of the means of livelihood. But to discover too much 'determinacy' in his theoretical system ought to damage his self-respect quite as much. For it is, after all, the aim of theory to reflect as closely as possible the conditions of the real world, and we all know from daily experience that in the real world many problems are indeterminate in the economist's sense.

Robinson concludes:

> It is a great merit in the *General Theory of Employment* that it allows us to believe that the general level of prices is

determined very largely by arbitrary human decisions, and yet saves our self respect by leaving us such problems as the determination of the level of real wages and the amount of employment to be discussed by the methods of pure economic analysis.[23]

In light of these views and her own attempt at its diagrammatic representation, it seems that Robinson did not object to a diagrammatic approach to the *General Theory per se*. Rather she objected to the 'determinateness' of the IS–LM diagram and equations; equations which were originated and first used by others in the General Theory group – Harrod and Meade.

Another prominent member of the earlier 'Cambridge Circus' and what I have termed the General Theory group was Richard Kahn, who, in his retrospective book *The Making of Keynes' General Theory* (1984), bitterly attacked the IS–LM approach. According to Kahn, Keynes's letter to Hicks about his IS–LM paper was, in effect, critical. Kahn explains, 'Keynes's rebuke' was 'too mild' and it 'left Hicks unrepentant'. Kahn asserts that the outcome of this has been 'that elementary teaching of Keynesian economics has been a victim of IS–LM and related diagrams and algebra. It is tragic that Keynes made no public protest when they began to appear'. Kahn concluded that he believed 'that the IS–LM scheme has very seriously confused the development of economic thought.'[24]

As I have tried to show, however, it is my view that Keynes's 1937 *Quarterly Journal of Economics* article, with its re-emphasis on uncertainty or, as Robinson would put it 'indeterminacy' was, in fact, Keynes's considered reaction to the IS–LM approach as a whole and the IS–LM interpretations of Harrod, Hicks and Meade respectively. To be brief, Keynes neither accepted the IS–LM approach outright – as Hicks and others thought he did – nor did he reject it outright, as Robinson, Kahn and the post-Keynesians would have it. Rather, he was ambivalent or, as I would prefer to put it, agnostic, preferring not to reject specifically the variant interpretations of his *General Theory* – made by the members of his General Theory group and others, such as Hicks, Champernowne, Reddaway and Kaldor – in order to get, as he put it in his 1937 *Quarterly Journal of Economics* paper, his 'simple fundamental' and 'basic ideas' across.[25]

## IS–LM and the economics profession:
## 'revealed preference' and 'trained intuition' or 'chimera'?

In his study of the development of Keynes's monetary thought (1976), Patinkin asserted that 'to judge from the subsequent rapid acceptance of the Hicks–Modigliani IS–LM model as the standard interpretation of the *General Theory* – the revealed preference of the profession is actually for the more formal style of presentation of the analysis that Keynes used in his 1934 draft, as against his presentation in the final form of the *General Theory*.' Moreover, as I mentioned in the introduction, Solow – citing Tobin – described the IS–LM approach as essentially the 'trained intuition' of the economics profession. In light of the wide divergence of opinion about the IS–LM interpretation of Keynes amongst Keynesians, and its rejection as a valid analytical tool by both the new classical expectationists and advocates of the long-period monetarist position, it is debatable whether IS–LM is now either the 'revealed preference' or 'trained intuition' of the economics profession.[26]

But more is involved here than the academic debate on the analytical efficacy of the IS–LM approach. In my view, the very nature of cognition, concept formation and development and choice-theoretic decision in economics are involved. For, as Robinson noted fifty years ago, economists have a predilection for discovering 'determinacy' in the problems they choose to deal with. As she put it:

Some writers, brought up in the tradition of 'methodological pessimism', consider this task of such importance that they attempt no other. After counting up the number of equations and the number of independent variables involved in a problem and triumphantly pointing out that the two numbers are equal, so that the solution of the problem is determinate, they are quite content to let the matter rest, without making any attempt to tell us what the solution is. Others, taking a less humble view of their function are apt to resort to special pleading to show that some problem which they desire to solve can in fact be completely dealt with by the methods at their disposal, and to display unreasonable hostility to anyone who attempts to maintain the contrary opinion.[27]

This is exactly the trap fallen into by those adhering to the Patinkin–Tobin–Solow view of IS–LM, on the one hand, and those supporting the Kahn–Robinson view, on the other. This is because – despite the predilection of economists for imposing order and certainty and thereby 'determinacy' on their cognitive processes – the IS–LM approach is, in my view, neither a chimera nor Keynes's central message. Rather, as I have tried to show above, it is only one 'suggested interpretation' of Keynes's *General Theory*.[28]

And, in light of the evidence, I think that Keynes himself would probably have supported this view of the IS–LM approach. Indeed, Harrod and Austin Robinson – two of those close to Keynes and representative of the divergence of opinion regarding the IS–LM approach in the General Theory group – were in complete agreement as to Keynes's overall notion of the formation and development of his own concepts and approach to economics. At the first 'Keynes Seminar' held at Keynes College, University of Kent in 1972, Harrod spoke of 'Keynes's theory and its applications'. He said:

One talks nowadays of Keynes's theory; but he had many theories in the course of his life. We don't know whether in a very long-term horizon some of his earlier theories may not prove to be more important than what we now think of as 'Keynes's theory' in the singular – theories which he expounded in such books as *Indian Currency and Finance*, his *Tract on Monetary Reform* and *A Treatise on Money*; these books are laced with very interesting and important theories.

Harrod then gave his interpretation of the way Keynes would have adapted his views to the most recent contingencies, events and developments.[29]

Austin Robinson summed up Keynes's intellectual disposition in concise and lucid terms:

Maynard taught us to question, to think for ourselves, to accept nothing and to be absolutely ruthless when we tried to see our way through problems – to question and question. Now I get rather frightened in this generation, and I hate it as much as I believe he would have hated it, when people, like preachers in a pulpit, start trying to preach a sermon (which nearly always says something entirely different) by beginning by quoting a text from the Holy Writ of Maynard. Maynard certainly never looked on the *General Theory* as his last work in economics . . . Maynard's intellectual development would not have stopped short at the *General Theory*; he had taught us how to go on and on thinking; and I believe that if he were here today, what he'd be saying to you is: 'Forget the *General Theory*. That was a stage in the development of economics; it's not the last word in economics. Go on, and think for yourselves, and unless you are thinking for yourselves you're not doing your job as economists'.[30]

As I have attempted to show in this book, it was, however, the IS–LM approach that actually became 'the Holy Writ' of modern macroeconomics and most interpreters of Keynes after 1937, rather than one 'suggested interpretation' of Keynes's *General Theory*; so much so that neither its origins nor development had even been the subject of previous detailed study.

### The IS–LM enigma in comparative perspective

There are a number of instances in modern economics that parallel the IS–LM case. For example, in 'The Inflation–Unemployment Trade-off: A Critique of the Literature' (1978) in the *Journal of Economic Literature*, which ostensibly reviewed all the material published on the topic of the 'Phillips curve' to that date the authors curiously omitted reference to two works on the trade-off between inflation and unemployment – those of Pigou (1945) and Brown (1955) – which predated Phillips's famous 1958 article. In his paper 'The Relationship between Unemployment and the Rate of Change of Money-wage Rates in the United Kingdom, 1861–1957', Phillips also did not refer to these works. Indeed, this was the case in most papers on the topic published in the late 1950s and early 1960s.[31]

In his 1945 volume *Lapses from Full Employment*, Pigou observed that trade unions 'must choose between high rates of wages and lower rates of unemployment'. A decade later, Arthur Brown, in his important book *The Great Inflation 1939–51* identified 'the nature and conditions' characterizing the relationship between the level of unemployment and what he called the 'price–wage spiral' during the periods 1881–1914 and 1920–51 in the

United Kingdom and 1921–48 in the United States. Brown even presented 'scatter' type diagrams illustrating what he took to be an inverse relationship between the annual change of wage rates and unemployment both in the United Kingdom and United States cases for the respective sub-periods.[32]

And yet, it took fifteen years for Brown's contribution to be recognized, and then, it seems, to be overlooked again by most of the economics profession. In 1970, in a survey of 'Empirical Models of Inflation in the UK' for the United Kingdom Department of Employment, D. V. Jones wrote 'the existence of a relationship between the rate of change of wages and unemployment in the UK was first commented upon by Brown and received its first detailed investigation by Phillips.' This somewhat laconic statement exemplified the limited degree to which the major contribution made by Arthur Brown to the development of what has come to be known as the 'Phillips curve' is recognized. Moreover, the earlier theoretical contribution of Pigou is also hardly ever cited by anyone dealing with 'Phillips' type relationships, including Phillips himself – with the exception of Arthur Brown, who gave it due recognition in his seminal work. From 1958 onwards then, it was the 'Phillips curve'' – as Hicks's IS–LM diagram had done some two decades before – that caught the imagination of the economics profession. Indeed, it seems that Phillips, as well as Hicks, had 'done a Marshall' – as Brown put it when explaining the reaction of those economists who attended the 1936 Oxford conference where the IS–LM diagram was first presented.[33]

To sum up, then, the following points may be made. First, we can see the marked importance of diagrams and the ability of this method of representing and interpreting a theory to take precedence over either its verbal exposition or equational representation by referring to a number of examples in economics. While diagrammatic representation of natural phenomena has even been termed 'working conceptual hallucinations' by some, there is still analytical and for that matter, pedagogical efficacy in using diagrams to convey the message of equational representation of complex systems or processes.

Secondly, in economics, diagrams usually take the form of what are called curves or schedules which can map either the functional form of equational representation of economic phenomena or notional constructs based upon them. But the steps from verbal exposition to equational and diagrammatic representation of theories are not necessarily taken by the same person or group of people. Indeed, the final stage leading to diagrammatic representation can be, in some cases, a major breakthrough in economic thought, or at least the addition of a powerful instrument or tool to the economist's 'analytical tool-kit'. The example of 'Marshall's discovery of the demand function' and its subsequent representation in diagrammatic form in the framework of his famous 'scissors' diagram is a case in point, even though Cournot, among others, had already set down the principles regarding the nature of demand. Other instances are much less well known, for example the case of the Phillips curve and the ideas underlying the 'Lewis diagram', which A. K. Dasgupta had developed as early as 1949 and published – albeit not in an academic journal – prior to Lewis's classic paper in which he presented his diagram in the Manchester School (1954).[34]

Thirdly, in light of the material presented in this book, if economics aspires – as some would have it – to become a 'science' or even a 'scientific discipline' for that matter, then economists, and especially those who deal with the history of economic thought, must focus on the origins and development of the core concepts of modern economics which they talk about, utilize and teach. Indeed, what may be needed is a new methodology especially for those historians of economic thought who tend to focus upon the 'grand picture' rather than upon the interaction between people and the origin and development of economic concepts, i.e. a grounded history of economic thought.[35]

When I started my study of the history of IS–LM, Frank Hahn called me a 'hagiographer' – one who deals with 'ancient' and 'sacred' personalities, documents and texts. Perhaps a bit of 'grounded hagiography' would do wonders for those who deal with the history of economic thought.

# Notes

## Introduction

1 See Solow (1984, p. 14) and Dornbusch and Fisher (1984, p. 100). On 'Bastard Keynesianism', see Joan Robinson (1962, pp. 690–2).

2 In his Hicks Lecture, Solow (1984, p. 14) overlooked the fact that Meade's paper appeared in the February 1937 issue of *Review of Economic Studies*, and that a summary of it only appeared in *Econometrica* in October 1937! On the distinction between 'J. R.' and 'John' Hicks, see Hicks (1975, p. 365) where he said 'clearly I need to change my name . . . J. R. [was] a "neo-classical" economist now deceased . . . John [is] a non-neo-classic who is quite disrespectful towards his "uncle".'

3 Solow's statement (1984, p. 15) seems to imply that Harrod's paper (1937a) and Meade's (1937a) differ from Hicks's (1937). As I show below, however, they all comprise the 'Harrod–Hicks–Meade' IS–LM approach.

4 The list of participants appears in the April issue of *Econometrica*, (1937, p. 198), while a summary of Meade's paper appears in Phelps-Brown's conference report in the October issue (1937, pp. 361–2).

5 On these points, see Jammer (1982, pp. 63–5, 68–71).

6 Hicks's account of the construction of his diagram (1937, p. 153) is repeated here since it is the earliest version extant. Horwich (1964, pp. 519, 522–4) made an interesting point about 'the Keynesian dichotomized money supply' not being used by Hicks to derive his LL curve in his book on the trade cycle (1950, pp. 140–1).

7 The importance of Hicks's original version of the derivation of his diagram (1937, pp. 153, 156) will become clear when it is compared with his later versions of its derivation, for example, in Hicks (1979c; 1980).

8 The importance of Hicks's use of the marginal efficiency of capital curve (1937, pp. 156–7) will become clear in chapter 1.

9 Hicks's generalization of the LL curve (1937, p. 157) enabled him to introduce the possible effects of monetary policy, rather than remain stuck in the 'liquidity trap' of the ungeneralized version of the LL curve which he presented earlier in his article (1937, pp. 153–4).

10 Hicks's claim (1937, pp. 156, 158) to have 'invented' the 'little apparatus' he presented in his IS–LM paper seems to refer to his diagram only, since, as we will show, the equations were not originated by Hicks but by Harrod.

11 On these points see Tobin (1980, p. 80).

12 See Harrod (1937a, p. 592) reprinted in Harris (1949); page references to reprint.

13 Champernowne (1936, pp. 211–14) and Reddaway (1936, p. 35) are examples of variations on Harrod's IS–LM equations and Hicks's diagram. Kaldor (1937, pp. 752–3) is one of the earliest examples of the application of the IS–LM approach, while Lange (1938, pp. 12–13) is the forerunner of both Modigliani's neo-classical synthesis (1944), i.e. IS–LM in 'real terms' and the Keynes–Lange system of Timlin (1942), Clower (1965) and Leijonhufvud (1968).

14 See Keynes (1937a, pp. 211–12).

15 See Keynes (1937b, p. 151).

16 See, for example, Hicks (1973, p. 10) and Kahn (1984, pp. 160, 249).

17 See the collection of Hicks's works *The Economics of John Hicks*, edited by Helm (1984, p. 1), where Helm also refers to 'Hicksian economics'. Helm claims that Hicks's IS–LM diagram was a 'reformulation' of the 'core of Keynes's *General Theory*' (1984, p. 1) and that Hicks's interpretation of Keynes's *General Theory* 'has become part of the received tradition, and was accepted by Keynes and many, but by no means all, of his followers' (1984, p. 5). In a note to this statement, Helm takes Harrod to task for only one reference to Hicks in Harrod's biography of Keynes (1951). In Helm's words 'In Harrod's life of Keynes . . . Hicks receives one obscure footnote only. Since Hicks's interpretation had already become a standard one, this is odd in the extreme!' (1984, p. 5). In this context, however, it should also be remembered that in his 1937 article Hicks cited neither Harrod's nor Meade's papers.

## Chapter 1

1 See the Tarshis Lecture notes – dated 14 November 1932 – and the lecture notes compiled by Marvin Fallgatter of 'J. M. Keynes, The Monetary Theory of Production' (Michaelmas term, October–December 1933). These notes have been reproduced by Prof. Tom Rymes (1983, pp. 34–5). I am indebted to him for allowing me to cite them here. On Bryce's notes, see Patinkin (1976, p. 79).

2 The distinction must be drawn between the earlier 'Cambridge Circus' of 1931 and what I call here the General Theory group, which consisted of Joan and Austin Robinson, and Richard Kahn in Cambridge, and Roy Harrod and James Meade in Oxford. Meade was also a member of the 1931 Circus, but Harrod was not. As for Harrod's Trade Cycle group, this was wholly Oxford-based, and distinct from the Oxford Economists Research Group (OERG), which was led by Henderson, although a number of college lecturers and staff of the Oxford Sub-faculty of Economics and Institute of Economics were members of both groups. On the 'Circus', see for example, Patinkin (1976), Kahn (1985), A. Robinson (1985). On the OERG, see Lee (1981). Also see Keynes (1936).

3 See Meade (1936) and the second edition of his book (1937b, pp. 10, 16–18, 26–9). I shall be citing from Meade's replies to Robertson in chapter 6. I am indebted to Prof. James Meade for permission to cite from his letters to Robertson, and to Prof. S. Dennison for permission to cite from Robertson's letters.

4 Interview with Prof. James Meade, 29 November 1985. On the Harrod–Keynes correspondence in 1935, see Keynes's *Collected Writings* (1971–82) – cited below as JMK with volume number – (JMK XIII, pp. 546–61). Also see Harrod (1938, pp. 383–412, esp. pp. 402–5).

5 See Thomson (1962, pp. 641–70, esp. pp. 655–6).

6 It was Keynes who emphasized uncertainty, as can be seen, for example, in his letter to Henderson dated 28 May 1936 (JMK XXIX, pp. 221–2). In this he wrote 'the rate of interest is, on my theory, essentially an uncertainty phenomenon' and that 'in a world ruled by uncertainty with an uncertain future linked to an actual present, a final position of equilibrium, such as one deals with in static economics, does not properly exist.' Keynes also set the tone for considering his book as 'revolutionary' and a complete break with its predecessors in his preface to the *General Theory* (1936, pp. v–viii). This was repeated by Robinson, for example, in her paper 'What has become of the Keynesian Revolution?' (1975, p. 125) and in her collection of essays *What are the Questions?* (1980, p. 56). She also accused Keynes of overlooking the 'point of his revolution' and 'fudging' his *General Theory* position on expectations and 'calculable risk' approach to uncertainty, which he only put right, in her view, in his *Quarterly Journal of Economics* restatement of the *General Theory*, when he recognized the importance of history as compared with equilibrium (1975, p. 125; 1980, p. 57). Maurice Dobb also deals with this problem (1973, p. 10).

7 See Harrod (1937a; 1969). Also see Meade (1975).

8 See for example, Shackle (1968, pp. xvii–xviii).

9 On Joan Robinson's objection to IS–LM, by which she claims

'generations of students have been taught to misinterpret the *General Theory*' see (1971, pp. 82–5; 1980, p. 10). Also see Kahn (1984, pp. 160, 249).

10 For an account of the period 1830–1930 and the 'abstract ideas' at its centre, see Thomson (1962, pp. 655–66).

11 In Robinson's opinion 'uncertainty' was not Keynes's central theme in his *Quarterly Journal of Economics* (1937a) restatement of the *General Theory* (1975, p. 125). But Robinson has overlooked here the issue of determinacy as compared with indeterminacy she raised almost four decades before (1937a). Also see Kahn (1984, pp. 160, 249).

12 It appears strange to today's generation of economists how quickly things got into print in the 'early days'; see for example, Solow's comments in his Hicks Lecture (1984, pp. 13–14). In view of the fact, however, that Keynes had seen Harrod's paper in late August 1936, and Meade's in mid-September 1936, as we will show, as well as Hicks's, which he saw in mid-October 1936, it is almost certain that he used his February 1937 platform to reply to them also.

13 Interview with Prof. Arthur Brown, 31 October 1985.

14 Interview with Prof. George Shackle, 23 October 1985.

15 See chapter 6 below.

16 See JMK (XIII, pp. 548–52).

17 Ibid., pp. 553, 557.

18 See JMK (XIV, p. 84).

19 Ibid., pp. 85–6.

20 See Harrod (1937a, p. 592).

21 See Harrod (1969, p. 174).

22 See Harrod (1937a, pp. 595–6).

23 Ibid., pp. 595, 601–2.

24 See Hicks (1937); Patinkin (1976, p. 75); JMK (XIV, pp. 80–3).

25 Meade (1937a) reprinted in Harris (1949), page references to Harris reprint.

26 Meade (1975, pp. 82, 83, 87).

27 Meade (1937a, pp. 609–10, 615).

28 Ibid., pp. 615–18.

29 Ibid., pp. 608, 610, 616. Also see Keynes (1936, p. 193).

30 Ibid., p. 610.

31 Meade (1975, p. 83).

32 Harrod (1937a, pp. 597, 602).

33 See Keynes (1936, pp. 183–4).

34 See Pasinetti (1974), Hicks (1976b; 1980).

35 See Patinkin (1976, p. 76).

36 See JMK (XIV, pp. 73–9).

37 Ibid., pp. 79–81.

38 Ibid., 83–4.

39 As noted above, Solow recognized the identical nature of the equations

in his Hicks Lecture (1984, p. 14), but didn't ask how and why?

40 Both the equations and diagram are part of the Harrod–Hicks–Meade IS–LM approach. It is indeed curious that Solow (1984) did not raise the point of 'multiple discovery' of the equations in the IS–LM papers, having recognized that they were identical. But, as he did not cite the fact that Meade's paper (1937a) was even published, it is doubtful that this possibility would have crossed his mind when he was preparing the first annual Hicks Lecture.

41 The letter is in Meade's papers at the British Library of Economics (LSE), File 2/4/46. Because it did not indicate the year in which it was written, the letter was found, misfiled, among earlier correspondence from Hicks to Meade. From its contents, it is clear that it was written by Hicks on 6 September 1936.

42 See JMK (XIV, p. 81). An additional problem regarding Hicks's published version of his IS–LM paper can be cleared up at this point by reference to a letter from Hicks to Robertson, dated 1 November 1936. In his letter, Hicks writes:

> On this 'historical' question, I have been reading most of your authorities and they seem to bear out a view to which I was coming rather while writing my paper and since, which I would like tentatively to suggest to you. It is that one may make a distinction between
>
> 1 the view that an increase in the supply of money must be followed by a general rise in incomes to restore equilibrium, but that in the process of reaching this adjustment there is a temporary redistribution of income in favour of classes with a strong propensity to save, and this may lower the rate of interest
>
> 2 the view that an increase in the supply of money is immediately followed by a temporary 'equilibrium' in which incomes are not much raised, but the rate of interest sufficiently reduced to persuade people to hold the additional stock of money. In a way, the difference between these views need be no more than a difference about the nature of equilibrium, and there is no reason why we should not find a place for lots of equilibria!
>
> But – provided we do not stop too long at the temporary equilibrium – the second method has the advantage of making the whole process more determinate. I think the first method is typical of Marshall, and of much of your own work; the second is already beginning to lift its head in Pigou and Lavington, and reaches maturity (perhaps over-ripeness!) in the General Theory. But I know how merely symbolic such a statement must be.

In the published version of his IS–LM paper, Hicks cites the approaches of Lavington and Pigou as setting the stage for Keynes in so far as they had shown, according to Hicks, that the 'demand for money depends upon the rate of interest' (1937, p. 51). Hicks continues:

> Like Lavington and Professor Pigou, Mr. Keynes does not in the end believe that the demand for money can be determined by one variable alone – not even the rate of interest. He lays more stress on it than they did, but neither for him nor for them can it be the only variable to be considered. The dependence of the demand for money on interest does not, in the end, do more than qualify the old dependence on income (1937, pp. 152–3).

Hicks then presents his equational interpretation of what he takes to be Keynes's *General Theory*, claiming that in this case 'Mr. Keynes takes a big step back to Marshallian orthodoxy, and his theory becomes hard to distinguish from the revised and qualified Marshallian theories, which, as we have seen, are not new' (1937, p. 153).

It seems, therefore, that after seeing Harrod's equations and developing his diagram, Hicks wanted to put his approach in the perspective of earlier approaches to the problem, and it was Robertson who put him on to the 'authorities' in order to get around the 'historical question' of the basis for his IS–LM approach, which Robertson was in agreement with.

43  I am indebted to Prof. James Meade for allowing me to study his pre-war correspondence in order to recount the stages in the development and publication of his IS–LM paper and the reactions to it.

44  Keynes's postcard to Meade, in Meade's papers, File 2/4/71, dated 14 September 1936. Harrod to Meade, letter dated 12 September 1936 in Meade's papers, File 2/4.

45  Tinbergen to Meade, letter dated 18 September 1936, in Meade's papers, File 2/4/110.

46  Frisch to Meade, letter dated 8 October 1936, in Meade's papers, File 2/3/70.

47  Ursula Hicks to Meade, letter dated 30 November 1936, in Meade's papers, File 2/4/53.

48  Interview with Prof. James Meade, 29 November 1985.

49  See JMK (XIV, p. 86).

50  Ibid., p. 81. Also see Keynes to Harrod, letter dated 7 October 1936 (from 46 Gordon Sq., Bloomsbury, London), cited in Hamish Riley-Smith's *Catalogue of the Papers of Sir Roy Harrod* (1982), number 66.

51  See the April issue of *Econometrica* (1937, p. 198). Also see Phelps-Brown (1937), JMK (XIV, p. 84); Prof. G. Shackle, letter to author dated 17 October 1985.

52 Phelps-Brown (1937, pp. 361–83).
53 See April issue of *Econometrica* (1937, p. 198).
54 Letter from Prof. Colin Clark to author, dated 7 November 1985; interview with Prof. George Shackle, 23 October 1985.
55 Letter from Prof. Ludwig Lachmann to author, dated 12 November 1985; letter from Prof. Sir H. Phelps-Brown to author, dated 18 October 1985; also see Phelps-Brown (1937, pp. 361–3).
56 I am indebted to Prof. Arthur Brown for allowing me to reproduce this here.
57 See diagram and text in Brown's notes.
58 Interview with Prof. Arthur Brown, 31 October 1985; also see Hicks (1937, pp. 153, 157).
59 Interview with Prof. Arthur Brown, 31 October 1985.
60 Brown notes, p. 2; also see JMK (XIV, p. 84) and Hicks (1937, p. 159).
61 Hicks (1939, p. 4 and note 1; 1980, p. 140).
62 Tinbergen to Meade, letter dated 18 September 1936, in Meade's papers, File 2/4/110.
63 Phelps-Brown (1937, pp. 362–3).
64 On this, see Hicks (1973, pp. 2, 10).
65 Ibid., p. 11.
66 Interview with Prof. Arthur Brown, 31 October 1985; interview with Prof. David Champernowne, 13 November 1985; letter from Prof. Sir John Hicks to author dated 2 December 1985.
67 Interview with Prof. Arthur Brown, 31 October 1985; interview with Prof. James Meade, 29 November 1985.
68 Interview with Prof. James Meade, 29 November 1985.
69 Letter from Dr Herbert Robinson to author, dated 20 November 1985.
70 Letter from Prof. Ludwig Lachmann to author, dated 12 November 1985.
71 See Hicks (1937, p. 158).
72 Ibid., pp. 156, 158. Also see Keynes (1936, p. 242) and Hicks (1973, pp. 8, 11).
73 Interview with Prof. George Shackle, 23 October 1985; interview with Prof. Arthur Brown, 31 October 1985. According to Hicks (1973, p. 8), Keynes wrote him a note in June 1935 in which Keynes said 'The channels through which my ideas are reaching you sound rather alarming! Probably you will gather the tendency but do not take the details too seriously!' Hicks then interpreted the 'channels' Keynes referred to as follows 'These no doubt were notes on the lectures that Keynes had been giving in Cambridge – notes which were beginning to circulate at the LSE' (1973, p. 8). But according to Hicks himself, he didn't pay much attention to these notes. As he put it 'I knew no more of the details until I was asked, very much to my surprise, to review

the *General Theory* for the Journal [*EJ*] (on its publication in January 1936).' (1973, p. 8). Again, Hicks's memory has proved to be 'treacherous' here, since the *General Theory* was only published in February 1936. But more importantly, it is doubtful whether Hicks digested Keynes's simultaneous equation approach in his 1933–4 lectures, or if he actually saw notes of them, for he then would either have mentioned it in his review of the *General Theory*, or reviewed the *General Theory* using an IS–LM approach in June 1936. On these points, see also Hicks (1936b).

74 Hicks (1937, p. 147). Interview with Prof. Lord Kaldor, 23 November 1985. Also see Kaldor (1937).
75 See Shackle (1967, p. 267).
76 Interview with Prof. George Shackle, 23 October 1985.
77 Interview with Prof. Arthur Brown, 31 October 1985.
78 Interview with Prof. George Shackle, 23 October 1985.
79 Interview with Prof. Arthur Brown, 31 October 1985.
80 Interestingly enough, Kregel (1985, p. 82) recently asked whether Harrod's *General Theory* diagram was the basis for Hicks's IS–LM diagram, referring to 'the famous meeting in Oxford in which Keynes's theory was enshrined in static form in terms of Hicks's IS–LM (which largely reflected the diagram that Keynes had borrowed from Harrod's defence of supply and demand)'. As I shall show below, however, while the IS–LM diagram can be derived from Harrod's *General Theory* diagram, this can only be done in conjunction with Harrod's IS–LM equations and involves a series of sophisticated thought-experiments which only a mathematically inclined economist – like Hicks – could do. Thus, it is not surprising that Hicks wrote his own paper and constructed his IS–LM diagram only after seeing Harrod's and Meade's papers and the equational system they contained.
81 See Robinson (1980, pp. 56, 112–113). It is interesting to note here that in her *Essays in the Theory of Employment* (1937a, p. 2), Robinson attacked Champernowne's IS–LM-type treatment (1936) of the wage–employment nexus, and said that 'Mr. Champernowne . . . adheres, on the whole, to the Pigovian school.' She returned to attack Hicks's IS–LM in her book *Economic Heresies* (1971, pp. 82–4) as 'the quantity theory in its purest form', and again attacked Hicks in *What Are The Questions?* (1980, p. 10), but never focused her sights on either Harrod or Meade.
82 Hicks (1936a, pp. 131–2, 140).
83 Ibid., pp. 130, 136.
84 Hicks (1936b, pp. 238, 242; 1937, p. 152). Also see Hicks (1976a, pp. 207, 209).
85 Hicks (1979a; 1983).
86 Harrod (1937a, pp. 604–5).

87 Harrod (1938, pp. 403, 407, 412).
88 See Harrod (1937a; 1938; 1939).
89 Harrod (1969, pp. 162–6, 169, 174).
90 On the 'reconciling role' of 'generalized economic analysis', see Dobb (1973, pp. 10–11).

## Chapter 2

1 See Harrod (1969, pp. 162–3). The fundamental contributions of Maurice Allen to the development of modern economic thought have not been dealt with previously. An example that can be cited briefly at this point is Robertson's letter of 19 May 1933 to Keynes about revising an article by Robertson that was to appear in the *Economic Journal*. In this letter, Robertson said that he would possibly be able to put 'some of the points more clearly' after sending the proofs for comments by Allen. Robertson asked for three copies of the proofs of his article so that he could have one for himself, one to 'try on' Pigou, and one 'to try it on . . . my one faithful disciple Maurice Allen'; JMK (XXIX, p. 23). William Maurice Allen, born in 1908, took his B.Sc. (Econ.) at the LSE in 1929. He was a lecturer at LSE and at New College, Oxford, 1930–1. He was a fellow and tutor in economics at Balliol College, Oxford, 1931–48, and University Lecturer in Economics, Oxford, 1947. From 1947–9, he was Assistant Director of Research, IMF. In 1950, he was an advisor to the Bank of England. He became a governor of LSE in 1951 and was on the council of the Royal Economic Society in 1953. He was a visiting fellow at Nuffield College, Oxford from 1954–62. He was Executive Director, Bank of England, from 1964–70.
2 See Harrod (1969, pp. 163–6). I am indebted to Maurice Allen for permission to reproduce portions of his essay here. It is to be found in the pre-war correspondence of Prof. James Meade, File 2/3/29.
3 See Hicks (1936b). Also see JMK (XIV, p. 70) and Reddaway (1936, pp. 28, 31–3).
4 Reddaway (1936, pp. 34–5; 1964, p. 109).
5 Reddaway (1936, p. 35).
6 Interview with Prof. Brian Reddaway, 8 November 1985. Also see Reddaway (1937) and Lange (1938, p. 12).
7 Lange (1938, p. 12).
8 Ibid., pp. 12–14.
9 See Keynes (1938, p. 321).
10 Lange (1938, pp. 19–20).
11 Ibid., pp. 20–3.
12 Ibid., pp. 27–9.
13 Hicks (1980, pp. 141–2). Also see Shackle (1982, p. 438).
14 See Champernowne (1936). Interview with Prof. David Champernowne,

13 November 1985; letter from Champernowne to author, 9 November 1985; letter from Champernowne, 24 November 1985.

15 Letters from Champernowne to author, 9 November and 14 November 1985.

16 Interview with Prof. Champernowne, 13 November 1985; letter from Champernowne, 24 November 1985. Also see Champernowne (1936, p. 211).

17 Champernowne (1936, pp. 211, 213–14).

18 Interview with Prof. Champernowne, 13 November 1985; letter from Champernowne to author, 14 November 1985. Also see Champernowne (1936, pp. 211, 216).

19 Champernowne (1936, p. 216).

20 Interview with Prof. Champernowne, 13 November 1985; letter from Champernowne to author, 14 November 1985; letter from Champernowne, 24 November 1985.

21 See Harrod (1951, p. 317) and Phelps-Brown (1980, pp. 7–8). Also see H. Riley-Smith (1982, pp. 120–1). The evidence for this may be found in Harrod's letters to Meade dated 13 and 16 January and 4 May 1936, to be found in Prof. Meade's pre-war correspondence, File 2/4/25. The reference to Charles Hitch is to be found, for example, in a letter from Harrod to Meade dated 7 February 1937, to be found in Meade's pre-war papers, File 2/4/30.

22 See Brown (1985, pp. 8–9); also see JMK (XIII, p. 553).

23 Interview with Prof. Arthur Brown, 31 October 1985.

24 Harrod (1939a); interview with Prof. Arthur Brown, 31 October 1985.

25 On Marshack, see H. Riley-Smith (1982, p. 121). Marshack's manuscript has remained unidentified until now, since he signed it 'T. M', according to Riley-Smith. But Marshack always initialled his drafts in that way; his 'J' looking like a 'T'. On the Keynes–Harrod correspondence regarding the nature of warranted growth, see Young (1975); also see Kregal (1980).

26 Matthews to Harrod, 2 January 1964 in H. Riley-Smith (1982, p. 93).

27 See Goodwin (1982, pp. vii–viii) and Tinbergen (1937, pp. 89–91).

28 I wish to thank Prof. Robin Matthews for providing me with copies of Harrod's letters to him. Also see Harrod (1937a, pp. 604–5).

29 See JMK (XIV, p. 84). Also see a letter from Harrod to Meade dated 7 February 1937 in the Meade papers, File 2/4/30. In this letter Harrod wrote 'At our Trade Cycle group the other night Hitch made a point which if right is surely important. He argued that it is the value, not the volume of capital output which is important . . . as touching the absorption of saving.' Also see Harrod (1937b).

In recent correspondence with the author, Prof. Tinbergen has clarified a number of points concerning his May 1937 review of Harrod's *Trade Cycle* and their meeting at the September 1936 Oxford conference. Prof. Tinbergen thinks that 'it is certainly possible' that he talked with Harrod about the book and his intended review of it at the September 1936 conference. But Prof. Tinbergen stresses that 'in my review I wanted to be critical of theories not formulated mathematically and to state that without introduction of a lag the formulae for the two relations Harrod mentions do not produce a cyclical movement of the variables. These ideas were my own.' Letter from Prof. Jan Tinbergen to author, 8 June 1986; also see Tinbergen (1937).

30 See Harrod (1939a; 1939b, p. 299).

## Chapter 3

1 See Hicks (1936b) and Harrod (1937a, pp. 594–7, 602–3).
2 See Keynes (1936, p. 180); also see Kregal (1985, p. 82) and chapter 1, note 80.
3 Letter to author from Prof. Sir John Hicks, 2 December 1985.
4 Champernowne (1936, p. 213); interview with Prof. Champernowne, 13 November 1985; letter to author from Prof. Sir John Hicks, 2 December 1985; letter from Prof. Champernowne, 24 November 1985.
5 Letter to author from Prof. Hicks, 5 December 1985.
6 Letter to author from Prof. Hicks, 16 December 1985.
7 On these points, see Hicks (1974; 1979a, b; 1980, p. 141).
8 Hicks (1974, pp. 6–7, 31).
9 Hicks (1979b, p. 200 and 1979a, p. 73).
10 See the exchange between Hawtrey and Hicks in the Manchester School over Hicks's review of Hawtrey's book *A Century of Bank Rate*, in Hawtrey and Hicks (1939b, pp. 144–56, esp. p. 153). Also see the Hawtrey–Hicks correspondence on *Value and Capital* in the Hawtrey papers at Churchill College, Cambridge, and Hawtrey's review of *Value and Capital* (1939a).
11 See Hicks (1973, p. 2; 1979c, p. 990).
12 As for Hicks's mention of the possible relevance of the French translation of the draft of the mathematical appendix of *Value and Capital* in 1937, this is not relevant here, as Bowley showed in his review (1938, pp. 513–15).
13 Letter from Prof. Champernowne, 24 November 1985; also see Champernowne (1936, pp. 211, 214).
14 Hicks (1980, pp. 141–2).
15 Lerner (1937, pp. 350–1), reprinted in Lerner (1953a); page references to reprint.
16 Lerner (1936; 1938), reprinted in S. Harris (ed.) (1949); also see Lerner (1951, p. 265) cited in Hansen (1953, pp. 148–9); letter to author from Prof. Ludwig Lachmann, 12 November 1985.

17 Lerner (1938, pp. 639–40, 653) reprinted in Harris (1949); page references to reprint.
18 Lerner (1939, pp. 265, 269), reprinted in Lerner (1953a); page references to reprint.
19 Lerner (1939, p. 269).
20 Lerner (1939, pp. 269, 272); Pigou (1938).
21 Lerner (1944, pp. 334–40; 1953b, pp. 8–9, 11).
22 Lerner (1951, p. 265); also see Hansen (1953, pp. 148–9).
23 Hansen (1953, pp. 150–1).
24 Presley (1979, p. 143).
25 Lerner (1974, pp. 38–9).
26 Lerner (1939, p. 272) and Lerner (1936, p. 446).
27 Kaldor (1937, p. 752).
28 Ibid., p. 748.
29 Ibid., p. 752.
30 Ibid., p. 752.
31 Interview with Prof. Lord Kaldor, 23 November 1985.
32 Ibid.; also see Pigou (1938, p. 134) and Kaldor (1937, p. 753).
33 Pigou (1938, pp. 134, 138).
34 I am indebted to Prof. Lord Kaldor for allowing me to photocopy the letters from Prof. Sir Dennis Robertson to him and to cite his letters to Robertson, and to Prof. S. Dennison for permission to cite Sir Dennis Robertson's letters here. The letter from Hicks to Kaldor is in the Kaldor papers. Also see JMK (XIV, pp. 240–67).
35 See JMK (XIV, p. 254); also see Robertson to Kaldor, 19 October 1937; Kaldor to Robertson, 23 October 1937; Hicks to Kaldor, 23 October 1937; also see JMK (XIV, p. 254), where in Keynes's letter to Robertson dated 20 October 1937 he writes 'Many thanks for sending me your note about Pigou. I have also heard from him, he much preferring Kaldor's criticism to mine!'; on Kahn's letter and Keynes's reply, see JMK (XIV, pp. 260, 262).
36 JMK (XIV, pp. 266–7).
37 Ibid., p. 267.
38 Interview with Prof. Lord Kaldor, 23 November 1985; also see Kahn (1984, pp. 160, 249).
39 See Hansen (1936, p. 686).
40 Hansen (1938, pp. 13–34). The passages cut from his 1936 version are numerous. See, for example, Hansen (1936, pp. 675–6, 680, 682–3) and compare with (1938, pp. 27, 34).
41 Hansen (1936, p. 676; 1938, pp. 27, 34). It should be noted here that Winch (1969, pp. 193, 380) also recognized Hansen's 'conversion' but did not ask why?
42 Hansen (1949, preface).
43 Ibid., pp. 71–2, 77.
44 Kaldor (1937), Modigliani (1944). Also see Hansen (1941; 1947); Dornbusch and Fisher (1984, p. 100).

45 Hansen (1949, p. 72).
46 Ibid., pp. 81–2.
47 Letter from Robertson to Meade dated 9 May 1937, in Meade's papers, File 2/4/94.
48 Hansen (1947a, pp. 133–4, 138; 1947b, pp. 197–8). Also see Hansen (1941; 1953).
49 Hansen (1953, pp. 143–4).
50 Ibid., pp. 146–7.
51 Ibid., pp. 147–8.
52 Ibid., p. 148.
53 Ibid., pp. 151, 154–5. It should also be noted that at about this time, Lindhal published a variant interpretation of Keynes's *General Theory*; see Lindhal (1954). Moreover, Lindhal used a four-quadrant diagram developed earlier by Scott (1951), which later became another 'standard' – albeit usually unattributed – textbook interpretation of 'the Keynesian system'.
54 Modigliani (1944; 1963, p. 79); also see Lange (1938) and Timlin (1942).
55 Timlin (1942, pp. 1, 8).
56 Ibid., p. 8.
57 Ibid., p. 7.
58 Modigliani (1944, p. 45).
59 Ibid., p. 46.
60 Ibid., pp. 46–7, 66–7, 73–5.
61 Modigliani (1963, pp. 79, 81); also see Lucas (1981a, p. 276).
62 Letter from Champernowne, 24 November 1985.

## Chapter 4

1 Hawtrey (1937, p. v).
2 I wish to thank Prof. Don Moggridge for allowing me to quote from Hawtrey's letters to Harrod, and I am most grateful to Lady Harrod for allowing me to cite Sir Roy Harrod's letters to Hawtrey. The correspondence is to be found in the Hawtrey papers at Churchill College, Cambridge. Also see Hawtrey (1937, p. 125) and Robertson (1937).
3 Robertson (1937, pp. 125–6); also see Harrod (1936, pp. 124–5).
4 Harrod (1937a; 1969).
5 Harrod (1937a, pp. 601, 603–4).
6 Harrod (1969, pp. 168, 171–3).
7 Harrod (1937a, pp. 596, 601).
8 Harrod (1969, p. 174).
9 Hawtrey (1952).
10 Keynes (1936, p. 1980).

11 JMK (XIII, pp. 546–61).
12 Ibid., pp. 550, 544–55, 557.
13 Hansen (1953, p. 147); also see JMK (XIII, p. 555).
14 Hawtrey (1937, preface).
15 Hawtrey (1952, preface, p. vi).
16 Ibid., p. vi.
17 Hawtrey, (1937, p. 6; 1952, p. 5).
18 Hawtrey (1937, pp. 198–9; 1952, p. 182).
19 Hawtrey (1937, pp. 3–4, 264).
20 Ibid., pp. 228–30.
21 Hawtrey (1952, p. 3).
22 Keynes (1936, p. 376); also see Hawtrey (1952, pp. 215–16).
23 Hawtrey (1952, p. 219).
24 Harrod (1936, pp. 180–1, 194).
25 Harrod (1969, p. 203).

## Chapter 5

1 See Hicks (1939; 1945, pp. 2, 5); also see Hansen (1949).
2 See Harrod (1939; 1948) and Hicks (1949; 1950, pp. 6–7, 137–47).
3 See Hicks (1949, pp. 106–7, 109–10).
4 Ibid., p. 109.
5 See Harrod (1939) and Hicks (1950, pp. 3–6, 6–7).
6 See Harrod (1938; 1939; 1948, pp. 3–4, 10–11, 13–14).
7 See Hicks (1950, p. 137).
8 Ibid., pp. 137–47.
9 Ibid., pp. 138–9.
10 Ibid., pp. 141–3.
11 Ibid., p. 143.
12 Ibid., pp. 145–6.
13 Ibid., pp. 147–51.
14 Ibid., pp. 4–5.
15 Hicks (1979c, p. 990; 1980, pp. 141–2).
16 Hicks (1945, p. 6; 1949; 1950, pp. vi, 4–6, 90, 99); also see Frisch (1933).
17 Frisch (1933); Harrod (1936; 1948); Hicks (1945, p. 6; 1949; 1950).
18 Hicks (1974, p. 7; 1977, pp. 177–81; 1979c, p. 989).
19 Clower (1965, p. 273).
20 Ibid., p. 270; also see Hicks (1974, pp. 6–7).
21 Lange (1938); Timlin (1942); Clower (1965, pp. 275, 279, 289).
22 Clower (1965, pp. 287–90); Lange (1938, pp. 14, 22–3); Timlin (1942).
23 See Leijonhufvud (1967, pp. 298–9; 1968; 1969).
24 Clower (1965, p. 289); also see Leijonhufvud (1967, pp. 301, 308–9).

25 Clower and Leijonhufvud (1975, p. 184); also see Lange (1938), and Timlin (1942).
26 Leijonhufvud (1967, p. 298); also see Clower and Leijonhufvud (1975, pp. 182–3).
27 Leijonhufvud (1983a; 1984, pp. 37–8).
28 Ibid., pp. 69–71, 85–6.
29 Timlin (1942, pp. 13–17).
30 Hicks (1967, pp. vii, 143); also see Leijonhufvud (1968, p. 4).
31 Hicks (1967, pp. 145–6); it should be noted that Hicks here is using 'real' income expressed, in his terms, as Y/W. Also see Hicks (1979c, p. 990; 1980, pp. 141–2).
32 Hicks (1967, pp. 147–50).
33 See Weintraub (1958; 1959; 1960; 1977); Robinson (1971); Davidson (1972); Pasinetti (1974); Minsky (1975).
34 Robinson (1971, pp. 82–5).
35 Letter from Robertson to Meade, 9 May 1937, cited above, in the Meade papers, File 2/4/94.
36 Robinson (1971); Davidson (1972).
37 Hicks (1973, pp. 9–10; 1974, p. 6).
38 Pasinetti (1974, p. 46).
39 Pasinetti (1983, p. 208).
40 See Robinson (1971; 1980); Minsky (1975); Weintraub (1976; 1977); Hicks (1979a, p. 73; 1980).
41 Hicks (1980); Kahn (1984; pp. 160, 249); Robinson (1971); Pasinetti (1974). But also see Moggridge (1976, pp. 165–7) and Harcourt (1980) for substantive critiques of IS–LM.
42 See Leijonhufvud (1983b); also see Samuelson (1983, pp. 212–17).
43 See Tobin (1980, p. 73) and interview with Tobin in Klamer (1984, pp. 98, 101).
44 Tobin (1980, pp. 21–2, 40–2; 1983, p. 36).
45 Meltzer (1981, pp. 51–5).
46 Meltzer (1983a, pp. 75, 78).
47 Meltzer (1983b, pp. 52–5, 58, 64–5).
48 Ibid., pp. 67–8.
49 See for example Meltzer (1981, p. 40); Shackle (1968); Davidson (1980); Kregal (1983); also see Garegnani (1979); Bharadwaj (1983) and the works of Eatwell (1983); Milgate (1983) and Pasinetti (1981); Harcourt (1987) deals with the distinction between the post-Keynesians.
50 See Tobin (1980); Modigliani (1944; 1963); Friedman (1970; 1971; 1974); also see the works of Meltzer (1981; 1983a, b); Lucas (1981a); Sargent and Wallace (1975); Phelps (1968); also see Leijonhufvud (1976, p. 71).
51 See Samuelson (1983, p. 216); Tobin (1980, pp. xii, 21, 36–7; 1983, p. 36); Tobin interview in Klamer (1984, p. 101); also see Meltzer

(1983b, pp. 52, 67–8), the papers by Lucas (1981a, pp. 280–1; 1981b) and the interview with Lucas in Klamer (1984, pp. 34–5, 40–2, 55–6); also see Leijonhufvud (1984, pp. 38–9).

52 Leijonhufvud (1983b, pp. 184–5); also see Keynes (1936, pp. 50–1).
53 Rutherford (1984, p. 383); Shackle (1984); Colander and Guthrie (1981, p. 219); Davidson (1972); also see Torr (1987).
54 See for example Meltzer (1983b, pp. 58, 64–5); also see Kahn (1984, pp. 160, 249) and Robinson (1971, pp. 82–5).

## Chapter 6

1 See Solow (1984, p. 25); Patinkin (1983); Blaug (1985, p. 92).
2 Solow (1984, p. 14).
3 Ibid.
4 See Hicks (1937); Lange (1938, p. 12); Timlin (1942, p. 8); Modigliani (1944, p. 46); Samuelson (1947, p. 276); Klein (1950; 1968, p. 193).
5 See Hansen (1949; 1953); Weintraub (1959; 1960, p. 62), reprinted in R. Ball and P. Doyle (eds), (1969), page references to reprint; Horwich (1964, pp. 512–28); Leijonhufvud (1968, p. 31).
6 See Clower (1960; 1965) and Leijonhufvud (1968; 1969); also see Lange (1938) and Timlin (1942); see also Winch (1969, pp. 190–3, 380) and Shackle (1967, p. 267).
7 See for example Robinson (1971, pp. 82–5) and Davidson (1972); also see Pasinetti (1974, pp. 46–7), Minsky (1975, pp. 32–8) and Klein (1950; 1968).
8 Moggridge (1976, pp. 165–7); Patinkin (1976); Deane (1978, pp. 188–9); also see Johnson (1976, pp. 242–3).
9 Coddington (1979); Hicks (1973, p. 2; 1979c, p. 990).
10 See Tobin (1980, p. 73); Morgan (1981); also see Hicks (1980); Lucas (1981a, p. 276) and Meltzer (1981, p. 37; 1983a; 1983b, p. 67); also see Leijonhufvud (1983a, pp. 64–5; 1983b) and Klamer (1984, p. 3) and Solow (1984, pp. 14–15, 25); Pasinetti (1983, p. 208).
11 See Harrod (1937a; Meade (1936; 1937a, b) and Hicks (1937). Both Champernowne's and Reddaway's use of generalized IS–LM-type simultaneous equations (and, in the former case, diagrams), were probably based upon Keynes's lectures of 1932–4, since they were both Keynes's students. See Lekachman (1964, pp. vii–viii). Harrod's equations were those specifically used by Hicks to draw the SILL diagram, as attested to by his letter to Meade of 6 September 1936 cited above.

Some confirmation of the problematic nature of Hicks's accounts of the origin of the diagram can be seen in his latest published reference to it, see Hicks (1986, p. 7) where he says 'I suppose that even at the moment when I first drew out that famous diagram, I had a suspicion that all was not well with it. For when I next ran into something like its problem, in *Value and Capital* . . . I avoided it.'

12 Meade (1937b) and Robinson (1937a, b).

13 Letter from Kahn to Harrod cited in Riley-Smith (1982, p. 91).

14 Letter from Harrod to Durbin, 7 February 1936; I am grateful to Prof. Liz Durbin for sending me a copy of this letter. Letter from Robertson to Harrod, 22 July 1936, cited in Riley-Smith (1982, p. 101).

15 Letter from Robertson to Kaldor, 16 February 1939; I am grateful to Prof. Lord Kaldor for allowing me to photocopy this letter and to Prof. S. Dennison for permission to cite it here.

16 Interview with Kaldor, 23 November 1985; also see Catalogues of the London School of Economics (1936–7, pp. 118–20; 1938–9, pp. 110–11).

17 See Kaldor (1937); letters from Robertson and Hicks to Dobb, written in May and June 1937; I am grateful to Brian Pollit for providing me with this material from the Dobb papers, and to Prof. S. Dennison for permission to cite Robertson's letters.

In his letter of 25 June 1937, which ended the exchange, Robertson wrote to Dobb:

I have just dug this correspondence out of its lair. Apologies for having kept it so long

1 . . . I don't think I'm convinced by Hicks' argument that the issue depends on whether or not people expect the wage change to be permanent. Let us suppose that they do. Even so, it seems to me that while it is true that a stable situation could be reached if all other prices fall 5% and employment was unchanged, it is equally true that a stable situation will be reached if all other prices do not fall 5% and employment is increased. And unless Hicks can show some reason why the former should come about rather than the latter, I don't think he has proved his point (I think even Keynes agrees that if the wage cut is expected to be temporary, it may stimulate employment, just as I should agree that if it is expected to be repeated it may check employment. One must, I think, try to reach a rational answer first on the assumption that the cut is expected to be permanent and then introduce other expectations or further complications).

2 I'm not sure that I've understood your point. But I don't think it can be said that in Keynesese 'a rise of interest rates is virtually synonomous with (or even always associated with) an increase in investment.' True, an increase in investment tends to raise interest rates through an increase in M1, but that as I understand, may be counteracted if there is a sufficient

decline in 'liquidity preference proper' or a sufficient increase in the supply of money. But I don't pretend to be clear as to what he does now hold about this.

18 Meade (1937a; 1937b, pp. v–vi, 10, 16–18, 26–9); Robinson (1937a, b).
19 I am very grateful to Prof. S. Dennison for providing me with copies of Meade's letters to Robertson, and to Prof. Meade for permission to quote from his letters to Robertson. Presley (1979, pp. 186–91, 207–15), recognized intuitively the reasons for Robertson's support for IS–LM and the input Robertson provided to Hicks's IS–LM paper regarding the 'historical question' and 'authorities', i.e. Marshall, Lavington and Pigou, that Hicks refers to, both in his letter to Robertson of 1 November 1936 and the published version of his IS–LM paper; see Hicks (1937, pp. 151–2).
20 This confirms Prof. Meade's point, made in his interview with me, that his book *Economic Analysis and Policy* (1936; 1937b) was based on his IS–LM approach to Keynes's *General Theory*; see Meade (1937a).
21 Robinson (1937b, pp. v, 8–12, 16–17, 28–9, 70–1); Pasinetti (1974, pp. 36–9).
22 Robinson (1937a; 2nd edn 1947, pp. 119, 126–33).
23 Ibid., pp. 171–2, 174.
24 Kahn (1984, pp. 160, 249).
25 See Keynes (1937a, pp. 211–12); also see the Keynes–Robinson correspondence in Robinson (1937a, b), in JMK (XIV, pp. 148–50) and JMK (XXXIX, pp. 184–6).
26 Patinkin (1976, p. 76); Solow (1984, pp. 14–15).
27 Robinson (1937a; 1947, pp. 171–2).
28 Rubinstein et al. (1984, pp. 26–9); Patinkin (1980, p. 24).
29 Harrod (1974, pp. 3–11).
30 A. Robinson (1974, p. 101).
31 Santomero and Seater (1978); Pigou (1945); Brown (1955); Phillips (1958).
32 Pigou (1945, p. 72); Brown (1955, pp. 99–101).
33 Jones (1970, p. 16); Brown (1955, p. 90).
34 See Shackle (1953, pp. 10–12); Hicks (1979d, p. 55). It is ironic that Hansen, commenting on Marshall's predecessors noted that they 'were fumbling around in the dark because they never grasped the concept of a demand schedule . . . Not until Marshall did the demand function play a significant role in economic analysis. Yet Cournot (and perhaps others) had formulated the principle before'; see Hansen (1948a, p. 135). For an earlier exposition of the Phillips-type relationship, see for example Irving Fisher (1933), *Inflation?* (George Allen and Unwin, London) chapter 5. I want to thank Prof. M. Blaug for referring me to Fisher's early work on this.

Also see Dasgupta (1965, pp. 29–37) and Lewis (1954, pp. 146, 150–2). Prof. A. K. Dasgupta has stressed in a recent interview with me (28 August 1986) that any economist with both a knowledge of 'the classics' and experience in underdeveloped countries could, and would have drawn the 'Lewis diagram' at the time.

35 See for example Glaser and Strauss (1967).

# Bibliography

## Abbreviations

This bibliography encompasses the articles, books and other material cited in the text and notes above. The abbreviations used are as follows:

| | |
|---|---|
| *AEJ* | *Atlantic Economic Journal* |
| *AER* | *American Economic Review* |
| *AJS* | *American Journal of Sociology* |
| *BLQR* | *Banca Nazionale del Lavoro Quarterly Review* |
| *CamJE* | *Cambridge Journal of Economics* |
| *CJEP* | *Canadian Journal of Economics and Political Science* |
| *EC* | *Econometrica* |
| *Econ* | *Economica (N.S.)* |
| *EJ* | *Economic Journal* |
| *EP* | *Economia Política* |
| *ER* | *Economic Record* |
| *HOPE* | *History of Political Economy* |
| *ILR* | *International Labour Review* |
| *JEI* | *Journal of Economic Issues* |
| *JEL* | *Journal of Economic Literature* |
| *JMK* | *Collected Writings* of John Maynard Keynes, with volume number |
| *JPE* | *Journal of Political Economy* |
| *JPKE* | *Journal of Post Keynesian Economics* |
| *JRSS* | *Journal of the Royal Statistical Society* |
| *MS* | *Manchester School* |
| *OEP* | *Oxford Economic Papers* |
| *QJE* | *Quarterly Journal of Economics* |
| *RES* | *Review of Economic Studies* |
| *REP* | *Revue d'économie politique* |
| *REcon. Stat* | *Review of Economics and Statistics* |

*Welt. Arch.*    *Weltwirtschaftliches Archiv*
*ZFN*    *Zeitschrift für Nationalökonomie*


References


Ball, R. and P. Doyle (eds) (1970), *Inflation* (Penguin, Harmondsworth).
Bharadwaj, K. (1983), 'On Effective Demand: Certain Recent Critiques' in J. Kregel (ed.), *Distribution, Effective Demand, and International Economic Relations* (Macmillan, London).
Blaug, M. (1985), *Great Economists since Keynes* (Wheatsheaf, Brighton).
Bowley, A. (1938), 'Review of Hicks' *Théorie mathématique de la Valeur*', *EJ* (vol. 48, September).
Brown, A. (1955), *The Great Inflation 1939–51* (Oxford Univ. Press, Oxford).
—— (1985), 'A Worm's-eye view of the Keynesian Revolution', unpublished manuscript.
Champernowne, D. (1936), 'Unemployment, Basic and Monetary: The Classical Analysis and the Keynesian', *RES* (vol. 3, June).
Clower, R. (1960), 'Keynes and the Classics: A Dynamical Perspective', *QJE* (vol. 74, May).
—— (1965), 'The Keynesian Counter-revolution: A Theoretical Appraisal' in F. Hahn and F. Brechling (eds), *The Theory of Interest Rates* (Macmillan, London); reprinted in R. Clower (ed.), (1969), *Monetary Theory* (Penguin, Harmondsworth).
—— (ed.), (1969), *Monetary Theory* (Penguin, Harmondsworth).
—— and Leijonhufvud, A. (1975), 'The Co-ordination of Economic Activities: A Keynesian Perspective', *AER: Papers and Proceedings* (vol. 65, May).
Coddington, A. (1979), 'Hicks's Contribution to Keynesian Economics', *JEL* (vol. 17, September).
Colander, D. and Guthrie, R. (1980), 'What do Rational Expectations mean?', *JPKE* (vol. 3, Winter).
Davidson, P. (1972), *Money and the Real World* (Macmillan, London).
—— (1980), 'The Dual-faceted Nature of the Keynesian Revolution', *JPKE* (vol. 3, Spring).
Dasgupta, A. (1965), *Planning and Economic Growth* (George Allen and Unwin, London).
Deane, P. (1978), *The Evolution of Economic Ideas* (Cambridge Univ. Press, Cambridge).
Dobb, M. (1973), *Theories of Value and Distribution* (Cambridge Univ. Press, Cambridge).
Dornbusch, R. and Fisher, S. (1984), *Macroeconomics*, 3rd edn (McGraw-Hill, Maidenhead).
Eatwell, J. and Milgate, M. (eds), (1983), *Keynes's Economics and the*

*Theory of Value and Distribution* (Gerald Duckworth, London).
Friedman, M. (1970), 'A Theoretical Framework for Monetary Analysis', *JPE* (vol. 78, March–April).
—— (1971), 'A Monetary Theory of Nominal Income', *JPE* (vol. 79, March–April).
—— (1974), introduction in R. Gordon (ed.), *Milton Friedman's Monetary Framework* (Univ. of Chicago Press, Chicago).
Frisch, R. (1933), 'Propagation Problems and Impulse Problems in Dynamic Economics' in *Essays in Honour of G. Cassel* (George Allen and Unwin, London).
Garegnani, P. (1978; 1979), 'Notes on Consumption, Investment, and Effective Demand: I and II', *CamJE* (vols 2, 3, December and March).
Glaser, B. and Strauss, A. (1967), *The Discovery of Grounded Theory: Strategies for Qualitative Research* (Aldine, Chicago).
Goodwin, R. (1982), *Essays in Economic Dynamics* (Macmillan, London).
Hansen, A. (1936), 'Mr. Keynes on Underemployment Equilibrium', *JPE* (vol. 44, October).
—— (1938), 'Keynes on Underemployment Equilibrium' in A. Hansen, *Full Recovery or Stagnation* (A. and C. Black, London).
—— (1941), *Fiscal Policy and Business Cycles* (Norton, London).
—— (1947), *Economic Policy and Full Employment* (McGraw-Hill, Maidenhead).
—— (1948a), 'The *General Theory* (2)' in S. Harris (ed.), *The New Economics* (Dennis Dobson, London).
—— (1948b), 'Keynes on Economic Policy' in S. Harris (ed.), *The New Economics* (Dennis Dobson, London).
—— (1949), *Monetary Theory and Fiscal Policy* (McGraw-Hill, New York).
—— (1953), *A Guide to Keynes* (McGraw-Hill, New York).
Harcourt, G. (1980), 'A Post Keynesian Development of the Keynesian Model' in E. Nell (ed.), *Growth, Profits and Property: Essays in the Revival of Political Economy* (Cambridge Univ. Press, Cambridge).
—— (1987), 'Post Keynesian Economics' in J. Eatwell et al. (eds), *The New Palgrave: A Dictionary of Economic Theory and Doctrine* (Macmillan, London).
Harris, S. (ed.), (1948), *The New Economics: Keynes' Influence on Theory and Public Policy* (Dennis Dobson, London).
Harrod, R. (1936), *The Trade Cycle* (Clarendon Press, Oxford).
—— (1937a), 'Mr. Keynes and Traditional Theory', *EC* (vol. 5, January); reprinted in S. Harris (ed.), *The New Economics* (Dennis Dobson, London).
—— (1937b), 'Review of Lundberg's *Studies in the Theory of Economic Expansion*, *ZFN* (vol. 8, August).
—— (1938), 'Scope and Method of Economics', *EJ* (vol. 48, September).
—— (1939a), 'An Essay in Dynamic Theory', *EJ* (vol. 49, March).

—— (1939b), 'Review of Hicks' *Value and Capital*' *EJ* (vol. 49, June).
—— (1948), *Towards a Dynamic Economics* (Macmillan, London).
—— (1951), *The Life of John Maynard Keynes* (Macmillan, London).
—— (1969), *Money* (Macmillan, London).
—— (1974), 'Keynes' Theory and its Applications' in D. Moggridge (ed.), *Keynes: Aspects of the Man and his Work* (Macmillan, London).
Hawtrey, R. (1937), *Capital and Employment*, 1st edn (Longman, London).
—— (1939a), 'Review of Hicks' *Value and Capital*', *JRSS* (vol. 102, part II).
—— (1952), *Capital and Employment* (Longman, London).
—— and Hicks, J. (1939b), 'Hicks' Review of Hawtrey's *A Century of Bank Rate*: Replies and Rejoinder', *MS* (vol. 10, October).
Helm, D. (1984), *The Economics of John Hicks* (Basil Blackwell, Oxford).
Hicks, J. (1936a), 'Economic Theory and the Social Sciences' in *The Social Sciences: Their Relations in Theory and Teaching*, proceedings of conference of Univ. of London Institute of Sociology, 27–9 September 1935 (Le Play House Press, London).
—— (1936b), 'Mr. Keynes' Theory of Employment', *EJ* (vol. 46, June).
—— (1937), 'Mr. Keynes and the "Classics"; A Suggested Interpretation', *EC* (vol. 5, April).
—— (1939), *Value and Capital* (Clarendon Press, Oxford).
—— (1945), 'La théorie de Keynes après neuf ans', *REP* (vol. 55, January–February).
—— (1949), 'Mr. Harrod's Dynamic theory', *Econ* (vol. 16, May).
—— (1950), *A Contribution to the Theory of the Trade Cycle* (Oxford Univ. Press, Oxford).
—— (1967), 'The Classics again' in J. Hicks, *Critical Essays in Monetary Theory* (Oxford Univ. Press, Oxford).
—— (1973), 'Recollections and Documents', *Econ* (vol. 40, February).
—— (1974), *The Crisis in Keynesian Economics* (Basil Blackwell, Oxford).
—— (1975), 'Revival of Political Economy: The Old and the New', *ER*, (vol. 51, September).
—— (1976a), 'Revolutions in Economics' in S. Latsis (ed.), *Method and Appraisal in Economics* (Cambridge Univ. Press, Cambridge).
—— (1976b), 'Some Questions of Time in Economics' in A. Tang et al. (eds), *Evolution, Welfare and Time in Economics* (Lexington, Mass.).
—— (1977), *Economic Perspectives* (Oxford Univ. Press, Oxford).
—— (1979a), *Causality in Economics* (Basic Books, New York).
—— (1979b), 'The Formation of an Economist', *BLQR* (vol. 32, September).
—— (1979c), 'On Coddington's Interpretation: A Reply', *JEL* (vol. 17, September).
—— (1979d), 'Is Interest the Price of a Factor of Production' in M. Rizzo (ed.), *Time, Uncertainty and Disequilibrium* (Lexington, Mass.).

—— (1980), 'IS–LM: An Explanation', *JPKE* (vol. 3, Winter).

—— (1983), 'Is Economics a Science?', mimeo.

—— (1986), 'Towards a more "General Theory" ', *EP* (vol. 3, April).

Horwich, G. (1964), *Money, Capital, and Prices* (Richard Irwin, Homewood, Ill.).

Jammer, M. (1982), 'Einstein and Quantum Physics' in G. Holton and Y. Elkana (eds), *Albert Einstein: Historical and Cultural Perspectives* (Princeton Univ. Press, Princeton, N.J.).

Johnson, H. (1976), 'General Theory: Revolution or War of Independence?', reprinted in H. and E. Johnson (eds), (1978), *The Shadow of Keynes* (Basil Blackwell, Oxford).

Jones, D. V. (1970), 'Empirical Models of Inflation in the UK' in Dept. of Employment, *Prices and Earnings in 1951–69: An Econometric Assessment* (HMSO, London).

Kahn, R. (1984), *The Making of Keynes's General Theory* (Cambridge Univ. Press, Cambridge).

—— (1985), 'The Cambridge "Circus" (1)' in G. Harcourt (ed.), *Keynes and his Contemporaries* (Macmillan, London).

Kaldor, N. (1937), 'Prof. Pigou on Money Wages in Relation to Unemployment', *EJ* (vol. 47, December).

—— (1983), 'Keynesian Economics after Fifty Years' in D. Worswick and J. Trevithick (eds), *Keynes and the Modern World* (Cambridge Univ. Press, Cambridge).

Keynes, J. M. (1936), *The General Theory of Employment, Interest and Money* (Macmillan, London).

—— (1937a), 'The General Theory of Employment', *QJE* (vol. 51, February).

—— (1937b), 'The Theory of the Rate of Interest' in A. Gayer (ed.), *Lessons of Monetary Experience: Essays in Honour of I. Fisher* (Rinehart, New York).

—— (1938), 'Mr. Keynes and Finance', *EJ* (vol. 48, June).

—— (1971–82), *Collected Writings*, D. Moggridge (ed.), (Macmillan, London); cited as JMK with volume number.

Klamer, A. (1984), *The New Classical Macroeconomics: Conversations with new Classical Economists and their Opponents* (Wheatsheaf, Brighton).

Klein, L. (1950; 1968), *The Keynesian Revolution*, 1st and 2nd edns (Macmillan, London).

Kregel, J. (1980), 'Economic Dynamics and the Theory of Steady Growth', *HOPE* (vol. 12, Spring).

—— (1983), 'The Microfoundations of the "Generalization of the General Theory" and "Bastard Keynesianism": Keynes' Theory of Employment in the Long and Short Period', *CamJE* (vol. 7, September–December).

—— (1985), 'Harrod and Keynes: Increasing Returns, the Theory of Employment and Dynamic Economics' in G. Harcourt (ed.), *Keynes and his Contemporaries* (Macmillan, London).

Lange, O. (1938), 'The Rate of Interest and the Optimum Propensity to Consume', *Econ* (vol. 5, February).

Lee, F. (1981), 'The Oxford Challenge to Marshallian Supply and Demand: The History of the Oxford Economists' Research Group', *OEP* (vol. 33, November).

Leijonhufvud, A. (1967), 'Keynes and the Keynesians: A Suggested Interpretation', *AER* (vol. 57); reprinted in R. Clower (ed.), (1969), *Monetary Theory* (Penguin, Harmondsworth).

—— (1968), *On Keynesian Economics and the Economics of Keynes* (Oxford Univ. Press, Oxford).

—— (1969), *Keynes and the Classics* (Institute of Economic Affairs, London).

—— (1976), 'Schools, "Revolutions", and Research Programmes in Economic Theory' in S. Latsis (ed.), *Method and Appraisal in Economics* (Cambridge Univ. Press, Cambridge).

—— (1983a), 'What was the Matter with IS–LM?' in J. Fitoussi (ed.), *Modern Macroeconomic Theory* (Basil Blackwell, Oxford).

—— (1983b), 'What would Keynes have thought of Rational Expectations?' in D. Worswick and J. Trevithick (eds), *Keynes and the Modern World* (Cambridge Univ. Press, Cambridge).

—— (1984), 'Hicks on Time and Money', *OEP* (vol. 36, supplement).

Lekachman, R. (ed.), (1964), *Keynes' General Theory: Reports of Three Decades* (Macmillan, London).

Lerner, A. (1936), 'Mr. Keynes's "General Theory of Employment, Interest and Money" ', *ILR* (vol. 34, October).

—— (1937), 'Capital, Investment, and Interest' reprinted in A. Lerner (1953a), *Essays in Economic Analysis* (Macmillan, London).

—— (1938), 'Alternative Formulations of the Theory of Interest', *EJ* (vol. 48, June); reprinted in S. Harris (ed.), (1948), *The New Economics* (Dennis Dobson, London).

—— (1939), 'Ex-ante Analysis and Wage Theory', *Econ* (vol. 4, November); reprinted in Lerner (1953a), *Essays in Economic Analysis* (Macmillan, London).

—— (1944), *The Economics of Control* (Macmillan, London).

—— (1951), *Economics of Employment* (McGraw-Hill, Maidenhead).

—— (1953a), *Essays in Economic Analysis* (Macmillan, London).

—— (1953b), 'On the Marginal Productivity of Capital and the Marginal Efficiency of Investment', *JPE* (vol. 61, February).

—— (1974), 'From the *Treatise on Money* to the *General Theory*', *JEL* (vol. 12, March).

Lewis, W. (1954), 'Economic Development with Unlimited Supplies of Labour', *MS* (vol. 22, May).

Lindhal, E. (1954), 'On Keynes' Economic System: Parts I and II', *ER* (vol. 30, May and November).

Lucas, R. (1981a), *Studies in Business Cycle Theory* (Basil Blackwell, Oxford).
—— (1981b), 'Tobin and Monetarism: A Review Article', *JEL* (vol. 19, June).
Meade, J. (1936), *Economic Analysis and Policy* (Oxford Univ. Press, Oxford).
—— (1937a), 'A Simplified Model of Mr. Keynes' System', *RES* (vol. 4, February); reprinted in S. Harris (ed.), (1948), *The New Economics* (Dennis Dobson, London).
—— (1937b), *Economic Analysis and Policy*, 2nd edn (Oxford Univ. Press, Oxford).
—— (1975), 'The Keynesian Revolution' in M. Keynes (ed.), *Essays on John Maynard Keynes* (Cambridge Univ. Press, Cambridge).
Meltzer, A. (1981), 'Keynes's *General Theory*: A Different Perspective', *JEL* (vol. 19, March).
—— (1983a), 'Interpreting Keynes', *JEL* (vol. 21, March).
—— (1983b), 'On Keynes and Monetarism' in D. Worswick and J. Trevithick (eds), *Keynes and the Modern World* (Cambridge Univ. Press, Cambridge).
Minsky, H. (1975), *John Maynard Keynes* (Macmillan, London).
Modigliani, F. (1944), 'Liquidity Preference and the Theory of Interest of Money', *EC* (vol. 12, January).
—— (1963), 'The Monetary Mechanism and its Interaction with Real Phenomena', *REcon. Stat* (vol. 45, supplement).
Moggridge, D. (1976), *Keynes* (Fontana, London).
Morgan, B. (1981), 'Sir John Hicks's Contribution to Economic Theory' in J. Shackleton and G. Locksley (eds), *Twelve Contemporary Economists* (Macmillan, London).
Nell., E. (ed.) (1980), *Growth, Profits and Property: essays in the revival of political economy* (Cambridge Univ. Press, Cambridge).
Pasinetti, L. (1974), *Growth and Income Distribution* (Cambridge Univ. Press, Cambridge).
—— (1981), *Structural Change and Economic Growth* (Cambridge Univ. Press, Cambridge).
—— (1983), 'Comment on Leijonhufvud' in D. Worswick and J. Trevithick (eds), *Keynes and the Modern World* (Cambridge Univ. Press, Cambridge).
Patinkin, D. (1976), *Keynes' Monetary Thought; A Study of its Development* (Duke Univ. Press, Durham, N.C.).
—— (1980), 'New Material on the Development of Keynes's Monetary Thought', *HOPE* (vol. 12, Spring).
—— (1983), 'Multiple Discoveries and the Central Message', *AJS* (vol. 89, September).
Phelps, E. (1968), 'Money Wage Dynamics and Labor Market Equilibrium', *JPE* (vol. 76, July).

Phelps-Brown, H. (1937), 'Report of the Oxford Meeting, 25–29 September, 1936', *EC* (vol. 5, October).
—— (1980), 'Sir Roy Harrod: A Biographical Memoir', *EJ* (vol. 90, March).
Phillips, A. (1958), 'The Relationship Between Unemployment and the Rate of Change of Money Wage Rates in the UK, 1861–1957', *Econ* (vol. 25, November).
Pigou, A. (1937), 'Real and Monetary Wage Rates in Relation to Unemployment', *EJ* (vol. 47, September).
—— (1938), 'Money Wages in Relation to Unemployment', *EJ* (vol. 48, March).
—— (1945), *Lapses from Full Employment* (Macmillan, London).
Presley, J. (1979), *Robertsonian Economics* (Macmillan, London).
Reddaway, W. B. (1936), 'Review of *The General Theory of Employment, Interest and Money*', *ER* (vol. 12, June).
—— (1937), 'Special Obstacles to Full Employment in a Wealthy Community', *EJ* (vol. 47, June).
—— (1964), 'Keynesian Analysis and a Managed Economy' in R. Lekachman (ed.), *Keynes's General Theory: Reports of Three Decades* (Macmillan, London).
Riley-Smith, H. (1982), *Catalogue of the Papers of Sir Roy Harrod* (Riley-Smith Booksellers, Norfolk).
Robertson, D. (1937), 'Review of Harrod's "*The Trade Cycle*" ', *CJEP* (vol. 3, February).
Robinson, A. (1974), 'Discussion of Opie: The Political Consequences of Lord Keynes' in D. Moggridge (ed.), *Keynes: Aspects of the Man and his Work* (Macmillan, London).
—— (1985), 'The Cambridge 'Circus' (2)' in G. Harcourt (ed.), *Keynes and his Contemporaries* (Macmillan, London).
Robinson, J. (1937a; 1947), *Essays in the Theory of Employment* (Macmillan, London; Basil Blackwell, Oxford).
—— (1937b), *Introduction to the Theory of Employment* (Macmillan, London).
—— (1962), 'Review of H. Johnson's "*Money, Trade and Economic Growth*", 1962', *EJ* (vol. 72, September).
—— (1971), *Economic Heresies* (Macmillan, London).
—— (1975), 'What has become of the Keynesian Revolution?' in M. Keynes (ed.), *Essays on John Maynard Keynes* (Cambridge Univ. Press, Cambridge).
—— (1980), *What are the Questions? And Other Essays* (Sharpe, Armonk).
Rubinstein, R. et al. (1984), *Science as Cognitive Process* (Univ. of Pennsylvania Press, Philadelphia, PA).
Rutherford, M. (1984), 'Rational Expectations and Keynesian Uncertainty', *JPKE* (vol. 6, Spring).
Rymes, T. (1983), Marvin Fallgatter's lecture notes of 'J. M. Keynes,

The Monetary Theory of Production, 1933'.

Samuelson, P. (1947), *Foundations of Economic Analysis* (Harvard Univ. Press, Cambridge, MA).

—— (1983), 'Comment on Leijonhufvud' in D. Worswick and J. Trevithick (eds), *Keynes and the Modern World* (Cambridge Univ. Press, Cambridge).

Santomero, A. and Seater, J. (1978), 'The Inflation–Unemployment Trade-off: A Critique of the Literature', *JEL* (vol. 16, June).

Sargent, T. and Wallace, N. (1975), 'Rational Expectations, the Optimal Monetary Instrument and the Optimal Money Supply', *JPE* (vol. 83, April).

Scott, I. (1951), 'An Exposition of the Keynesian System', *RES* (vol. 19, Winter).

Shackle, G. (1953), 'Economics and Sincerity', *OEP* (vol. 5, March).

—— (1967), *The Years of High Theory* (Cambridge Univ. Press, Cambridge).

—— (1968), *Expectations, Investment, and Income*, 2nd edn (Oxford Univ. Press, Oxford).

—— (1982), 'Sir John Hicks's "IS–LM: An Explanation": A Comment', *JPKE* (vol. 4, Spring).

—— (1984), 'Comment on Rutherford', *JPKE* (vol. 6, Spring).

Solow, R. (1984), 'Mr Hicks and the Classics' (First Hicks Lecture Oxford, 3 May 1984), *OEP* (vol. 36, supplement).

Thomson, D. (1962), *Europe since Napoleon* (Longman, London).

Timlin, M. (1942), *Keynesian Economics* (Univ. of Toronto Press, Toronto, Ont.).

Tinbergen, J. (1937), 'Review of Harrod's *Trade Cycle*', *Welt. Arch.* (vol. 45, May).

Tobin, J. (1980), *Asset Accumulation and Economic Activity* (the Jahnsson Lectures) (Basil Blackwell, Oxford).

—— (1983), 'Comment on Kaldor' in D. Worswick and J. Trevithick (eds), *Keynes and the Modern World* (Cambridge Univ. Press, Cambridge).

Torr, C. (1987), *Equilibrium, Expectations and Information* (Polity Press, Cambridge).

Weintraub, S. (1958), *An Approach to the Theory of Income* (Chilton, Philadelphia).

—— (1959), *A General Theory of the Price Level, Output, Income Distribution and Economic Growth* (Chilton, Philadelphia).

—— (1960), 'The Keynesian Theory of Inflation', *International Economic Review* (vol. 1); reprinted in R. Ball and P. Doyle (eds), (1970), *Inflation* (Penguin, Harmondsworth).

—— (1976), 'Revision and Recantation in Hicksian Economics: A Review Article', *JEI* (vol. 10, September).

—— (1977), 'Hicksian Keynesianism' in S. Weintraub (ed.), *Modern Economic Thought* (Univ. of Pennsylvania Press, Philadelphia, PA).

Winch, D. (1969), *Economics and Policy* (Collins–Fontana, London).
Young, W. (1975), 'Harrod, Keynes and the "Fundamental" Relationship', *AEJ* (vol. 3, Winter).
—— (1982), 'Time and Concept Formation in Economics', *JEI* (vol. 16, March).

# Index